AFRICAN FILM
Re-Imagining a Continent

AFRICAN FILM
Re-Imagining a Continent

Josef Gugler

Professor of Sociology
and Director of the Center
for Contemporary African Studies
University of Connecticut

Indiana University Press
BLOOMINGTON

David Philip
CAPE TOWN

James Currey
OXFORD

First published in 2003 in the United Kingdom by
James Currey Ltd
73 Botley Road
Oxford OX2 0BS

in North America by
Indiana University Press
601 North Morton Street
Bloomington, Indiana 47404-3797

and in South Africa by
David Philip, an imprint of New Africa Books (Pty) Ltd
99 Garfield Rd, Kenilworth, Cape Town

Manufactured in Great Britain

British Library Cataloguing in Publication Data
Gugler, Josef
    African film : re-imagining a continent
    1. Motion pictures - Africa - History
    I. Title.
    791.4'3'096

ISBN 0-85255-562-8 (James Currey cloth)
ISBN 0-85255-561-X (James Currey paper)

Library of Congress Cataloging-in-Publication Data
Gugler, Josef.
    African film : re-imagining a continent / Josef Gugler
        p. cm.
    Originally published: Oxford: J. Currey, 2003.
    Includes bibliographical references and index.
      ISBN 0-253-34350-X (alk. paper) -- ISBN 0-253-21643-5
    (pbk. : alk. paper)
    1. Motion pictures--Africa.   2. Africa--In motion pictures.
    I. Title.
    PN1993.5.A35G77 2003
    791.43'626--dc21

                         2003014797

    1 2 3 4 5 08 07 06 05 04 03
ISBN 0-253-34350-X (Indiana cloth)
ISBN 0-253-21643-5 (Indiana paper)

Frontispiece: Sotiguy Kouyaté in the role of Djéliba Kouyaté in *Keïta! The Heritage of the Griot*

**To the children of Africa
so prominently featured by many African directors**

The artist must in many ways be the mouth and ears of his people. In the modern sense, this corresponds to the role of the griot *in traditional African culture. The artist is like a mirror. His work reflects and synthesizes the problems, the struggles, and the hopes of his people.*

Ousmane Sembène ('Filmmakers and African Culture', Africa 71 (1977): 80)

Contents

17 films
in 17 sentences

Out of Africa 1985

Sydney Pollack draws on the writings of Isak Dinesen to present a nostalgic tale of the romantic entanglements of European settlers in a Garden of Eden.

Yaaba 1989

Idrissa Ouedraogo tells of villagers and their foibles in Burkina Faso.

Keïta! 1995

Dani Kouyaté introduces the *Sundjata*, the celebrated West African epic of the establishment of the Mali Empire, featuring the distinguished actor Sotigui Kouyaté.

Sambizanga 1972

Sarah Maldoror translates to the screen José Luandino Vieira's novel *The Real Life of Domingos Xavier*, depicting ordinary people resisting Portuguese rule in Angola.

Flame 1996

Ingrid Sinclair reconstructs the experiences of women guerrillas in Zimbabwe fighting the settler army as well as sexism in their own ranks.

The Gods Must Be Crazy 1980

Jamie Uys presents a very funny movie that shows the world according to the *apartheid* ideology of South Africa's white minority regime.

A Dry White Season 1989

Euzhan Palcy presents André Brink's novel of an Afrikaner who comes to confront repression at the time of the 1976 Soweto Uprising.

Mapantsula 1988

Oliver Schmitz and Thomas Mogotlane show the anti-*apartheid* protests of the 1980s in Soweto where a street tough comes to join the struggle.

Fools 1997

Ramadan Suleman has Patrick Shai portray a teacher dispirited, tormented, and courageous under *apartheid* in a story based on Njabulo Ndebele's novella.

Kongi's Harvest 1970

Ossie Davis takes Nobel Prize Winner Wole Soyinka's play of the corruption of power to the screen.

Xala 1974

Ousmane Sembène, Africa's most prominent director, tells of impotence and neo-colonialism in Senegal.

Tableau Ferraille 1997

Moussa Sene Absa presents Ismaël Lô, the popular Senegalese musician, in the role of an honest politician who falls victim to the corruption surrounding him.

The Blue Eyes of Yonta 1992

Flora Gomes depicts Guinea-Bissau two decades after the fight against the Portuguese colonial army brought independence.

Finzan 1990

Cheick Oumar Sissoko denounces widow inheritance, female genital mutilation, and corrupt government in rural Mali.

Kasarmu Ce 1991

Saddik Balewa contrasts the Islamic morality of a village with political corruption in Nigeria.

Kini and Adams 1997

Idrissa Ouedraogo scrutinizes friendship in rural Zimbabwe.

La Vie est belle 1987

Benoît Lamy and Mweze Ngangura feature Papa Wemba, the famous Congolese musician, in their tale of the country bumpkin who makes it on the Kinshasa music scene and gets his girl.

17 films

in **17** sentences

Place des Cinéastes Africains,
Ouagadougou, probably the world's
only monument dedicated
to filmmakers

This book has distant roots. Years of research and teaching in various parts of Africa were formative for me. From the very beginning I was fascinated with African literature. Later I developed a professional interest that was nurtured during my work at Bayreuth University. More directly this book arose out of a course on *Modern Africa: Re-Imagining Africa With Films and Novels* which I have taught regularly since 1991 at the University of Connecticut, and which has attracted increasingly large numbers of students. It is first of all due to my students who pressed me to embark on this enterprise and who then challenged me as they brought up the shortcomings of the successive drafts I shared with them.

Many people helped me along the way. I would like to thank most especially Bernth Lindfors who encouraged and assisted me time and again, Jeanick Le Naour whose generous hospitality at Cinémathèque Afrique and astute advice were invaluable, the team at Vues d'Afrique who gave me a cordial welcome at the African film festivals in Montréal, Oumar Cherif Diop who made me discover a dimension of the film *Xala* hidden from me, Françoise Pfaff whose thoughtful comments made this a better book, Robert Cancel and Mike Kirkwood who painstakingly went over the entire script and alerted me to my all too many mistakes, Kathy Kirkwood who magnificently integrated the illustrations with the text, and Lynn Taylor who went out of her way to put it all together. I am grateful to the directors who provided information and illustrations. I very much appreciate the help of the many individuals and organizations, acknowledged in the credits, that made the illustrations possible. My debts to Oliver Bartlet's *African Cinemas: Decolonizing the Gaze* and the extraordinary sources of information on African culture he has established around his review *Africultures* and the related website will be obvious to readers of this book. My thanks to Loretta Bass, Emmanuelle Bureau, Sophie Diagne, Harvey Feinberg, Rachel Gugler, Jonathan Haynes, Patricia Haward, Richard Lobban, Sicelo Makapela, Cornelius Moore, Bernard Nicolas, Monibo Sam, Marc Swiencicki and Nwachukwu Frank Ukadike who assisted me in various ways.

This book would not have been possible but for the support I received at the University of Connecticut. Lana Babij, Joseph Natale, and Lynn Sweet at the Interlibrary Loan Division responded with continued cheer to the rising flood of my requests and ever more difficult queries. Alex Bothell, John Collins, and Mohamed Faizal at the Graphic and Photo Division did not tire of responding with expertise and enthusiasm to my never-ending requests to process illustrative materials.

In spite of all the help so generously given, shortcomings remain, and I have to shoulder the responsibility for them. I would like to hear from readers of this book what is wrong with it. As I see and enjoy new African films I will find it hard to resist the temptation to continue this enterprise and embark on another edition.

The children of Africa are prominently featured by many African directors, for them all royalties are vested with UNICEF.

Josef Gugler, Storrs

Table 1 Basic Indicators for African Countries [1]

Countries	Year of Independence and colonial power [2]	Total population (millions) 2001	Urban population (%) 2000	GNP[3] per capita ($) 2001	GNP at PPP[4] per capita ($) 2001	Infant mortality (%) 2000	Illiterate men (%) 2000	Illiterate women (%) 2000
Angola	1975 P	14	34	500	1,550	128	—	—
Botswana	1966 Br	2	50	3,630	8,810	58	25	20
Burkina Faso	1960 F	12	19	210	1,020	104	66	86
Cameroon[2]	1960 G,Br,F	15	49	570	1,670	76	18	31
Congo/Zaïre	1960 Be	52	30	—	—	85	27	50
Côte d'Ivoire	1960 F	16	46	630	1,470	111	46	61
Ethiopia[2]		66	18	100	710	98	53	69
Ghana	1957 Br	20	38	290	1,980	58	20	37
Guinea-Bissau	1974 P	1	24	160	710	126	46	77
Kenya	1963 Br	31	33	340	1,020	78	11	24
Madagascar	1960 F	16	30	260	870	88	26	40
Malawi	1964 Br	11	15	170	620	103	26	53
Mali	1960 Fr	11	30	210	810	120	51	66
Mozambique	1975 P	18	40	210	1,000	129	40	71
Niger	1960 F	11	21	170	770	114	76	92
Nigeria	1960 Br	130	44	290	830	84	28	44
Senegal	1960 F	10	47	480	1,560	60	53	72
South Africa	1910 Br	43	55	2,900	9,510	63	14	15
Sudan	1956 Br, E	32	36	330	1,610	81	31	54
Tanzania[2]	1961 G, Br	35	28	270[5]	540[5]	93	16	33
Uganda	1962 Br	23	14	280	1,250	83	22	43
Zambia	1964 Br	10	45	320	790	115	15	29
Zimbabwe	1980 Br	13	35	480	2,340	69	7	15
Africa South of the Sahara		674	34	470	1,620	91	30	47
United States	1776 Br	284	77	34,870	34,870	7	—	—

1. Countries in Africa South of the Sahara with more than 10 million people and smaller countries where featured films are set.
2. Be(lgium), Br(itain), E(gypt), F(rance), G(ermany), P(ortugal). In World War I Germany lost Cameroon to France and Britain in 1916, mainland Tanzania to Britain in 1918. Italy occupied Ethiopia from 1936 to 1941.
3. Gross national product measures total value added from domestic and foreign sources claimed by residents.
4. Purchasing power parity converts currencies to U.S. dollars according to their purchasing power, i.e. one dollar has the same purchasing power over domestic GNP that the U.S. dollar has over U.S. GNP.
5. Mainland Tanzania.

Source: World Bank, 2002 World Development Indicators.

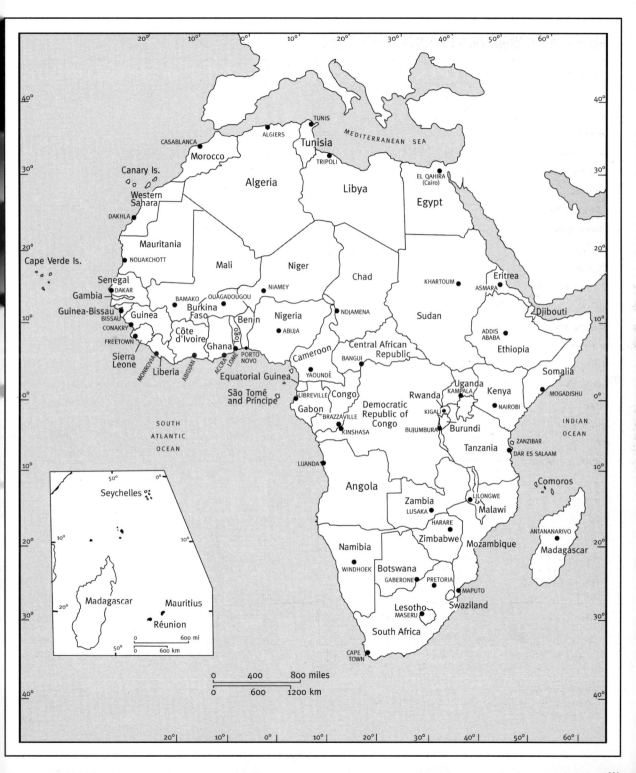

Le comédien dans la création et
la promotion du film Africain
FESPACO
18ème Edition
22 Février - 1er Mars 2003
www.fespaco.bf
Burkina Faso
Ouagadougou

Introduction

African films offer us a window on Africa, one that presents views quite different from those we usually see through the three windows on that continent readily available to Western viewers: television news, documentaries, and feature films produced in the West. Little news about Africa reaches Western audiences. At any one time no more than one or two African countries make the news. Even over the last ten years, widely distributed news stories covered probably only about a dozen African countries: the great majority of African countries never made it to our television screens. And the news tends to focus on disasters: droughts, epidemics, and war. It is the news of crises, it rarely touches on achievements, and it certainly does not portray everyday life in Africa. Crisis news is of course important in that it can play a major role in mobilizing public opinion. Television pictures of starving children in Somalia galvanized U.S. opinion to the point that reluctant politicians were persuaded to send troops to Somalia in 1992 to protect relief supplies against the predations of warlords – then, however, pictures of a few U.S. casualties turned public opinion around, the political establishment cravenly followed, and U.S. troops were withdrawn in 1994 without a thought for tens of thousands of Somalis left to die.

Documentaries tend to fall into one of two categories. One kind of documentary is an extension of the news and, like the news, tends to focus on disasters. Some such documentaries are superb. *Last Grave at Dimbaza*, shot clandestinely in South Africa by Nana Mahomo, was a dramatic account of the oppression of the *apartheid* regime and played a significant role in mobilizing foreign opinion. *Chronicle of a Genocide Foretold*, by Danièle Lacourse and Yvan Patry, is a heart-rending account of the massacre of more than half a million people in Rwanda in 1994 and a searing indictment of Western powers who stood by and let it happen. *The Language You Cry In*, by Alvaro Toepke and Angel Serrano, tells of the worst disasters befalling Africa, slavery and civil war, but it is first and foremost a moving account of the extraordinary story of how a song passed on from generation to generation over two centuries brings a woman from Georgia to the village of one of her ancestors in Sierra Leone.

Most television documentaries by and large dispense with the people of Africa to focus on the 'natural beauty' of Africa, on animals and landscapes. *National Geographic* provides a steady stream of magnificent images of picture-book Africa, an Africa that attracts tourists, but that

Before we started to make films, Europeans had shot films about the African continent. Most of the Africans we saw in those films were unable to set one foot in front of another by themselves. African landscapes were used as settings. Those films were based on European stories.
(Ousmane Sembène in an interview with Pfaff, 1984: 1)

Introduction

most Africans never get to see. When such documentaries do focus on Africans, they are also of the picturesque variety and emphasize the exotic. The few nomadic people of Africa appear time and again adorned with paint and beads. Still, there is beauty to admired. And there are demonstrations in cultural difference to be savored. Thus the young men of the Wodaabe, in Niger, recorded in Werner Herzog's *Herdsmen of the Sun* and a number of other documentaries, are magnificent as they apply makeup, braid their hair, dress up, and perform to court women in ways that strike Western viewers as an extreme case of 'female' coquetry.

Western feature films offer the third readily accessible window on Africa.[1] Since colonial days films produced in the U.S., Europe, and South Africa have propagated images of 'Black Africa' dominated by people of European descent with whom Western viewers could easily identify. The portrayals of Africans repeated and reinforced negative stereotypes: they appeared as barbaric, savage and bloodthirsty; as servants, mostly incompetent; or simply as part of the décor. Many of these films are akin to the 'beautiful Africa' documentaries: they show us a tourist paradise teeming with wild life, *Out of Africa* the finest example. Others take the intrepid white protagonist to challenging environments: the desert threatening excruciating death, the virtually impenetrable jungle where dangers lurk in the dark.

White superman in Africa and the white woman he saves are epitomized by the Tarzan movies. In 1912, with Western imperialism at its zenith and Europeans completing their self-assigned task of colonizing Africa, Edgar Rice Burroughs created Tarzan. Just six years later *Tarzan of the Apes* made it to the screen. In 1932 *Tarzan, the Ape Man* found his voice. Four decades after most of Africa has become independent, Hollywood continues to promote a white man dominating his African surroundings. The 47th Tarzan movie was released in 1998, and seventeen versions of Tarzan were available on the home video market at last count. He was given a new lease of life with the Disney release of an animated Tarzan in 1999, but this one altogether sidesteps the issue of how to depict Africans: 'no black natives are in evidence,' as one reviewer put it – given his racist language, we will do him the favor of letting him remain anonymous. Not only Tarzan movies, but most Western films set in Africa have similarly, if more subtly, put down Africans. We will start by looking at the recent example of *Out of Africa*, a great commercial success, highly praised by critics, and the recipient of seven Academy Awards, but our focus will be on films made by Africans opening a fourth window on Africa for us.

Albert Samama[2] in Tunisia was the first African to direct a film. In 1907 he produced a short documentary, *Tunis*, followed by *Tracteur Caterpillar labourant* in 1914. During World War I he filmed on the front lines for the French Army. In 1922 he shot a short feature, *Zohra*, and in 1924 a full-length feature film, *Ain el Ghezal*. His daughter Haydée Chikli featured as the female lead in both melodramas (Khlifi, 1970: 66–91). In Egypt, the production of feature films also began in the 1920s, and Cairo eventually emerged as the 'Hollywood of the Orient.' More than

1 For critical analyses of close to a century of American and British films set in Africa, see Cameron (1994) and Davis (1996), as well as the documentary *In Darkest Hollywood: Cinema and Apartheid* by Daniel Riesenfeld and Peter Davis.

2 Samama's name has also been transliterated as Chamama or Chemama, and he added Chikli, or Chikly, to it. *Ain el Ghezal* has also been rendered as *Ain al Ghazal* or *Aïn El-Ghazel*. I have not been able to consult Mansour's (2000) biography.

2,800 full-length films were produced in Egypt between 1924 and 1999, and 1,644 copies in 35mm were exported, nearly all of them to Arab countries, from 1988 to 1995 (Shafik, 2001; Thabet, 1998: 30–38; Youssef, 1995).

We will focus on Africa South of the Sahara.[3] The separation of North Africa from the rest of the continent in most scholarship is common as well as controversial. It is due, in part, to the requirement that a scholar of North Africa have a firm command of Arabic. But it also reflects genuine differences between the two regions and affinities across North Africa that extend into the Middle East. Certainly the development of what is invariably referred to as Arab cinema was very different from what happened South of the Sahara.

Afrique sur Seine (1957), is commonly taken to be the first film directed by a black African. Mamadou Sarr and Paulin Soumanou Vieyra, who had come from Senegal to study filmmaking, produced the short in Paris, reputedly because they were denied permission to film in an Africa still under colonial rule (Diawara, 1992: 23). In 1963 Ousmane Sembène completed *Borom Sarret*.[4] The short follows the driver of a donkey cart around Dakar and portrays the chain of disasters that befall him. It is sometimes referred to as the first feature film directed by a black African in Africa. However, Momar Thiam completed *Sarzan*, based on a story by Birago Diop, in Senegal that same year, and Mustapha Alassane had shot *Aouré* and *La Bague du Roi Koda* in Niger the year before. Indeed, a few shorts were produced much earlier, but they seem to have disappeared. In 1947 Raberono had shot *Rasalama*, documenting a ceremony on the centennial of Rasalama's death. Executed on the orders of Queen Ranavalo I, who was fighting the Christianization of Madagascar, she had become a Christian martyr (Sinda, 1998). In 1951 Albert Mongita shot *La Leçon de cinéma* on the golf course of what was then Léopoldville (now Kinshasa), the capital of the Belgian Congo.[5] Two years later another Congolese, Emmanuel Lubalu, shot *Les Pneus gonflés* (Otten, 1984: 22). Also in 1953 Mamadou Touré, from then French Guinea, directed *Mouramani*, based on an African folktale, in France (Vieyra, 1975: 15, 105). Eventually, in 1966, Sembène released a nearly full-length feature, *Black Girl*, which was to become a classic.[6]

Film production in Africa South of the Sahara is concentrated in South Africa and Nigeria. South Africa constitutes a major market: while poor by international standards, South Africa is much richer than any other African country, except for a couple of small island states. For many years its film production was actively promoted by substantial subsidies from the *apartheid* regime. Most South African productions were anti-African, perpetuating negative stereotypes about the continent while white minority rule lasted. We will consider the most successful of those films, *The Gods Must Be Crazy*. Two notable exceptions to the racist slant of the South African film industry were produced in semi-clandestine circumstances under false pretenses: Lionel Rogosin's *Come Back, Africa* and Oliver Schmitz's *Mapantsula* – we will discuss the latter as well as *Fools*, a film produced after the demise of *apartheid*.[7]

3 'Africa South of the Sahara,' while cumbersome, is preferable to the racist 'Black Africa' and the euro-centric 'sub-Saharan Africa.' Throughout this book, 'Africa' will stand as shorthand for Africa South of the Sahara.

4 The full scenario and an analysis of *Borom Sarret* are provided by Boughedir (1987: 57–73).

5 Five years later Albert Mongita was to complain that Congolese didn't get a chance to make films (Ramirez and Rolot, 1985: 429).

6 In spite of the daunting obstacles, a substantial body of African films emerged rapidly. By the late 1980s Françoise Pfaff (1988) could offer an introduction to 25 major filmmakers. That same year Nancy Schmidt's comprehensive bibliography provided 3,993 references to publications on African films and filmmakers. Her second bibliography added another 7,192 in 1994.

7 On films produced in South Africa, see Davis (1996) and Tomaselli (1988), as well as *In Darkest Hollywood*.

Introduction

Nigeria is Africa's most populous country, and the sheer size of its population constitutes a major market, or rather several major markets. The approximately 120 million people of Nigeria speak more than 200 different languages, but between about 20 and 40 million speak one of the major languages (Hausa, Yoruba, and Igbo)[8] as their first language or use it as a *lingua franca*. And while English, the official language, is understood only by a minority of Nigerians, they also number in the tens of millions. Ọla Balogun, Nigeria's most prominent filmmaker, alone produced eleven feature films between 1972 and 1982, the time of the Nigerian oil boom. Many of them, like the majority of Nigerian films, were shot in Yoruba for the more than 20 million speakers of that language. However, even the distribution of Nigerian films in English, or subtitled in English, has remained limited to the internal market; only a few have ever been released overseas – we will discuss *Kongi's Harvest* and *Kasarmu Ce*.[9] Over the last decade filmmaking has shifted to the production of video films produced in the hundreds every year. We will discuss this remarkable film industry in the concluding chapter.

Outside South Africa and Nigeria, local markets for African films are extremely limited. The population of most African countries is small, and few Africans have discretionary income to spend at the movie theater. In any case, African filmmakers have found it very difficult to penetrate established circuits of distribution in Africa (Barlet, 2000: 232–42). French and British companies controlling film distribution in African countries preferred to pass packages of inferior films through the African circuits. The Lebanese and Indians who owned most of the movie houses in West Africa were content to show cheap films from Hong Kong, India, and the U.S. (Diawara, 1992: 104–27). These imports came cheap because they made most of their money elsewhere. Unless African filmmakers had access to the South African and Nigerian mass markets, they had little choice but to reach out to more affluent Western markets. In the 1990s rapidly expanding video production in Nigeria and Ghana took over the mass market and confronted African filmmakers with even more severe competition, an issue to which we will turn in the last chapter.

Most of the African films reaching Western audiences offer images of Africa that are altogether different from the usual fare of Western films set in Africa. Africans invariably hold centre stage. Some films tell of African struggles for liberation, others offer critical perspectives on post-colonial developments. African filmmakers set out to *re-image* Africa, and Western viewers are given an opportunity to *re-imagine* the continent and its people.[10] As Cheick Oumar Sissoko put it in an interview with Hoffelt (2003:122, my translation):

> First of all we have to establish the image of Black People, to contribute to overcome this tragic absence of our images from the universe of images, so that we will finally recognize our place and our role, but also so that the North understands that we exist. We have a history, we have our cultures, we are people who have been organized, people who have known states, who have contributed to enrich world culture, who have participated in the two world wars, but all these contributions of Africa are obscured by the Occident all the time.

8 I am using the more recent spelling of the name of the third largest ethnic group in Nigeria, who previously were referred to as Ibo.

9 On films produced in Nigeria, see Balogun (1987), Ekwuazi (1991), Haynes (1995), and Ukadike (1994: 141–65). Hyginus Ekwuazi presents a number of Nigerian films and videos, directors, producers, and actors in Bankole Bole's documentary *Nigerian Cinema*.

10 African filmmakers were preceded by African writers, who responded to Western literature on Africa by *re-writing* Africa so that Western readers might transcend their preconceptions. The classic example is Chinua Achebe's *Things Fall Apart*, which has become a huge success: millions of copies have been sold in dozens of languages.

African films have usually been largely dependent on financial support from European sources: government agencies, non-governmental organizations, television networks, and a few commercial producers. Françoise Pfaff (1993) suggests that the impact of foreign finance varies according to its source. Films that obtain public funding have less commercial ambitions but are likely to suffer from tacit or manifest censorship or from self-censorship. Commercial interests, on the other hand, require profitability. They tend to seek multiple and varied publics and avoid hurting their political susceptibilities. In recent years non-governmental organizations based in Africa, but dependent on outside financial support, have begun to finance feature films for educational purposes. A notable example is Tsitsi Dangarembga's *Everyone's Child*, which focuses on the ravages of AIDS and the orphans the epidemic leaves behind.

The French government, in accordance with its policy of continued involvement in francophone Africa, has played a major role in supporting film production there (Barlet, 2000: 260–77). Since the early 1990s the European Union has taken on a similar role, but its support has also gone predominantly to the former French colonies. In consequence, the African films reaching us come primarily from these countries. Many have been produced in just two countries, Senegal and Burkina Faso. Specific circumstances explain why these two countries, small and extremely poor, should have taken a major place in African film production. Senegalese, in particular Paulin Soumanou Vieyra and Ousmane Sembène, pioneered African films, and Sembène, already known for his novels and short stories, was to gain world-wide renown with seven full-length feature films. Film production in Burkina Faso was encouraged by the establishment of the Institut Africain d'Education Cinématographique, the only film school in tropical Africa, which operated in the nation's capital Ouagadougou from 1976 to 1986, and by the Festival Panafricain du Cinéma de Ouagadougou (FESPACO), the African film festival held in Ouagadougou every two years since 1969. And the governments of both countries have provided some funding for film production.[11]

The distribution of even those films that seek to reach Western audiences has usually remained quite limited.[12] In the U.S. home video market, Inter Image Video pioneered the distribution of African films at low prices (one of our featured films, *Kasarmu Ce*, among them). The company failed to reach a larger public and has gone out of business recently. At this time, only one African film featured here, *La Vie est belle*, is promoted for the U.S. mass market, and it is priced at the high end. Six more are distributed in the U.S. by California Newsreel, the most important distributor of African films in the anglophone world. The audience for these films remains limited, and the videos are relatively expensive in spite of foundation support. Very few reach the market for video rentals and home videos, and screenings are by and large limited to festivals and college classrooms. Three more of the films featured here are distributed in the U.S. by New Yorker Films. Its videos are even more expensive and correspondingly limited in distribution.[13]

11 On film production in Burkina Faso see Tapsoba (2003); on FESPACO, see Diawara (1992: 128–39).

12 Some African films are distributed only in 16mm, a few others only on video, but most in both, and sometimes in 35mm as well. Film is more expensive than video, and less convenient to handle, but the quality of the projection is distinctly superior. However, film copies on rental are often quite worn out, and it requires the substantial investment of purchase to be assured of enjoying films to the fullest.

13 French versions of some of the films produced in francophone and lusophone countries are available in PAL and SECAM video from Médiathèque des Trois Mondes in Paris at low cost.

Introduction

I have included three more films even though they have only limited distribution, if any, at this time. *Kongi's Harvest* is based on an important play by Wole Soyinka, Africa's pre-eminent playwright and winner of the Nobel Prize in 1986.[14] *Fools*, derived from a novella by the prominent South African writer, Njabulo Ndebele, offers a complex post-*apartheid* perspective on life under *apartheid* in South Africa. And with *Kini and Adams* the distinguished director Idrissa Ouedraogo offers a fine example of filmmakers moving away from the common focus on social and political issues to an exploration of inter-personal relations. I meant to consider for inclusion *Love Brewed in the African Pot*, directed by Kwaw Ansah, the prominent Ghanaian filmmaker. This film enjoyed considerable success in Ghana and elsewhere in Africa, but I have not been able to view the film short of travelling to Ghana where the director holds the prints.

Multiple criteria may be adduced to label a film African. A film's setting, subject, perspective, and production stand out as important considerations. Nearly all the films featured here have been dependent on overseas finance, technicians and production facilities. Two films present the very perspectives that have distorted Western appreciation of Africa and serve to highlight the distorted perspectives on Africa conveyed by the films Western audiences are most likely to see. *Out of Africa*, a high-budget, hugely successful, Hollywood production, is utterly euro-centric. *The Gods Must Be Crazy* pretended that there is no racial conflict in South Africa; marketed with the claim that its *apartheid* fictions represented reality, its success on the international circuit surpassed all South African productions before or since and inspired a sequel as well as three Hong Kong feature films.

I have left aside African films that portray Africans in Europe and the U.S. They include a number of remarkable pioneering productions. *Afrique sur Seine*, one of the earliest films directed by a black African, follows an African student around Paris. The film is accompanied by a poetic commentary. It shows interracial couples and groups 'in spite of the machinations of men.' Ousmane Sembène's dramatic *Black Girl*, follows a maid from Dakar to her tragic destiny on the Côte d'Azur in France. Med Hondo's first full-length feature film, the avant-garde *Soleil O*, heavily loaded with symbolism, eventually dwells on the experience of immigrant workers in Paris. Jean-Marie Teno's heart-wrenching *Clando* moved from political repression in Cameroon in the 1990s to the expatriate community in Germany. And Moussa Touré's *Toubab bi* contrasted the integration African families provide for their members with the isolation suffered by some of the French a Senegalese visitor encounters in Paris. Most recently, Rachid Bouchareb's *Little Senegal* features Sotigui Kouyaté in the role of an elderly tourist guide at the Gorée slave dungeons prompted by a recurring dream to set out in search of the descendants of one of his kin sold into slavery two centuries ago. The film retraces the horrors of the slave trade, alludes to recent racially motivated killings in the U.S. and explores the difficult relationship between African-Americans and recent African immigrants.

14 Achebe's classic *Things Fall Apart* inspired Hans-Jürgen Pohland's *Bullfrog in the Sun*, subsequently retitled *Things Fall Apart*, which drew on Achebe's *No Longer At Ease* as well. It was also the source of two television series produced in Nigeria: an English version by the Nigerian Television Authority, and a different version for television in eastern Nigeria in Igbo. None of these attempts to trade on the extraordinary popularity of the novel has been a success.

Several other films focus on the slave trade. Med Hondo's *West Indies*, adapted from a play by Daniel Boukman, evokes the history of slavery in the Caribbean in the form of a musical. Haile Gerima's *Sankofa* is the highly dramatic, beautifully crafted fable of an African-American tourist who finds herself taken back in time to join slaves at Cape Coast Castle, in present-day Ghana, and who comes to endure the slave experience in the Caribbean. Roger Gnoan Mbala's *Adanggamon* focuses on the slave trade organized by an African despot.

African Film offers comprehensive accounts of seventeen films and touches on many more. Most African films give major play to social, cultural, and political issues, and I have emphasized these by my selection of featured films, by organizing this book in terms of five conflicts, and in privileging an analysis focused on society, culture, and politics. The featured films cover a wide range of topics, from new perspectives on Africa prior to the intrusion of the West, to the struggle against colonialism and white minority rule, to post-colonial issues of authoritarian rule, neo-colonialism, corruption, inequality, and the condition of the peasantry, with the position of women a recurrent theme. I conclude, though, with two films that move away from 'African' issues to resemble Western films focusing on personal relationships.

A few major political themes are not covered by the featured films. The imposition of colonial rule and the colonial experience have elicited little response from African directors. And while most African films situate themselves in the post-colonial period, and often focus on political issues, virtually no attention has been given to contemporary ethnic and religious conflicts, the ill-fated attempts to introduce socialism on the continent,[15] and the civil wars which have ravaged a number of African countries. Med Hondo did direct *Sarraounia*, the epic story of the confrontation between the Aznas of Niger, led by Queen Sarraounia, and French colonial troops. And Ousmane Sembène produced major films on French colonialism and religious conflict. His *Ceddo* focuses on Muslim and Christian missionaries and the slave trade; *Emitaï* recounts an historical incident of brutal repression when village women refused to deliver grain to the French colonial authorities in Senegal in 1942; and *Camp de Thiaroye* is based on the historic revolt of African soldiers mistreated while about to be discharged in 1944.[16] For the post-colonial period, Sembène's *Guelwaar* is unique in touching on the potential for religious conflict. I have preferred to feature Sembène's *Xala*, arguably his most important film, based on his eponymous novel.

Four of the films featured in this book are based on novels, three more on a play, an epic, or an autobiography. The transformation involved in bringing the written page, or the *griot's* recitation, to the screen invites special attention. I have focused on the different opportunities the various media provide and explored the specific agenda of the writers and directors, in particular the different audiences they intended to reach. I also discuss novels such as Chinua Achebe's *Things Fall Apart* and Shimmer Chinodya's *Harvest of Thorns* in relation to films that bear on the same topics.

15 The socialist alternative to Western-style development is the subject of two penetrating novels. Pepetela anticipated the constraints of socialism in independent Angola in *Mayombe*. Henri Lopes presented a critique of socialist practice in the Congo (Brazzaville) in *Sans Tam-tam*. Unlike writers and filmmakers elsewhere, Pepetela and Lopes wrote from within the ruling circle: Pepetela was Minister of Education at one time, Lopes Prime Minister.

16 *Camp de Thiaroye* illustrates the problematic of the fictional representation of specific historical events. In this case, Sembène and his co-director Thierno Faty Sow dramatized the action, and demonized colonialism, by taking considerable liberties with the historical record. In particular, the infamous massacre of the African soldiers, repatriated from Europe during World War II, was not perpetrated by tanks attacking sleeping men but by troops ordered to open fire when mutinous soldiers ran to fetch their weapons. For a discussion, see Gugler (2004).

Introduction

African film production over the last four decades has been substantial and there is considerable diversity in themes and styles. The diversity is still apparent across the films featured here even as it is attenuated by my predilection for films that address social, cultural, and political issues, leading me to omit such widely acclaimed films as Souleymane Cissé's *Yeelen* and Djibril Diop Mambety's *Hyenas*. Still, the orientation of many African filmmakers combines with the constraints they all experience to warrant generalizations that apply widely. They may be summarized *grosso modo* by highlighting the affinity between many African films and Italian neo-realism. The affinity is thematic: like their Italian counterparts at the end of World War II, African filmmakers after independence were intent on a critical examination of their societies. It is also grounded in the material context: at that time struggling production companies confronted Italian filmmakers with financial constraints not unlike those African film production has had to deal with to this day. There are thus striking parallels between many of the films produced two continents and several decades apart. As Oliver Barlet (2000: 21) spells out the kinship with Italian neo-realism: 'in many African films one finds an aesthetic close to news footage (documentary images, rejection of effects, unsophisticated editing), non-professional actors, the use of natural settings and a degree of improvisation.' If Western audiences tired of neo-realism's portrayal of everyday life after a few years, a major appeal of African films for Western viewers continues to reside in the window they open on the experiences of ordinary African people. We will conclude this introduction by examining in more detail some recurring characteristics of African films.

Ousmane Sembène began producing films in Wolof so as to make them accessible to his fellow Senegalese. More generally, authenticity as well as amateur actors have made an African language or a creole the language of choice. Other films use a European language, but often it is French or Portuguese rather than English. A number of films reproduce the common pattern of people switching between languages. African films have not been dubbed into English because their limited distribution does not warrant the cost. The viewer thus has to contend with several problems created by subtitles. Some, especially in older films, are hard to read. All necessarily provide only an abridged rendition of the dialogue whenever it becomes expansive. The quality of the translation sometimes leaves something to be desired. Most exasperatingly, the attention required to catch the subtitles distracts from the picture. There is a solution to that last problem: view the film a second time and disregard the subtitles!

African films, even when subsidized, have to be produced on extremely low budgets because of their limited markets – the budgets of fourteen African films featured here come, together, to less than half the $40 million budget of *Out of Africa*. Filmmakers are further constrained by the dearth of local technicians. The pool of experienced actors is slowly increasing, but there is little money to pay them. Directors are particularly hampered by the absence of local processing facilities. South

Africa is the only country South of the Sahara to have functioning film laboratories, and most films from tropical Africa continue to be processed in Europe. Directors usually do not get to view rushes while they are shooting. By the time they get to see the product of their labors, it is much too late to shoot afresh any unsatisfactory scenes. Finally, African filmmakers are acutely aware of the threat of censorship which hangs over them in most countries most of the time.

African directors invariably find themselves in extremely difficult situations; they produce their films against all odds; they are truly film-makers. One consequence is that they exert much more control over their productions than directors of high-budget films elsewhere. He, very rarely she, writes the script, seeks funding far and wide, recruits and trains the mostly amateur actors, and assembles the crew. African film is a *cinéma d'auteur,* and it comes at a price. After producing *Yaaba,* Idrissa Ouedraogo talked of having lost ninety per cent of his energy in the search for the money, the development of the story, and the creation of the setting (Bax, 1989). Saddik Balewa has spoken of the 'nightmare' of raising funds for *Kasarmu Ce,* characterized the conditions of filming as 'pure suicide,' and complained that he did not get to view most of the footage he shot until months later (Bandele-Thomas, 1991; Dalby and Givanni, 1993).

Les Fespakistes, by François Kotlarski and Eric Münch presents short comments by 50-odd filmmakers and actors at FESPACO 1999 and 2001. Mweze Ngangura spoke for many:

> I am a cineaste from the Congo [Kinshasa]. But I am a cineaste who comes from a country where there is no office whatsoever concerned with cinema, no institution whatsoever in charge of cinema. I am a cineaste who comes from a country where there are no producers. I am a cineaste who comes from a country where film distribution does not exist and where there is no movie theater that can project 35mm film. In spite of everything, I am a cineaste, and that's it. (my translation)

African films are different from Western films and television in other ways as well. Some of the differences reflect the different perspective African directors bring to bear on Africa – the very focus of our exploration. Others reflect the different cultural context. Perhaps most disconcerting to viewers used to Western films which have come to move ever faster, one dramatic event chasing after another, is the fact that many African films proceed in a much more leisurely manner. Their pace reflects the reality of societies where life usually is not as hectic as in modern industrial societies, but it also serves to give Western viewers time to take in unfamiliar settings, ideas, and actions. As Andrée Davanture, who edited many films for francophone African directors, observed: 'A fast-moving film imposes a way of looking on the viewers, a point of view, whereas a slow film allows them the freedom to see what they want to see, to involve themselves, to make discoveries' (Barlet, 2000: 171). Indeed, developments in African films often appear unpredictable to Western viewers in as much as they are unfamiliar with the context of different cultures, poor countries, and often repressive politics, and need time to familiarize themselves with the foreign environments.

Introduction

Most African films adopt a realistic mode. Ode Okore (1982: 290–1) has spelt out the implications in terms of camera work with reference to the *œuvre* of Ousmane Sembène, the man who has been called 'the father of African cinema':

> The deliberate slowness and simplicity ... characterizes all the films, particularly in the use of long takes. The attempt is partly to allow the audience enough time, and with minimum difficulty, to digest information and partly to reflect the reality of the slowness which characterizes much of African life. The need to maintain spatial and temporal realities also compels an unspectacular camera display. It will be seen, for instance, that almost throughout his camera remains at an eye-level – that is, no indulgence in high- or low-angle theatrics. For Sembène, man sees the world basically from two positions: either sitting down or standing up. This is basic reality, and anything else is mere contrivance. Similarly, his persistent use of tracking shots derives from a need to situate his characters within the same, unfragmented space. Indeed, Sembène's insistence on presenting time and space realistically is so strong that even the use of such an expressionistic cinematic code as montage is subordinated to it. Thus ... montage images are realized through, not Eisensteinian cross-cutting, but a *mise-en-scène*. Throughout, the narrative technique must be made to serve ... the purpose of the content, which is to reproduce a particular social reality. Indeed, the great necessity to present this social reality and to make it understandable to his African audience, his primary audience, and significantly too, the desire to make 'man' the center of his creative activity, forces Sembène to superordinate the cultural to the purely cinematic codes. It is in the consistent fusing of these recognizable elements in the narrative ... that his filmic aesthetics achieves its distinctiveness.

Other major characteristics that distinguish African films reflect different choices made by African directors in terms of subject and presentation. Western films tend to focus on individuals – while usually denying individuality to African characters. In contrast most African films, while establishing distinct individuals, move beyond them to give major play to social, cultural, and political issues. African films tend to focus on groups rather than individuals. Their camera typically operates at mid-range. As Cheick Oumar Sissoko commented when discussing his film *Finzan*:

> I avoided close-ups and a tight focus generally. I know American films do this, and I see it as a technique to idealize the individual. My intention was to show that people are never isolated. I didn't want to emphasize individuality. It's not one person but the group effort that influences events.
> I tried to give my characters individuality as well; Nanyuma is the most typical example. I wanted to show her sentiments, but I wanted to integrate that into her social reality. (Aufderheide, 1990: 30)

The absence of violence in most African films is striking after the usual U.S. fare. And indeed, after the violence of slavery, of colonialism, and of post-colonial conflicts, gratuitous violence seems obscene. Violence is shown in films on political struggles, and the violence there, in particular torture scenes, can be quite unsettling to Western audiences inured to different kinds of violence. In fact, cultural expectations are so ingrained that many Western viewers comfortable with extreme displays of violence in Hollywood movies are turned off by spitting in the final scene of Ousmane Sembène's classic *Xala*. As for explicit sex and nudity, African films qualify for parental guidance rating in this respect as well. African directors tell stories of love, but they are discreet. They operate within the strictures of Islam in some countries and of censorship in most. But there is also the issue that a film displaying bare-breasted women risks recalling the voyeuristic Western gaze on Africans. I do promise you beautiful and dignified people such as the children and 'grandma' in *Yaaba*, the *griot* in *Keïta*, the couple in *Sambizanga*, the first wife in *Xala*, the movie star to be and the musician already famous who serenades her in *Tableau Ferraille*, the 'most beautiful girl in town' in *The Blue Eyes of Yonta*, the hermit in *Kasarmu Ce*, the belle in *La Vie est belle*.

Enjoy re-imagining Africa!

References and Further Reading

Achebe, Chinua. 1958. *Things Fall Apart*. African Writers Series 1. London: Heinemann.

——. 1960. *No Longer At Ease*. African Writers Series 3. London: Heinemann.

Adanggamon. 2000. Film directed by Roger Gnoan Mbala, written by Jean-Marie Adiaffi and Yao Bertin Akaffou. Distributed in the U.S. by New Yorker Films. 90 minutes.

Afrique sur Seine (Africa on the Seine). 1957. Film directed by Mamadou Sarr and Paulin Soumanou Vieyra, scenario by Mamadou Sarr, commentary by Paulin Soumanou Vieyra and Mamadou Sarr. Produced by Le Groupe Africain du Cinéma (France). Available for viewing at Cinémathèque Afrique, Paris. 21 minutes.

Ain el Ghezal (Gazelle's Eye)/*La Fille de Carthage* (The Girl from Carthage). 1924. Film written, directed, and produced by Albert Samama-Chikli (Tunisia). The Centre National du Cinéma, Paris, has restored an incomplete 19 minute copy in 35mm.

Aouré (Wedding). 1962. Film written and directed by Mustapha Alassane. Produced by Myriam Smadja (Niger). Available for viewing at Cinémathèque Afrique, Paris. 30 minutes.

Aufderheide, Pat. 1990. 'Interview: Cheikh Oumar Sissoko,' *Black Film Review* 6 (2): 4–5, 30.

Balogun, Françoise. 1987. *The Cinema in Nigeria*. Enugu: Delta Publications.

Bandele-Thomas, 'Biyi. 1991. 'This Land is Ours.' *West Africa* 3857, 12–18 August: 1326–7.

Barlet, Olivier. 2000 (1996). *African Cinemas: Decolonizing the Gaze*. London/New York: Zed Books. Revised and updated translation, by Chris Turner, of *Les cinémas d'Afrique noire: Le regard en question*. Collection Images plurielles. Paris: L'Harmattan.

Bax, Dominique (1989) 'Dans mon village...' *Le Nouvel Afrique Asie* 1, 2 October, pages 41–2.

Black Girl/La Noire de... 1966. Film written and directed by Ousmane Sembène. Produced by Les Actualités Françaises (France) and Filmi Doomireew (Senegal). Distributed in the U.S. by New Yorker Films. 65 minutes.

Borom Sarret. 1963. Film written and directed by Ousmane Sembène. Produced by Filmi Doomireew (Senegal) and Actualités Françaises (France). Distributed in the U.S. by New Yorker Films. 22 minutes.

Boughedir, Ferid. 1987. *Le Cinéma africain de A à Z*. Cinémas d'Afrique Noire. Bruxelles: OCIC.

Boukman, Daniel. 1971. *Les Négriers, Pièce en 3 parties*. Honfleur: P. J. Oswald.

Bullfrog in the Sun/Things Fall Apart. 1971. Film directed by Hans-Jürgen Pohland. Produced by Nigram, Calpenny-Nigeria Films Ltd, and Cine 3.

Burroughs, Edgar Rice. 1912. 'Tarzan of the Apes.' *The All-Story*, October 241–372.

Cameron, Kenneth M. 1994. *Africa on Film: Beyond Black and White*. New York: Continuum.

Camp de Thiaroye. 1988. Film written and directed by Ousmane Sembène and Thierno Faty Sow. Produced by Société Nouvelle de Promotion Cinématographique (Senegal), ENAPROC (Algeria), and SATPEC (Tunisia). Distributed in the U.S. by New Yorker Films. 152 minutes.

Ceddo. 1976. Film written and directed by Ousmane Sembène. Produced by Filmi Doomireew (Senegal). Distributed in the U.S. by New Yorker Films. 120 minutes.

Chinodya, Shimmer. 1989. *Harvest of Thorns*. Harare: Baobab Books. African Writers Series. Oxford/ Portsmouth, NH/Ibadan/Nairobi/Gabarone: Heinemann.

Chronicle of a Genocide Foretold. 1996. Documentary directed by Danièle Lacourse and Yvan Patry. Distributed in the U.S. by First Run/Icarus Films. 141 minutes.

Clando (Clandestine). 1996. Film written and directed by Jean-Marie Teno. Produced by Les Films du Raphia (France), Zweites Deutsches Fernsehen (Germany), Arte (France), and Le Messager Film (France). Distributed in the U.S. by California Newsreel. 98 minutes.

Come Back, Africa. 1959. Film directed by Lionel Rogosin, written by Lionel Rogosin with Lewis Nkosi and William (Bloke) Modisane. Produced by Lionel Rogosin (USA). Distributed in North America by Villon Films. 83 minutes.

Dalby, Alexa, and June Givanni. 1993. 'Film Face of Africa.' *The Herald* (Glasgow), 11 May, 16.

Davis, Peter. 1996. *In Darkest Hollywood: Exploring the Jungles of Cinema's South Africa*. Johannesburg: Ravan Press; Athens: Ohio University Press.

Diawara, Manthia. 1992. *African Cinema: Politics & Culture*. Blacks in the Diaspora. Bloomington/Indianapolis: Indiana University Press.

Ekwuazi, Hyginus O. (1987) 1991. *Film in Nigeria*. Jos: Nigerian Film Corporation.

Emitaï. 1971. Film written and directed by Ousmane Sembène. Produced by Filmi Doomireew (Senegal). Distributed in the U.S. by New Yorker Films. 101 minutes.

Everyone's Child. 1996. Film directed by Tsitsi Dangarembga, written by Shimmer Chinodya. Produced by Media for Development Trust (Zimbabwe). Distributed in the U.S. by California Newsreel. 90 minutes.

Guelwaar. 1992. Film written and directed by Ousmane Sembène. Produced by Filmi Doomireew (Senegal), Galatée Films (France), and FR3 Film Production (France). Distributed in the U.S. by New Yorker Films. 105 minutes.

Gugler, Josef. 2004. 'Fiction, Fact, and the Responsibility of the Critic: *Camp de Thiaroye, Yaaba*, and *The Gods Must Be Crazy*.' *Focus on African Film*, edited by Françoise Pfaff. Bloomington: Indiana University Press.

Haynes, Jonathan. 1995. 'Nigerian Cinema: Structural Adjustments.' *Research in African Literatures* 26: 97–119.

Herdsmen of the Sun/Hirten der Sonne. 1989. Documentary directed by Werner Herzog. Produced by Werner Herzog Filmproduktion (Germany), Süddeutscher Rundfunk (Germany), and Arion Productions (France). Distributed in the U.S. by Kino International. 52 minutes.

Hoffelt, Sophie. 2003. 'Cheick Oumar Sissoko: "La tragique absence de nos images dans l'univers des images".' *CinémAction* 106: 122–3.

Hyenas/Hyènes. 1992. Written and directed by Djibril Diop Mambety. Produced by ADR Productions (France), Thelma Film (Switzerland), Maag Daan (Senegal), and MK2 Productions (France). Distributed in the U.S. by California Newsreel and Kino International. 113 minutes.

In Darkest Hollywood: Cinema and Apartheid. 1993. Documentary written, filmed, and edited by Daniel Riesenfeld and Peter Davis. Produced by Nightingale (USA) and Villon (USA). Distributed by Villon Films. 112 minutes.

Khlifi, Omar. 1970. *Histoire du cinéma en Tunisie*. Tunis: Société Tunisienne de Diffusion.

La Bague du Roi Koda (King Koda's Ring). 1962. Film written and directed by Mustapha Alassane. Produced by Myriam Smadja (Niger). Available for viewing at Cinémathèque Afrique, Paris. 24 minutes.

La Leçon de Cinéma (The Cinema Lesson). 1951. Film directed by Albert Mongita.

The Language You Cry In. 1998. Documentary produced and directed by Alvaro Toepke and Angel Serrano. Distributed in the U.S. by California Newsreel. 52 minutes.

Last Grave at Dimbaza. 1973. Documentary directed by Nana Mahomo. Produced by Morena Films (South Africa). 55 minutes.

Les Fespakistes. 2001. Documentary written and directed by François Kotlarski and Eric Münch. Produced by Couleurs Films (France), ArteFilm (France), Cityzen Télévision (France), and Cinécom Productions (Burkina Faso). 52 minutes.

Les Pneus gonflés (The Tires Inflated). 1953. Film directed by Emmanuel Lubalu.

Little Senegal. 2001. Film directed by Rachid Bouchareb, written by Olivier Lorelle et Rachid Bouchareb. Produced by 3B Productions (France). 98 minutes.

Lopes, Henri. 1977. *Sans tam-tam.* Yaounde: Editions CLE.

Love Brewed in the African Pot. 1981. Film written and directed by Kwaw Ansah. Produced by Film Africa (Ghana). 125 minutes.

Mansour, Guillemette. 2000. *Samama Chikly: Un Tunisien à la rencontre du XXe siècle.* Tunis: Simpact Editions.

Mouramani. 1953. Film directed by Mamadou Touré. 23 minutes.

Nigerian Cinema: Pioneers & Practioners. 2000. Documentary directed by Bankole Bole. Produced by the Nigerian Film Corporation. 45 minutes.

Okore, Ode. 1982. 'The Film World of Ousmane Sembène'. Ph.D. dissertation, Columbia University.

Otten, Rik, with Victor Bachy. 1984. *Le Cinéma dans les pays des Grands Lacs: Zaïre Rwanda Burundi.* Cinémas d'Afrique Noire. Brussels: OCIC; Paris: L'Harmattan.

Pepetela (Artur Carlos Maurício Pestana dos Santos). 1979. *Mayombe.* Lisbon: Edições 70. English translation by Michael Wolfers (1983) *Mayombe.* Harare: Zimbabwe Publishing House. African Writers Series. London/Ibadan/Nairobi: Heinemann.

Pfaff, Françoise. 1984. *The Cinema of Ousmane Sembene, A Pioneer of African Film.* Contributions in Afro-American and African Studies 79. Westport, CT/London: Greenwood Press.

——. 1988. *Twenty-Five Black African Filmmakers: A Critical Study, with Filmography and Bio-bibliography.* New York: Greenwood Press.

——. 1993. 'Impact de la co-production sur les composantes socioculturelles du cinéma d'Afrique francophone.' *Cinémas et liberté: Contributions au thème du FESPACO 93.* Paris/Dakar: Présence Africaine. 43–8.

Ramirez, Francis, and Christian Rolot. 1985. *Histoire du cinéma colonial au Zaïre, au Rwanda et au Burundi.* Annales – Série in-8° – Sciences Historiques 7. Tervuren: Musée Royal de l'Afrique Centrale.

Rasalama. 1947. Documentary directed by Raberono.

Sankofa. 1993. Film directed by Haile Gerima. Produced by Negod Gwad Productions (Ethiopia), Ghana National Commission, and DIPROCI (Burkina Faso). Distributed in the U.S. by Myphedu Films. 125 minutes.

Sarraounia. 1986. Film directed by Med (Mohamed Abib Médoun) Hondo, written by Med Hondo, Abdoulaye Mamani, and Abdoul War. Produced by Soleil O (France) and ORTN (Burkina Faso). Distributed in the U.S. by SPIA Media Productions. 121 minutes.

Sarzan. 1963. Film written and directed by Momar Thiam. Produced by Les Films Momar Thiam (Senegal). Available for viewing at Cinémathèque Afrique, Paris. 29 minutes.

Schmidt, Nancy J. 1988. *Sub-Saharan African Films and Filmmakers: An Annotated Bibliography/Films et cinéastes africains de la région subsaharienne: une bibliographie commentée.* London/New York: Hans Zell Publishers.

——. 1994. *Sub-Saharan African Films and Filmmakers, 1987–1992: An Annotated Bibliography.* London/Melbourne/Munich/New Jersey: Hans Zell Publishers.

Shafik, Viola. 2001. 'Egyptian Cinema', in Oliver Leaman (ed.) *Middle Eastern and North African Film.*

London/New York: Routledge. 21–129.

Sinda, Thierry. 1998. '2400 ans d'inventions mondiales finalisées par l'Occident/2400 Years of Global Inventions Culminating in the West: Le cinématographe.' *La Feuille* 7: 21–54.

Soleil O (O Sun) 1970. Film written and directed by Med (Mohamed Abib Médoun) Hondo. Produced by Soleil O (France). 102 minutes.

Tapsoba, Clément. 2003. '1980–2000: Les très riches années du cinéma burkinabè.' *CinémAction* 106: 124–35.

Tarzan of the Apes. 1918. Film directed by Scott Sidney. Produced by National Film (USA) 63 minutes.

Tarzan, the Ape Man. 1932. Film directed by W.S. Van Dyke, adaptation by Cyril Hume, dialogue by Ivor Novello. Produced by Metro Goldwyn Mayer (USA). Distributed in the U.S. by Swank Motion Pictures. 99 minutes.

Thabet, Madkour. 1998. *Industrie du film egyptien.* Série Prisme 3. Cairo: Département de l'Information Culturelle Etrangère, Ministère Egyptien de la Culture.

Tomaselli, Keyan. 1988. *The Cinema of Apartheid: Race and Class in South African Film.* Sandton: Century-Hutchinson; New York/Chicago: Smyrna/Lake View Press.

Toubab bi. 1991. Film written and directed by Moussa Touré. Produced by Valprod (France). Available for viewing at Cinémathèque Afrique, Paris. 100 minutes.

Tracteur Caterpillar labourant (Caterpillar Tractor Tilling). 1914. Documentary written, directed, and produced by Albert Samama-Chikli (Tunisia). The Centre National du Cinéma, Paris, has restored a 3 minute copy in 35 mm.

Tunis. 1907. Documentary written, directed, and produced by Albert Samama-Chikli (Tunisia). The Centre National du Cinéma, Paris, has restored a 2 minute copy in 35 mm.

Ukadike, Nwachukwu Frank. 1994. *Black African Cinema.* Berkeley/Los Angeles/London: University of California Press.

Vieyra, Paulin Soumanou. 1975. *Le Cinéma africain: Des origines à 1973.* Paris: Présence Africaine.

West Indies: Les Nègres marrons de la liberté. 1979. Film directed by Med (Mohamed Abib Medoun) Hondo. Produced by Soleil O (France), Yanek Sces (Mauritania), RTA (Algeria), IPC, ONCM (Mauritania). 110 minutes.

Yeelen (Brightness) 1987. Film written and directed by Souleymane Cissé. Produced by Les Films Cissé (Mali). Distributed in the U.S. by Kino International. 105 minutes.

Youssef, Ahmed. 1995. 'Une genèse cosmopolite.' *Egypte, 100 ans de cinéma*, edited by Magda Wassef. Librairie du Premier Siècle du Cinéma. Paris: Editions Plume and Institut du Monde Arabe. 52–73.

Zohra. 1922. Film written, directed, and produced by Albert Samama-Chikli (Tunisia). The Centre National du Cinéma, Paris, has restored a 10 minute copy in 35 mm.

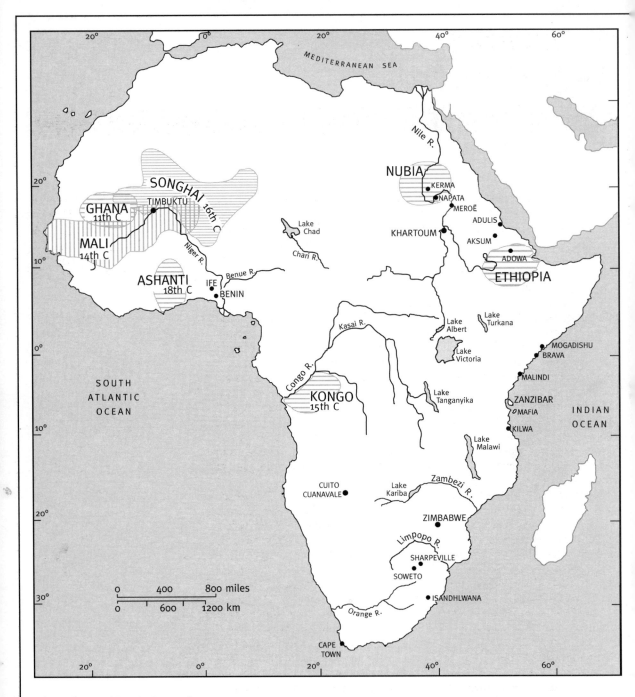

*Africa, showing historic sites, early
cities, pre-colonial African states and
major rivers and lakes*

1 Recovering the African Past

The desertification of the Sahara, about five millennia ago, created the world's largest desert. It all but isolated those living south of it from the rest of the world. Henceforth most contact with other peoples would occur on the coast. An account by the Greek historian Herodotus suggests that Phoenicians, under orders of Egypt's Pharaoh Necho, were the first to circumnavigate the continent, starting out at the Red Sea and returning through the Strait of Gibraltar in about 600 BCE.

Arab merchants have traded along the East African coast for two millennia. From the mingling of Africans and Arabs the Islamic Swahili culture arose. Based on cities on islands and along the coast, the Swahili traded with Arabia, Persia, India, and China, as well as the African interior. Coins were minted in Kilwa, Zanzibar, Mafia, and Mogadishu. A fifteenth-century Arab manual provides detailed sailing instructions for the very same East–West route the Phoenicians presumably took. Swahili, a north-eastern Bantu language rich in loan words from Arabic and several other languages, became the mother tongue of many coastal peoples and the *lingua franca* in a vast hinterland which by the nineteenth century reached as far as the present-day Congo (Kinshasa) and Zambia. After independence Swahili became the official language of Tanzania.

From Arab sources the Chinese had a pretty decent map of East Africa by the twelfth or thirteenth century. In 1417 Zheng He, Grand Eunuch of the Three Treasures, set out on his fifth great voyage West to escort home envoys from Malindi, Mogadishu, and Brava and bestow rewards on their rulers. They reached the East African coast the following year. A sixth expedition came in 1421–2. Some of its ships may have reached the Cape of Good Hope. A seventh expedition visited East Africa in 1431–3. But then the Emperor restricted shipping to the coastal waters of China.

The Chinese had little interest in Africa. The Arab slave trade remained circumscribed most of the time, and Arab rule was imposed only in a few small locations. It was Europeans who engendered the two traumatic experiences that profoundly affected Africa South of the Sahara over the last four centuries: the trans-Atlantic slave trade and colonial rule. Slavery and trading in slaves were common in many societies in Africa and elsewhere since time immemorial. However, the extent of the trans-Atlantic slave trade was without parallel: perhaps as many as 13 million people were taken from Africa to work in the

The colonialists have a habit of telling us that when they arrived in Africa they put us into history. You are well aware that it's the contrary – when they arrived they took us out of our own history. Liberation for us is to take back our destiny and our history. (Amílcar Cabral, quoted by Gabriel, 1973: 28)

plantations of the Americas, if they did not die *en route*. Many more died and entire communities were devastated in the wars that served to procure the human merchandise. And in the Americas, slavery entailed the master claiming racial superiority over the slave.

The Pope had decreed that the Spanish should explore to the West, the Portuguese to the East. Thus the Portuguese embarked on their voyages down the West African coast. In 1444 Portuguese reached the Cape Verde Islands, the western-most point of Africa. By 1460 they had established trade in gold and slaves along the coast as far as Sierra Leone. In 1483 they reached the Congo River and encountered the Kongo Kingdom. In 1488 they rounded the Cape of Good Hope, and in 1498 Vasco da Gama reached India whose lucrative spice trade had motivated much of Portuguese as well as Spanish exploration. But by 1526 Afonso, the Christian King of the Kongo, would write to his fellow sovereign, the King of Portugal, to complain of Portuguese merchants corrupting his people with Western merchandise bartered for slaves: '... it is *our will that in these Kingdoms there should not be any trade of slaves nor outlet for them* (Paiva-Manso, (1877) 1964: 192; emphasis in the original).

In 1807 the British banned the slave trade and then pressured other nations to sign anti-slave treaties. As the trade gradually came to an end in the nineteenth century, 'legitimate' trade flourished – palm oil greased the machines of the Industrial Revolution. At the same time, European missionaries ventured ever further inland to spread the Holy Word. Western European governments had been reluctant to get themselves involved in Africa, but they were prodded by traders as well as missionaries, and suddenly found themselves in competition with each other: the 'Scramble for Africa' was on, and nearly all West European countries joined in – Britain and France nearly went to war over conflicting claims in the Sudan in 1898.

In 1884–5 the European powers had met in Berlin and agreed on the rules for dividing up the African continent amongst themselves. Ironically Germany, the host of the proceedings, was to lose all its colonies in World War I. Its African colonies – Burundi, Cameroon, Namibia, Rwanda, the mainland of Tanzania, and Togo, to use their present-day names – became trust territories under the League of Nations and subsequently the United Nations. Their administration was entrusted to the powers who had conquered them during the war: Belgium, Britain, France, and South Africa. In practice they were treated little different from the territories their new masters controlled already.

Eventually the imperial powers took over virtually all of Africa. Liberia and Ethiopia, then known as Abyssinia, were the only exceptions. African-American settlers had landed on the Liberian coast in 1822, the first of some 15,000 to settle there. The colony was declared independent in 1847, and the United States provided it with a measure of protection when European powers coveted it subsequently. Menelik II, the Christian Emperor of Abyssinia, annihilated an Italian army of 20,000 men at Adowa in 1896, and the Italians sued for peace. Ethiopia, as it came to be called, remained independent, except for an

Italian occupation, imposed with tanks and airplanes, from 1936 to 1941.

Much of the European occupation of Africa involved deceit and a show of force. Traders or government agents persuaded African rulers to sign treaties they did not fully understand. The Italian version of the 1889 Treaty of Wichale differed from the Amharic version in giving Italy a protectorate over Abyssinia. When Africans showed their discontent, the invaders used 'gunboat diplomacy': a show of force. Africans did win battles at Adowa and elsewhere. In 1879, the Zulu army made short shrift of a thousand British riflemen with two guns camped at Isandhlwana. In 1885, the army of Muhammad Ahmad ibn Abdullah, the Mahdi, took Khartoum, defended by Charles George Gordon and six thousand men. In spite of such victories, the European powers succeeded in imposing colonial rule everywhere except Liberia and Ethiopia.

As a rule, European invaders easily crushed African resistance. Most battles were altogether lopsided as the invaders' superior weapons devastated even vastly larger forces: the European powers had agreed in the Brussels convention of 1890 not to sell their new weapons to Africans. The Maxim machine-gun had been patented in 1884, and Hilaire Belloc was to rhyme, in a poem entitled 'The Modern Traveller':

> Whatever happens, we have got
> The Maxim Gun, and they have not.

Also, the invaders recruited troops locally and trained them. They were usually well organized and disciplined. In contrast, their adversaries, even when they managed to obtain the newly introduced breech-loading and repeating rifles, found it difficult to use them to good effect.

The boundaries the European powers imposed cut across societies and cultures. With the assumption of colonial control European voices came to dominate the discourse about Africa: to this day they shape our image of Africa. Imperialists proclaimed superiority over the colonized. Henceforth they would affirm that Africa had no history, that they were enlightening the 'Dark Continent,' that they were there on a civilizing mission, that they were carrying the 'white man's burden,' as Rudyard Kipling, the troubadour of British imperialism, put it.

Africa, the cradle of mankind, has of course a long history (see map on page 16). In recent years more and more of that history has been pieced together from archeology, oral history, local writing where it was established – most famously the Timbuktu chronicles written in Arabic by Ibn al-Mukhtār and al-Saʿdī in the seventeenth century, and the writing of visitors such as Ibn Battūta who travelled along the East African coast and across the Sahara in the fourteenth century.

The earliest African cities have been unearthed along the middle Nile in present-day Sudan. Kerma, in Nubia, goes back to the third millennium BCE. After 730 BCE the Nubians conquered Egypt and ruled it for 60 years. When the Assyrian conquest of Egypt pushed them back to the south, the kings moved first to Napata, also known as Kush, and then to Meroë, mentioned in the fifth century BCE by Herodotus, who had travelled as far as Aswan.

Recovering the African Past

Aksum, in the highlands of Northern Ethopia, was an important trading center by the first century. Through the Red Sea port of Adulis it reached the Mediterranean and South Asia. Aksumite rulers issued coinage from the late third to the early seventh century and repeatedly waged military campaigns on the Arab peninsula. Aksum produced a fair body of written material, and, after the conversion to Christianity of the 'King of Kings' Ezana in the fourth century, the Bible and various literary works were translated from Greek, Arabic, and Syriac into Ge'ez. The medieval Ethiopian kingdoms, based on an expanding landowning class, connect Aksum with the modern world: the last 'King of Kings,' Emperor Haile Selassie of Ethiopia, was deposed in 1974.

The introduction of the camel opened up the era of the trans-Sahara trade about two millennia ago, and West Africa became the world's most important supplier of gold. When the Ghana Kingdom is first mentioned by Arab writers in the eighth century, it is referred to as the 'Gold Country.' Eventually Ghana declined, and early in the thirteenth century the Mali Empire arose. A century later Malian emperors exchanged embassies and gifts with the Sultan of Morocco. The pilgrimage of Emperor Mansā Mūsā to Mecca, in 1324–5, made the Empire famous in the world of Islam. He visited the Mamluk sultan of Egypt on his way. And he persuaded the Spanish poet and architect Abū Ishāq al-Sahilī, the Ismaili missionary al-Mu'ammar Abū 'Abdallāh ibn Khadīja al-Kūmī, and four shurafā' (descendants of the Prophet) to return with him to Mali. During the period of its greatest expansion, in the fourteenth century, Mali came to extend from the Atlantic eastward past the great bend of the Niger River. In the fifteenth century the Songhai Empire began to take on a pre-eminent role in the region. Now Timbuktu had its golden age as the rulers of Songhai made it their second capital. Scholarship at the mosque university of Sankoré, in contact with North Africa and Egypt, included many disciplines of the Islamic sciences: grammar, exegesis of the Koran, doctrinal theology, traditions of the Prophet, jurisprudence, the philosophy of jurisprudence, rhetoric, and logic. A large number of commentaries, transcribed by foreigners and locals, were studied with scholars who specialized in different disciplines. Ahmad Baba is reported to have lost as many as 1,600 volumes during the Moroccan invasion that brought the empire to an end in 1591.

The bronze and terracotta sculptures of the Yoruba and from Benin, in south-western Nigeria, have become world-famous. Some, from Ife, the first Yoruba state, date perhaps as early as the 12th century. When the Portuguese first visited Benin in 1485, it was a well-established state, with a large army conducting long campaigns far afield. Several tens of thousands inhabited the capital, Benin. A great many artisans worked for the King of Benin and major chiefs. They produced their finest sculptures from the fifteenth to the seventeenth centuries.

We might pursue our journey to visit other African states once prominent, but these examples suffice to help us to re-imagine Africa, to counter Western images of Africa established as master claimed superiority over slave, as European powers proclaimed their right to rule

Africa. Recent scholarship on African history enables us to correct some of the worst distortions as we learn of wealthy traders, mighty rulers, and flourishing civilizations. Still, most people in Africa, as elsewhere in the world until quite recently, were farmers, cattle herders, or hunter-gatherers. Even as we delight in African prowess, we need to start out re-imagining Africa by discovering the humanity and individuality of common people who are omitted from oral epics and written chronicles. Chinua Achebe's classic *Things Fall Apart* made us appreciate how custom, culture, and change characterize village society. Shortly we will examine a film that similarly makes us partake of village society. Another will introduce us to one of the great epics recalling a renowned empire. Like African literature these films take us beyond the stereotypes of the Other. But before we move beyond these stereotypes, we will discuss *Out of Africa,* perhaps the most prominent example of Western cinematic approaches to Africa.

References and Further Reading

Achebe, Chinua. 1958. *Things Fall Apart*. London: Heinemann.

Belloc, Hilaire. 1907. *Cautionary Tales*. London.

Blier, Suzanne Preston. 1998. *The Royal Arts of Africa: The Majesty of Form*. New York: Harry N. Abrams; Upper Saddle River, NJ: Prentice Hall.

Connah, Graham. (1987) 2001. *African Civilizations. Precolonial Cities and States in Tropical Africa: an Archaeological Perspective*. Second edition. Cambridge/New York/Cape Town: Cambridge University Press.

Freund, Bill. (1984) 1998. *The Making of Contemporary Africa: The Development of African Society Since 1800*. Second edition. Boulder, CO: Lynne Rienner.

Gabriel, Teshome H. 1973. 'Tribute to a Fallen Comrade'. *Ufahamu* 3 (3): 25–9.

Ibn Battūta. 1355. *Tuhfat al-nuzzar fī gharā'ib al-amsār wa-'ajā'ib al-asfār*. English translation of accounts of travels in East and West Africa by Said Hamdun and Noel King (1975) *Ibn Battuta in Black Africa*. London: Rex Collings.

Ibn al-Mukhtār. 1665 (1913). *Ta'rīkh al-fattāsh*. French translation by O. Houdas and M. Delafosse, *Tarikh el-Fettach ou chronique du chercheur pour servir à l'histoire des villes, des armées et des principaux personnages du Tekrour*. Documents Arabes relatifs à l'histoire du Soudan 3. Paris: Ernest Leroux.

Levtzion, Nehemia. (1973) 1980. *Ancient Ghana and Mali*. London: Methuen. Reprint with additions. New York/London: Africana Publishing.

Paiva-Manso, Visconde de. 1877. *Historia do Congo (Documentos)*. Lisbon. English transl. of extracts by Basil Davidson (1964) *The African Past: Chronicles from Antiquity to Modern Times*. Boston/Toronto: Little, Brown.

Pakenham, Thomas. 1991. *The Scramble for Africa 1876–1912*. London: George Weidenfeld & Nicolson; New York: Random House.

Pearson, Michael N. 1998. *Port Cities and Intruders: the Swahili Coast, India, and Portugal in the Early Modern Era*. Baltimore, MD: Johns Hopkins University Press.

Pouwels, Randall 2000. 'The East African Coast'. In Nehemia Levtzion and Randall Pouwels (eds) *The History of Islam in Africa*. Athens: Ohio University Press; Oxford: James Currey; Cape Town: David Philip. 251–71.

Reader, John. 1998. *Africa: A Biography of the Continent*. London: Hamish Hamilton; New York: Knopf.

al-Sa'dī. 1655. *Ta'rīkh al-sūdān*. English translation by John O. Hunwick (1999), *Timbuktu and the Songhay Empire: Al-Sa'dī's Ta'rīkh al-sūdān down to 1613 and other Contemporary Documents*. Islamic History and Civilization: Studies and Texts 27. Leiden/Boston/Köln: Brill.

Snow, Philip. 1988. *The Star Raft: China's Encounter with Africa*. New York: Weidenfeld & Nicolson.

BASED ON A TRUE STORY.

ROBERT REDFORD   MERYL STREEP

A SYDNEY POLLACK Film

OUT OF AFRICA

A MIRAGE Production "OUT OF AFRICA"
KLAUS MARIA BRANDAUER
Co-Producer TERRY CLEGG Executive Producer KIM JORGENSEN Associate Producer JUDITH THURMAN and ANNA CATALDI Music by JOHN BARRY
Screenplay by KURT LUEDTKE Produced and Directed by SYDNEY POLLACK

A UNIVERSAL Picture

Out of Africa 1985
Settler Romance in Nature Paradise

Out of Africa is the most successful film ever to be set in Africa. The nostalgic tale of Karen Christentze Dinesen, who married a friend to escape from her native Denmark and become Baroness Blixen, who joined the emerging settler class in Kenya just before the outbreak of World War I,[1] and who went hunting with her lover Denys Finch Hatton in the magnificent setting of the Rift Valley, attracted a much larger public than those already entranced by her writings. Renowned actors such as Meryl Streep, Robert Redford, and Klaus Maria Brandauer further enhanced the film's appeal. The khaki chic of Meryl Streep set off a fashion trend (Conant, 1986), and Dinesen's *Out of Africa* made the U.S. and British bestseller lists. With the help of a budget of close to $40 million that ensured excellent 'production values', Sydney Pollack had created an outstanding film. Seven Academy Awards, including best picture, and numerous other awards in the U.S. and elsewhere, gave the film wide recognition. World-wide box office receipts have surpassed $200 million. *Out of Africa* continues to be shown regularly on the Disney Channel, and it is readily available in just about every video store.

Out of Africa is the most important recent example of the 'beautiful Africa' approach to Africans in the West. The film takes us to the Garden of Eden,[2] it presents Europeans as the masters of that universe, and it has Western viewers identify with them and their view of the land and the people. *Out of Africa* finds a plausible scenario for images of white dominance by its choice of time and place. The film is set in an early phase of colonialism – indeed, this part of East Africa was still a British 'protectorate' when Karen Blixen first arrived. And it takes us to one of the few settler colonies: the comfortable climate and fertile lands attracted European settlers to what came to be known as the 'White Highlands.' The film poster, repeated in most countries with little variation, invites us to join the bliss of Meryl Streep and Robert Redford lounging in the Garden of Eden. It has been so popular as to become the only poster of any of the films featured here to be reproduced commercially. *Out of Africa* presents an Africa long gone, focuses on a setting where Europeans live off the labor of Africans who have been dispossessed of their land, and shows contented Africans serving their white masters: the farm workers sing happily as they harvest the coffee for their mistress. We are far from Tarzan, but the white man – and the white lady – continue to be the dominant figures in the Western image of Africa.

We are treated to similar pictures from a time long gone, when dispossessed Africans labored for their white masters – happily, we are supposed to believe – in another outstanding and immensely successful Hollywood film: *Gone With the Wind* held the record of having grossed the

[Western films put] us in the background, which is where we are in Western history. Africans are betrayed on the screen ... They are part of the landscape and they are used for a function – like to bring an orange juice to the master – and they walk out of the scene. We are never human beings. We are underdeveloped characters. Our sex life, our feelings of love or hatred are not explored because they don't see us as part of a society. (Haile Gerima quoted by Pfaff, 1977: 28)

1 The film has Karen Dinesen arrive in Kenya in 1913 and stay for about a decade. Actually, she disembarked in Mombasa in January 1914 and, after several trips to Europe, finally left in 1931. Foreshortening her stay may have served to enhance the drama of the story. And putting her arrival a year earlier highlighted that she arrived before the outbreak of World War I in August 1914.

2 East Africa is of course quite literally the Garden of Eden where the human species originated about 1.8 million years ago.

Recovering the African Past

most money ever for half a century. The difference is that by the 1980s the racism of the film classic was widely recognized and rejected,[3] whereas a similar account from Africa was widely praised – in the West. But how does the portrayal of Farah Aden, Kamante Gatura, and Chief Kinanjui look to their great-grandchildren? To the one perhaps studying colonialism at the University of Nairobi right now?

Out of Africa offers a variety of perspectives on the colonial experience, or more precisely on the experience of one of the few colonies where Europeans settled in substantial numbers, appropriated the land to themselves, and made Africans work their estates. These perspectives range from the conservative to the patronizing to the domineering. But they are all European perspectives, and they invariably take the master status of Europeans for granted. Denys Finch Hatton stands for nostalgia and benign neglect: 'Don't turn Africans into little Englishmen,' 'we are only passing through.' Chief Kinanjui is portrayed as a conservative preoccupied with retaining his power. His 'The British can read – and what good has it done them?' is good for laughs that drown out the obvious rejoinder that they have managed to establish themselves in power in foreign lands. Baron Blixen's 'The servants are wonderful' illustrates Haile Gerima's observation: white cinema goers are treated to the vicarious experience of belonging to the master race. And Baroness Blixen represents the gentle face of paternalism, or rather maternalism: some education, some health care, some land for 'my Gikuyu.'[4] It is left to the anonymous settler who gets into an argument with Baroness Blixen and a fight with Barclay Cole on New Year's Eve to suggest the vulnerability of the colonial regime. He is opposed to educating Africans – perhaps he understands that educated Africans will challenge the colonial dispensation and cease to be such wonderful servants.[5]

Indeed, at about that time educated Africans began to assert themselves. In 1921 they established the Kikuyu Central Association. Jomo Kenyatta became its Secretary in 1928, demanding land reform and political rights for Africans. He went to England in 1930, got a Ph.D. at the London School of Economics, and published his dissertation *Facing Mount Kenya*, an account of Gikuyu society, in 1938, just one year after the appearance of Karen Blixen's *Out of Africa*, published under the semi-pseudonym Isak Dinesen. Perhaps we cannot expect the retired settler to have been sensitive to these developments, but we should expect such sensitivity from Hollywood, many years after Kenyatta had become the first President of independent Kenya in 1963, at a time of growing protests against the racism of *apartheid* South Africa.[6]

A few elements in the film remind the keen observer that Africans were no longer all that 'traditional' even in the early days of colonialism. Young Kamante speaks English. When conversing with Farah and Baroness Blixen, Chief Kinanjui does not speak his own Gikuyu language but instead uses Swahili, the East African *lingua franca*, a fact lost on most Western viewers and one that the film does not care to convey. And some of the servants are practicing Islam, another major world religion

3 On the distortions of the historical record in *Gone With the Wind*, see Chadwick (2001: 189–98).

4 I am using the more recent spelling of the name of the largest ethnic group in Kenya who previously were referred to as Kikuyu.

5 Instead of acknowledging the challenge educated Africans posed for colonialism, Western fiction usually ridiculed them. The classic example is Joyce Cary's *Mister Johnson*, recently resurrected on the screen. The all too many similar treatments of educated African-Americans are painful to remember, but at least they are a thing of the past.

6 Just about the time *Out of Africa* was released Hollywood began to produce several films denouncing the *apartheid* regime.

*Farah Aden and Baroness Blixen
arrive at the army camp*

come from foreign lands. But these are minor elements lost in a flood of images of other races serving Europeans. The devotion of African servants, and Indians at the club, to their masters is all the more striking when compared with Blixen's relationship with her grumpy American foreman. The Africans in *Out of Africa* only exist in relation to their masters. If Farah appears, rather implausibly and in fact contrary to her account, unattached to family and kin, this reinforces the image of his exclusive devotion to his mistress. The distance between the races is extreme: Denys does not talk with his companion; Barclay 'thinks' that his mistress is fond of him. Only in the relationship between the lonely Baroness Blixen and Farah does the film ever so tentatively begin to bridge the gap between the races.[7]

The scene of Blixen arriving with the supply wagon at the army camp tellingly conveys it all. The camera shows an exhausted and disheveled woman: we are made to see the hardship she endured. There is no suggestion that the Africans who made the trek possible suffered like her, or indeed that the journey was harder on them: they walked, while she rode on her horse. Her servants had risked their lives as a matter of course, while her American foreman had told her in no uncertain terms that ferrying war supplies was not part of his contract.[8]

Out of Africa takes white superiority and dominance for granted. Instead of problematizing race relations, it makes gender into the salient issue. From the historical record and from her writings, Karen Blixen appears as an independent and assertive woman, and gender is not a

7 Claire Denis's *Chocolat* offers a quite different, sensitive portrayal of the colonial context and interracial relations as the director recalls her childhood in Cameroon in the 1940s.

8 Here as elsewhere the film dramatizes: in real life Baroness Blixen made several much less adventurous supply treks over shorter distances.

Chief Kinanjui: the Hollywood portrayal of the fellow-aristocrat Baroness Blixen described

9 In Charles Kiselyk's documentary *A Song of Africa* Streep takes a feminist stance against Pollack on certain issues.

10 The contrast between Karen Blixen's 'feudal mirage' and the historical context in Kenya is elucidated by Kennedy (1987).

11 Ngũgĩ wa Thiong'o, Kenya's foremost writer, presents some of the evidence for such a harsh assessment (Ngũgĩ, 1993: 132–5, also in some of his earlier essays). JanMohamed (1983: 49–77, 186–7) emphasizes Blixen's deep involvement with and genuine concern for Africans in his appreciative discussion of her autobiographical writing, and takes issue with Ngugi.

major explicit theme in her *Out of Africa*. The film, in contrast, shows a much weaker woman, dependent on men, with Meryl Streep playing the entranced girl to Robert Redford, the gallant man of adventure. He is made to initiate her into hunting and to prompt her to start writing – Karen Blixen's stories had been published, and she had hunted game before she ever met Finch Hatton.[9] Hollywood, however, responded to the heightened concern with gender issues in the West at the time the film was produced. Thus the film gives great play to her being escorted from the men's bar at the Muthaiga Club when she first arrives in Nairobi, then invited in for a drink on her final departure. When she arrives at the army camp the men watch in silence as it sinks in that she is as tough as the strongest among them. But, of course she has not become one of them. She has complained previously that it is a men's war, and she leaves quietly the next morning without so much as awakening her husband. When in the end she implores the new Governor to recognize that 'Kenya is a hard country for women,' viewers are asked to forget how privileged she was, and that colonial Kenya was a hard country for Africans.

Out of Africa is explicitly based on the writings of Blixen. Her *Out of Africa* eloquently conveys the charmed existence of the early settlers, the sense of discovery and adventure, her experiences of love gained and lost.[10] Reading her is, however, a doubly unsettling experience. While her racism is not altogether unexpected, its depth still comes as a shock.[11] It is even more unsettling to discover that the Africans she tells us about have considerable stature, quite unlike the people the film shows us. Hollywood, in 1985, thought fit to diminish these Africans so as to convey an image of simple Africans serving sophisticated (listen to that Mozart playing!) white masters.[12]

Most striking is the transformation Hollywood wreaked on Chief Kinanjui to show us an old man cloaked in cow-hide emerging from a miserable hut, shuffling around with an attendant who has a blanket knotted over his shoulder, and bowing to the white lady. In her book, Blixen presents him as a fellow-aristocrat. He sometimes came over to see her, 'in a gorgeous fur-cloak [of blue monkey skins], accompanied by two or three white-haired senators and a few of his warrior-sons' (Dinesen, 1937: 142).[13] We learn that he ruled over more than 100,000 people, and that he eventually visited her in a fancy car acquired from the American Consul.[14]

Farah speaks broken English in the film, but from Blixen we learn that Farah spoke English and French well. He had joined her on the boat in Aden when she first came to Kenya, and he accompanied her on the train to Mombasa on her final departure. He had married and brought his bride from Somalia to the farm; along with her came her mother, her younger sister, and a young cousin. He handled the plantation's accounts. After Blixen's departure he established a small shop and became one of the city's notables. Malik Bowens, who plays Farah, visited his family, which had become very influential in Nairobi (Rouchy, 1986).

Kamante, in Blixen's account, 'had all the attributes of genius' (Dinesen, 1937: 36). The Prince of Wales complimented the Baroness on the Cumberland Sauce Kamante had prepared. After she had returned to Denmark, Kamante had letters sent to her regularly. His mistress was greatly embarrassed when he was imprisoned for having taken the Mau Mau oath in the 1950s rebellion against the British settlers. Eventually he provided stories and illustrations for a book (Kamante Gatura, 1975). He came out on location one day when the film was shot,[15] but he was living in dire poverty (Kramer, 1986; Critchfield, 1994: 239–40; Dedet, 1986).[16]

The visit of the Prince of Wales alerts us to the fact that the Blixen estate was much more important than the film lets on. Baroness Blixen and her overseas partners owned 6,000 acres, and she employed several Europeans. Blixen was running a major business enterprise based on cheap labor. If she failed – because the soil, rainfall, and altitude were ill-suited for coffee – most settlers did very well under the colonial dispensation. Lord Delamare, lord of a million acres, was indeed their leader, but as far as Africans were concerned, he was anything but the friendly gentleman: he ruthlessly pursued settler interests against them. Hollywood chose to offer us a nostalgic tale of happy Africans serving Europeans absorbed in their romantic entanglements. As for the great-grandchildren of Farah, Kamante, and Chief Kinanjui, President Jomo Kenyatta may well have spoken for them when he commented after seeing the film: 'We are not amused' (Kramer, 1986: 27).

12 *A Song of Africa* offers an instructive discussion of the music choices made by John Barry, with some interference by Sydney Pollack. Barry acknowledges that he used African elements only once and briefly, during the Masai sequence.

13 *A Song of Africa* has period photos of Farah, Kamante, and Juma, but not of Chief Kinanjui.

14 Pollack was a stickler for authenticity when it served to enhance exoticism. Gikuyu no longer perforate and elongate their earlobes, so the extras were outfitted with drooping latex ears specially produced in England (Universal Studios, 1985).

15 Kamante is shown visiting the location in *A Song of Africa*.

16 Cooper (1991) details many of the liberties Pollack took with both the historical record and Baroness Blixen's accounts. She shows in particular how Africans were progressively omitted at each successive stage: autobiography, first film script, final script, shooting, and editing. Eventually much of the interaction between Blixen and her servants was eliminated, while some incidents between Blixen and Farah were recast in the film as exchanges between her and Finch Hatton. The 'shooting script' is provided by Luedtke and Pollack (1987). Pollack has claimed that he had read everything and emphasized the power and remarkable dignity of the Africans chosen to play Farah, Kamante, and Chief Kinanjui (Henry, 1986). He has also commented on the problems of producing a film based on literary material, incidentally mentioning that the young boy Kamante became Blixen's renowned chef, but he offers only economy and dramatic effect as explanations for omissions and outright inventions (Luedtke and Pollack, 1987: x). We are left to wonder about the role of Judith Thurman, Blixen's foremost biographer, who is credited as associate producer and appears in *A Song of Africa*.

References and Further Reading

Cary, Joyce. 1939. *Mister Johnson*. London: Michael Joseph.

Chadwick, Bruce. 2001. *The Reel Civil War: Mythmaking in American Film*. New York: Alfred A. Knopf.

Chocolat. 1988. Film directed by Claire Denis, written by Claire Denis and Jean-Pol Fargeau. Distributed in the U.S. by New Yorker Films. 105 minutes.

Conant, Jennet. 1986. 'Out of Africa: The Movie Has Inspired a Ruggedly Romantic Look.' *Newsweek*, 17 February, page 61.

Cooper, Brenda K. 1991. 'Through the Eyes of Gender and Hollywood: Conflicting Rhetorical Visions of Isak Dinesen's Africa.' Ph.D. dissertation, Ohio University.

Critchfield, Richard. 1994. *The Villagers. Changed Values, Altered Lives: The Closing of the Urban–Rural Gap*. New York/London/Toronto/Sydney/Auckland: Doubleday.

Dedet, Christian. 1986. 'Kamante, le petit pâtre kikuyu.' *Le Matin*, 26 March.

Dinesen, Isak. 1937. *Out of Africa*. London: Putnam; New York: Random House.

A Dry White Season, see pages 80–9.

Gone With the Wind. 1939. Film directed by Victor Fleming, written by Sidney Howard. Produced by Metro Goldwyn Mayer (USA). Distributed in the U.S. by Swank Motion Pictures. 231 minutes.

Henry, Michael. 1986. 'Entretien avec Sydney Pollack sur *Out of Africa*.' *Positif* 302: 4–8.

JanMohamed, Abdul R. 1983. *Manichean Aesthetics: The Politics of Literature in Colonial Africa*. Amherst: University of Massachusetts Press.

Kamante Gatura. 1975. *Longing for Darkness: Kamante's Tales from* Out of Africa. *With Original Photographs (January 1914–July 1931) and Quotations from Isak Dinesen (Karen Blixen)*. Collected by Peter Beard. New York/London: Harcourt Brace Jovanovich.

Kenyatta, Jomo. 1938. *Facing Mount Kenya: The Tribal Life of Gikuyu*. London: Secker and Warburg.

Kramer, Jane. 1986. 'The Eighth Gothic Tale.' *New York Review of Books* 33: 21–7.

Kennedy, Dane. 1987. 'Isak Dinesen's African Recovery of a European Past.' *Clio* 17: 37–50.

Luedtke, Kurt, and Sydney Pollack. 1987. *Out of Africa: The Shooting Script*. New York: Newmarket Press.

Mister Johnson. 1991. Film directed by Bruce Beresford, written by Bruce Beresford and William Boyd. Distributed in the U.S. by Kino International. 105 minutes.

Ngũgĩ wa Thiong'o. 1993. *Moving the Centre: The Struggle for Cultural Freedoms*. London: James Currey; Nairobi: EAEP; Portsmouth, NH: Heinemann.

Out of Africa. 1985. Film directed by Sydney Pollack, written by Kurt Luedtke. Produced by Universal Studios (USA). Distributed in the U.S. by Swank Motion Pictures. 161 minutes.

Pfaff, Françoise. 1977. 'Toward a New Era in Cinema "Harvest 3000 Years."' *New Directions* 4 (3): 28–30.

Rouchy, Marie-Elisabeth. 1986. 'Out of Africa.' *Le Matin*, 23 March.

A Song of Africa. 1999. Documentary produced, written, and directed by Charles Kiselyk. Produced by Universal Studios Home Video (USA). Part of DVD of *Out of Africa*. 49 minutes.

Thurman, Judith. 1982. *Isak Dinesen: The Life of a Storyteller*. New York: St Martin's Press.

Universal Studios. 1985. Press kit 'Out of Africa.'

Yaaba (1989)

Friendship in the Village that Time Forgot

Yaaba is based on tales of my childhood
and on that kind of bedtime story-telling
we hear just before falling asleep...
(Ouedraogo, 1989)

Recovering the African Past

1 For an enthusiastic account of the cinematic qualities of *Yaaba*, see Cardullo (1991).

2 The former Upper Volta was rebaptized Burkina (Mossi for 'land of honest men') Faso (Dioula for 'democratic republic') by Thomas Sankara. Gaining power in a military coup in 1983, he was one of the rare army officers to initiate genuine reforms. They were short-lived as he was assassinated in 1987 by his fellow coup-makers who claimed that his rule had become arbitrary.

3 *Yaaba* brought Ouedraogo international recognition, and he has referred to it as his beginning in cinema (Ruelle, 1997), but he had previously directed another feature film, *Yam Daabo*.

4 *Aficionados* of *ouali*, the game popular under various names all the way from West Africa to East Africa and beyond as far as the Philippines, can catch a glimpse of it being played in the foreground of an early scene as the villagers carry food to the family that has lost its granary.

5 In this respect *Yaaba* follows a pattern established by Gaston Kaboré in *Wênd Kûuni*, the pioneering attempt to 'Africanize' film language by unfolding at a measured pace consonant with the time-honored customs and seasonal rhythms of African village life (Cham, n.d.). *Yaaba* also shares key elements with the story of *Wênd Kûuni* – the young boy and the girl, the woman accused of witchcraft and chased away, the impotent man deserted by his wife – but they are developed quite differently. And while Kaboré invites an ethnographic gaze, Ouedraogo presents differentiated characters in depth and explores their relationships.

6 Throughout I translate foreign currencies into US\$ at the average exchange rate in the year preceding the release of the film.

With *Yaaba* Idrissa Ouedraogo created one of the finest African films.[1] A beautifully filmed morality tale of superstition and intelligence set in Burkina Faso, it touchingly conveys the humanity of its characters and offers a message of tolerance.[2] *Yaaba* became one of the most successful African films. It won the International Critics' Prize at the Cannes Film Festival, the Special Prize of the FESPACO Jury, and the Sakura Gold Prize at the Tokyo International Film Festival. And it is one of the few African films to have achieved substantial commercial distribution: it ran for 25 weeks in Paris and sold 285,000 seats in France (Barlet, 2000: 258).[3]

Yaaba distinguishes itself from Western films set in Africa by a whole set of characteristics that make it a distinctly African film: characters, setting, pacing, language, music, and last, but certainly not least, finance. *Yaaba* introduces us to a range of individual African characters – some we come to know quite well, and the camera makes us see the beauty in the faces of simple villagers. Unlike the African landscapes where Western films are set, *Yaaba*'s Sahel setting holds no particular attractions or excitement: the fauna is sparse; we never get to see any game; the desert does not threaten excruciating death, even if droughts are a recurring calamity; nor are there any dangers lurking in the dark. Instead Ouedraogo introduces us, with a good deal of humor, to life in an African village.[4] We see simple dwellings and begin to comprehend complex relationships. We witness cooperation and conflict in a family that extends beyond parents and their children. Kougri advises his younger brother Tibo to get married again; and when Nopoko is dying, it is Kougri rather than her father who deals with the charlatan and the healer Taryam. When Razougou tries to persuade Koudi to leave her husband, she responds 'it's a family matter.' We get a sense of community as the villagers unite to assist a family that has lost its food supplies, dance to celebrate a wedding, and mourn a dying child. And we come to appreciate what it means to be cast out by such a community, like Sana, or to be marginalized, like Noaga.

In stark contrast to Western films, *Yaaba* follows a slow peasant mode: Ouedraogo uses long shots as the camera leisurely pans the wide open landscape, following the slow progress of characters dwarfed by the vast expanse: Sana, for example, on her way to Taryam.[5] All speech in *Yaaba* is in Moré, the language of the Mossi villagers portrayed. Indeed, if viewers are so inclined, they can learn some Moré as they count with Bila and Nopoko, the two children, playing games; they can pick up a greeting, and perhaps a couple of insults too; they will certainly remember that *yaaba* means grandmother. The music in *Yaaba* is credited to the late Francis Bebey, a well-known writer, poet, and composer-performer from Cameroon. Used sparingly, it accompanies but never intrudes. Gentle music accompanies the interludes when long shots take in the countryside. A faster rhythm introduces the few dramatic scenes.

Like all African films, *Yaaba* is a low-budget production: it cost 6 million French francs (Barlet, 2000: 227), then about \$1 million.[6] If many African films suffer from shortcomings that can be traced to financial constraints, Ouedraogo, at any rate, managed to produce a first-rate film. He accomplished this feat by taking on the roles of both writer and director, by shooting the film in Tougouzagué, a village a few miles from his birthplace, and by recruiting villagers and his relatives to act – Bila and Nopoko are cousins of his wife – and getting them to act naturally.[7]

Yaaba was a low-budget production, but it still required finance from overseas sponsors – like most African films produced outside Nigeria and South Africa. In this case financial support came from France, Switzerland, and Germany. Whatever Ouedraogo's preferred audience, this sponsorship presumably determined that the film should aim to reach a Western audience. Anybody familiar with the crowds of children in African villages is left to wonder whether presenting Bila and Nopoko as single children is intended to obviate the difficulty Western viewers could have in distinguishing them from their siblings, whether it is all that common for Mossi peasant women to have the final say as Bila's mother does, whether the drunkard-wife-lover triangle is more the classic French film scenario than Mossi village reality, whether the close-ups of the lovers are meant to play to Western sensibilities.

The parsimonious dialogue complemented by body language – gestures, laughter, raspberries – is the hallmark of Ouedraogo's cinema of minimalism (Diawara, 2000). It may be seen as a concession to foreign viewers who tire of subtitles, but such an argument would overlook the multiplicity of languages in all but a very few African countries. Ouedraogo trained at the Institut Africain d'Education Cinématographique in Ouagadougou. He then produced educational documentaries for Burkina Faso before continuing his film studies in France at the Sorbonne and the Institut des Hautes Etudes Cinématographiques. He has explained that these documentaries led him to work on image and setting: they had neither commentary nor dialogue because they were intended to be shown in a country where people speak 42 different languages and only a minority know French (Jousse and Saada, 1989).

Ouedraogo (1989) tells us that he based *Yaaba* on tales of his childhood, and the film portrays a village out of history. Nothing takes the viewer to precolonial times, nor is there any indication of a colonial presence. Ouedraogo himself put the village squarely in the present: 'This village lives as I show it in the film, there is no reconstitution, everything was shot in natural settings' (Gavron, 1989). But he also acknowledged: 'the reality of Africa today is not as untouched as in my film' (Bernard 1989, my translations).[8] If the setting is contemporary, the isolation of the village belongs to a distant past. Burkina Faso is one of the world's poorest and least urbanized countries, but its villagers pay taxes, send many of their children to school, and are likely to be able to access a clinic, however limited its resources. Market relations reach well beyond the big tree in walking distance where a few people gather with the local products we see in *Yaaba*. Because of the poverty, temporary migration to richer neighboring countries such as the Ivory Coast and Ghana, where many migrants find work in plantations, has become an established pattern for several generations. By now an estimated ten per cent of

7 Ouedraogo is a common name in Burkina Faso, and not every Ouedraogo appearing in the credits is a relative of the director.

8 Ouedraogo discusses the move from his early documentaries, which foregrounded the relationship between village and the city, to films such as *Yaaba* in *Idrissa*, a documentary on his life and work by Malick Sy.

Idrissa Ouedraogo, Noufou Ouedraogo, and Fatimata Sanga during the shooting

9 The film poster emphasizes isolation by showing the three principal characters lost in the barren landscape. Tougouzagué, of course, is anything but an isolated village, witness *Parlons grand-mère*, Djibril Diop Mambety's documentary of the filming of *Yaaba*.

Burkinabé, predominantly men, work outside the country at any one time. Yet there is no indication that any migrant ever returned to this village, no trace of anything he might have sent, or brought, or be using now, no transistor radio, not even a single T-shirt. A village such as this would be hard to find in Africa today – or anywhere else, for that matter.[9]

An alternative interpretation of *Yaaba* that situates it in the distant past has to contend with elements in the film that indicate a contemporary setting. For one thing, coins are common: the charlatan demands them, the beggar collects them, the children wager them. Of course, coins were introduced into this region with the trans-Sahara trade many centuries ago, but that their value should be so low that children and beggars have them indicates a contemporary setting. So do some elements of clothing. The squats Bila is made to do by his father come right out of the French school system – we will see them again, in school, in *Keïta!* And the body language Bila uses to insult a group of women looks of recent, imported vintage too.

The portrayal of village life in *Yaaba* bears comparison to the most widely read African novel, Chinua Achebe's *Things Fall Apart*. In response to Western accounts that diminish and stereotype Africans, both stories depict differentiated individuals in their full humanity. And they avoid the temptation to romanticize the African past that characterized earlier attempts to present an African perspective such as Camara Laye's novel *The Dark Child* and Ababacar Samb's film *Jom*. Instead they reveal village beliefs and customs that temper any enthusiasm that the modern viewer/reader might feel about the past. The key difference between *Yaaba* and *Things Fall Apart* lies in Achebe's situating his novel explicitly at a specific historical juncture. This was a time when the village's relations with the outside world took on new dimensions with the intrusion of Christian missions, the introduction of Western education, greatly expanding trading opportunities, and the imposition of colonial rule. The novel provides a more comprehensive and detailed account of village society, introducing the reader to religion, village government, farming, and custom; it refutes the notion of unchanging 'traditional' societies; and it memorably conveys the riches of an oral culture. In contrast, *Yaaba* fails to give any sense of the village's political structure. And the pointers to religion are confusing. Apparent monogamy and a curse which appears as 'May you go to hell' in the English subtitle suggest a village profoundly Christian, but Bila's father Kougri as well as Sana speak of 'gods' in the plural.[10]

As Manthia Diawara (1992: 162) has pointed out, the isolation of the village in *Yaaba* ignores complex social, political, and historical issues. Instead, the plot turns on superstition and human foibles and becomes a plea for tolerance. Western viewers are unlikely to connect Sana's outcast position to her history as an orphan who lacked family support. Rather, they are encouraged, once again, to assign superstition to the Other while taking their own supposed rationality for granted. The constancy of the two friendships – between the two children, and between Bila and Sana – assures us that we are witnessing a society in harmony but for superstition and personal failings.[11] The occasional quarrels between Bila and Nopoko dissipate quickly with a joke and a smile: they make us anticipate their lovers' quarrels to come in just a few years' time. And the tension created between Bila's parents by his mother's affirmative role is contained by her humor and his father's acquiescence.

Presenting the village as isolated since time immemorial makes *Yaaba* particularly attractive to Western audiences that are interested in such a different culture, but would rather not be reminded of the West's role in slavery and colonialism, of the West's continued dominance in the contemporary world, and of the manifold problems plaguing contemporary Africa. Western viewers may appreciate their good luck in not experiencing village poverty, but in *Yaaba* that poverty is taken for

10 The 'traditional' village becomes caricature in Gaston Kaboré's *Zan Boko*. After 27 minutes of a variety of village scenes that suggest that life goes on in time-honored ways, and give no hint that it might have been affected by the outside world, we suddenly discover the highrises of contemporary Ouagadougou, the capital of Burkina Faso, looming over the village.

11 Ouedraogo tells a very different story of friendship in his most recent film, *Kini and Adams*, which we will discuss towards the end of our exploration.

Recovering the African Past

It's a witch.

Tibo, Noaga, and Kougri listen to the charlatan

granted; its causes are not at issue.[12] We see the barren landscape of the Sahel, but people have food reserves to share when a family's granary burns down. Sana is destitute because she has been outcast, not because of a general state of poverty. Nopoko, Bila, and Sana are beautifully drawn, but the film's focus on them raises a further issue. Their very status, two children and an old destitute woman, invite the patronizing Western gaze: Western viewers are encouraged to strike, once again, a posture of benevolence *vis-à-vis* Africans.

Yaaba may be understood as a political parable. The scene of the villagers meeting with the charlatan conveys it well. The charlatan may be seen to act like a corrupt politician: he demonizes Sana, who has correctly diagnosed Nopoko's condition, and he wants her to be exiled; he asks for a sacrificial offering to be enjoyed by himself and his acolyte – note his assistant's smile when he demands a bull. Noaga may be seen as representative of the African intellectual, albeit in a village setting. He is more knowledgeable than the other villagers: he does not share their superstition about Sana, denounces the charlatan, and knows that Taryam can heal Nopoko. But the African intellectual is disowned by the masses, and his good counsel is discarded time and again: he is politically impotent and desperate. Noaga finds solace in drink. If you grant him such a symbolic role, then, as he lays Sana to rest, you can see him burying good old mother Africa. And you can see young Africa, the beautiful Koudi, deserting the man of reason to run off with a con man. Such an interpretation takes us far from the film's explicit story. And I do not know that Ouedraogo intended such a second layer of meaning.

Yaaba shares with most African films a realism in plot that distinguishes it from much Western film production. This realism is particularly striking in a dénouement that brings neither happy ending

12 The parallels between *Yaaba* and *Pather Panchali*, Satyajit Ray's classic portrayal of village life in India, are striking. While *Pather Panchali* does situate its story historically, it resembles *Yaaba* in that the political conflicts of the day – land ownership and taxation – are barely alluded to, and caste is never at issue. Instead a humanistic message underlies both films. And they share a sense of serenity: the story unfolds slowly, and the camera lingers on people and dwells on their natural surroundings. At the same time both directors avoid the trap of romanticizing village life. They tell of the quarrels of adults and contrast them with the complicity between a marginalized old woman and two children. In each film the old woman dies alone, and the link between old and young is broken when a child touches the seated woman and discovers that she is dead. Gupta (1994: 41–3) further details such parallels and suggests that *Yaaba* be seen as a tribute to *Pather Panchali*.

nor great drama: the lovers elope, Sana dies quietly in her sleep, and Ouedraogo keeps us at a distance as he compresses much of her burial in a single long shot which lasts nearly two minutes. The woman who saved Nopoko's life has remained an outcast, Noaga has been abandoned by his wife, and the camera lingers on the children who run into the distance and, we may presume, a more tolerant future. *Yaaba* is an African production, altogether different from Western films situated in Africa, even as it reaches out to Western audiences.

Yaaba introduces Western viewers to African peasants and their village context, but the picture remains incomplete because the film fails to convey the full reality of an African countryside that is connected in multiple ways with the wider world today. The film cannot be taken as the depiction of a contemporary African village. Nor should we assume that what *Yaaba* conveys about life in one village represents the African village: villages vary a great deal across the continent, as we shall see.

References and Further Reading

Achebe, Chinua. 1958. *Things Fall Apart*. London: Heinemann.

Barlet, Olivier. 2000 (1996). *African Cinemas: Decolonizing the Gaze*. London/New York: Zed Books. Revised and updated translation, by Chris Turner, of *Les cinémas d'Afrique noire: Le regard en question*. Collection Images plurielles. Paris: L'Harmattan.

Bernard, Jean-Jacques. 1989. 'Un plongeon en Afrique.' Première, 149: 29.

Cardullo, Bert. 1991. 'Rites of Passage.' *The Hudson Review* 44: 96–104.

Cham, Mbye. n.d. (1991). 'A Fable for Modern Africa.' *Library of African Cinema: a Guide to Video Resources for Colleges & Public Libraries*. San Francisco: Resolution Inc./California Newsreel. Page 29.

Diawara, Manthia. 1992. *African Cinema: Politics and Culture. Blacks in the Diaspora*. Bloomington/Indianapolis: Indiana University Press.

——. 2000. 'The Iconography of West African Cinema.' In June Givanni (ed.) *Symbolic Narratives/African Cinema: Audiences, Theory and the Moving Image*. London: British Film Institute. 81–9.

Englebert, Pierre. 1996. *Burkina Faso: Unsteady Statehood in West Africa. Nations of the Modern World: Africa*. Boulder, CO and Oxford: Westview Press.

Gavron, Laurence. 1989. 'Ouedraogo et sa "grand-mère" d'Afrique.' Libération, 12 May: 35.

Gupta, Dhruba. 1994. *African Cinema: a View from India*. Celluloid Chapter Documentations. Jamshedpur: Celluloid Chapter.

Idrissa. 2001. Documentary directed by Malick Sy. Produced by Canal France International (France) and Stella Films (France). 52 minutes.

Jom, the Story of a People/Jom ou l'histoire d'un peuple. 1981. Film directed by Ababacar Samb Makharam, written by Babacar Sine and Ababacar Samb Makharam. Produced by Baobab Films (Senegal). Distributed in the U.S. by New Yorker Films. 80 minutes.

Jousse, Thierry, and Nicolas Saada. 1989. 'Pourquoi juge-t-on les gens? Entretien avec Idrissa Ouedraogo.' *Cahiers du Cinéma* 423: 7–9.

Keïta! see pages 36–43.

Kini and Adams, see pages 181–6.

Laye, Camara. 1954. *L'Enfant noir*. Paris: Plon. English translation by James Kirkup and Ernest Jones, 1954, *The Dark Child*. New York: Farrar, Straus and Giroux. Also published as *The African Child*.

Ouedraogo, Idrissa. 1989. 'Synopsis,' in press booklet, 'Yaaba.'

Parlons grand-mère. 1989. Documentary directed by Djibril Diop-Mambety. Produced by Diproci (Burkina Faso), Thelma Film (Switzerland), and Maag Daan (Senegambia). Distributed in France by Médiathèque des Trois Mondes, Paris. Available for viewing at Cinémathèque Afrique, Paris. 34 minutes.

Pather Panchali. 1954. Film written and directed by Satyajit Ray. Produced by Government of West Bengal (India). Distributed in the U.S. by New Yorker Films. 112 minutes.

Ruelle, Catherine. 1997. 'Entretien avec Idrissa Ouedraogo,' in press booklet 'Kini and Adams.'

Wênd Kûuni/Le Don de Dieu (God's Gift). 1982. Film directed by Gaston Kaboré, written by Marie-Jeanne Kanyala. Produced by Direction du Cinéma (Burkina Faso). Distributed in the U.S. by California Newsreel, Kino International, and Mypheduh Films. 70 minutes.

Yaaba. 1989. Film written and directed by Idrissa Ouedraogo. Produced by Arcadia Films (France), Les Films de l'Avenir (Burkina Faso), and Thelma Film (Switzerland). Distributed in the U.S. by New Yorker Films. 90 minutes.

Yam Daabo/The Choice. 1986. Film written and directed by Idrissa Ouedraogo. Produced by Films de l'Avenir (Burkina Faso). Distributed in France by Médiathèque des Trois Mondes, Paris. 80 minutes.

Zan Boko. 1988. Film written and directed by Gaston Kaboré. Produced by Bras de Fer (Burkina Faso). Distributed in the U.S. by California Newsreel. 94 minutes.

Keïta! 1995
Transmitting the *Sundjata* to the Next Generation

The griot *animates life; he manages to push people, to motivate them. He is an inspiration. (Sotigui Kouyaté 1994: 22, my translation)*

1 Ahmadou Kourouma's novels *Monnè, outrages et défis* and *En attendant le vote des bêtes sauvages* present themselves as the oral history of a kingdom in a country that in many respects resembles Guinea (Conakry). They range from the imposition of colonial rule to recent tyranny. Like the *griot*, Kourouma at times uses repetitions as if to affirm incontrovertible facts. At other times he presents parallel accounts, ambiguities, and unreal exaggerations which convey the indeterminate character of all history. Readers are thus compelled to reconstitute, interpret, and evaluate

Sundjata Keïta established the Mali Empire in the early thirteenth century. Much of what we know about this period in West African history comes to us through oral history. The primary source is the *Sundjata*, the epic tale of the many trials and heroic exploits that eventually made Sundjata Emperor of Mali. It is the most important of various epics that continue to be told in many parts of Africa.[1] The film poster reminds us of the importance of listening in the transmission of this oral history – the film's working title was *Keïta: from Mouth to Ear.* Throughout the Mandeng cultural area, which spans much of West Africa, audiences take pride in their history as they listen to the story of their hero and marvel at the supernatural feats of their forebears.[2] Such epics are told by the *djéliba*, as they are called locally, or to use the term coined by the French colonizers, the *griot* (man) or *griotte* (woman). They constitute a caste, the calling passing from parents to sons and daughters. The *griot* may be seen as the West African counterpart of Europe's bard in pre-literate days. He is historian, advisor, the voice of the high and mighty, mediator, master of ceremonies, and praise singer; and he propels men into action.

1 (cont.) the past for themselves, to create their own histories and possibly share in the author's irony.

Mongo Beti's *Remember Ruben* and Ngũgĩ wa Thiong'o's *Petals of Blood* also draw on the mode of the oral epic to present the history of an African country from pre-colonial days to the post-colonial experience, but their critical stance is devoid of ambiguity. Mongo Beti tells of the impact of colonialism, German and French, in Cameroon, of armed struggle and neo-colonialism. Ngũgĩ wa Thiong'o relates the imposition of British rule in Kenya, the Mau Mau rebellion, and the emergence of an African capitalist class.

2 If *Keïta* conveys a sense of oral history, embellished by myth, a number of African films tell of a mythical past. Their drama propelled by myth, they have been successful with Western audiences. The most prominent example is Souleymane Cissé's *Yeelen*, Jury Prize at Cannes. It presents a Bamana story of the power struggle between father and son, magicians both.

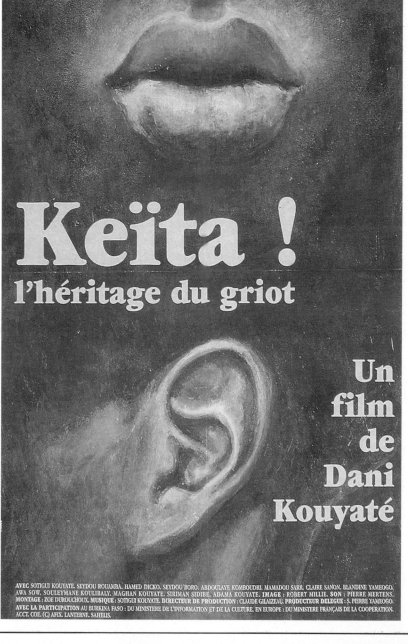

AFIX Productions / Les Productions de LA LANTERNE / SAHELIS Productions
présentent

Keïta !
l'héritage du griot

Un
film
de
Dani
Kouyaté

AVEC SOTIGUI KOUYATE, SEYDOU ROUAMBA, HAMED DICKO, SEYDOU BORO, ABDOULAYE KOMBOUDRI, MAMADOU SARR, CLAIRE SANON, BLANDINE YAMEOGO, AWA SOW, SOULEYMANE KOULIBALY, MAGHAN KOUYATE, SIRIMAN SIDIBE, ADAMA KOUYATE. IMAGE : ROBERT MILLIE. SON : PIERRE MERTENS. MONTAGE : ZOE DUROUCHOUX. MUSIQUE : SOTIGUI KOUYATE. DIRECTEUR DE PRODUCTION : CLAUDE GILAIZEAU. PRODUCTEUR DELEGUE : S. PIERRE YAMEOGO. AVEC LA PARTICIPATION AU BURKINA FASO : DU MINISTERE DE L'INFORMATION ET DE LA CULTURE. EN EUROPE : DU MINISTERE FRANÇAIS DE LA COOPERATION. ACCT, COE, (C) AFIX, LANTERNE, SAHELIS.

Recovering the African Past

3 Oral history is modified by time and setting. The versions of the *Sundjata* told today, more than seven centuries after the events, vary considerably. Belcher (1999: 89-113) provides a comparison of 27 versions recorded across West Africa since 1892. *Keïta* is loosely based on the version Mamadou Kouyaté presented to Niane (1960) who cast his translation in prose. For a quite different, comprehensive recording, see Johnson and Sisòkò (1992), a word-for-word translation in the original poetic form.

4 Sotigui Kouyaté professes his vocation as a *griot* in Monique Loreau's *Names Live Nowhere* as he presents stories of two Senegalese in Bruxelles and tells of the experiences of some other Africans in Europe. Supernatural events provide the dramatic elements of his tales. He is the subject of a documentary, Mahamat Saleh Haroun's *Sotigui Kouyaté, un griot moderne*.

5 The kora is a stringed instrument with a large calabash, not unlike a harp. The balafon is a xylophone made from gourds and wooden keys.

6 Ola Balogun's rendering of the *Sundjata* in his documentary *River Niger, Black Mother* takes the story further, up to the victory of Sundjata over the Sosso. His presentation comes closer to an oral performance: the narrator's telling of the story is accompanied by a *griot* reciting key passages, the song of women, and the play of instruments, while central events are enacted in a stylized fashion. H. Parker James and Lynda Shaffer are preparing a CD ROM on the *Sundjata* that will provide a full oral presentation in English. For further information: p.james@neu.edu.

7 The *Sundjata* reflects and reinforces the continuing significance of Mali and its emperors in the Mandeng region. When the French Sudan became independent in 1960, it adopted the empire's name, and a descendant of the emperors, Modibo Keïta, became the

Keïta! The Heritage of the Griot weaves together three strands: it evokes the past as told in the *Sundjata*,[3] it depicts the present of a middle-class family living in Ouagadougou, and it conveys the art of the *griot* transmitting the wisdom of ages to the next generation. Dani Kouyaté, the director, trained at the Institut Africain d'Education Cinématographique in Ouagadougou, then continued his studies in France at the Sorbonne and the Ecole Internationale d'Anthropologie. He produced several shorts before this, his first full-length feature. His father Sotigui Kouyaté plays the central role of Djéliba Kouyaté. Members of the Kouyaté family have served as *griots* to the Keïta lineage since at least the thirteenth century. The Kouyatés are guardians of the Keïta clan traditions, and their knowledge enjoys special authority in Mandeng culture. A Keïta noble will feel financial obligation toward a Kouyaté, and a Kouyaté will not hesitate to turn to a Keïta for help (Belcher, 1999: 10). The relationship of the Kouyatés with the Keïtas is conveyed by their very name, which translates as 'there is a secret between you and me.'

Sotigui Kouyaté is a distinguished *griot*, actor, and performer who has worked with Peter Brook in theater and film. He has appeared in more than two dozen films, most recently as Jacob in *Genesis* and as Alloune in *Little Senegal*.[4] In *Keïta!* he transformed his character, rendering Djéliba Kouyaté more forceful than the old dying man Dani Kouyaté had imagined (Barlet, 2002). Sotigui Kouyaté also performs the music. His voice may be heard leading some of the songs, and he plays simple melodies on single instruments: the kora and the flute (which would often accompany a *griot*'s recital, as might the balafon or the drum).[5] His counterpart, the teacher Drissa Fofana, is played by Abdoulaye Komboudri, a popular comedian in West African film and television. Dani Kouyaté shot the film in Ouagadougou, the capital of Burkina Faso; in Sindou, renowned for its dramatic landscape; and in Ouahabou, where Sotigui Kouyaté grew up and learnt his profession as a *griot* from his father and one of his spiritual fathers, Babou-lou Bathiono (Anonymous, 1995). *Keïta!* received the Best First Film Prize at FESPACO and the Junior Prize at the Cannes Film Festival.

An oral presentation of the *Sundjata*, accompanied by music, takes many hours, and filming the huge battles it relates would have been expensive. *Keïta!* presents us with the first third of the epic, up to the point when Sundjata Keïta is forced into exile from the Kingdom of Mandé to which he lays claim.[6] This part of the *Sundjata* deals with the extraordinary portents that preceded the birth of the hero, his severe handicap, and his superhuman strength. It is a story of morals and the occult rather than great deeds. The film has Djéliba Kouyaté tell the story to Mabo Keïta who, as his name indicates, is a descendant of the Emperor but now, at the end of the twentieth century, lives in the city.[7] The scenes depicting the events of the past are visually distinct from this frame story: they feature detailed, deeply focused images in warm colors.

Keïta! starts out with the Mandeng myth of the creation of the world at Wagadu. As all living beings came together, one man proclaimed that the world could not go on like this: 'I want to be your king.' And the people responded: '*Konaté*,' which translates as 'We do not hate you.' Maghan Kon Fatta thus became Konaté, King of Mandé. Sundjata descends from this royal lineage on his father's side.[8] In Sindou towering rocks provide a striking backdrop. Kouyaté's depiction of the court avoids the temptation to aggrandize the past, but seems to underplay the stature of the King. We would expect to see more retainers and wonder that there are no horsemen in evidence.[9]

On his mother's side, Sundjata descends from Sogolon. She is the adopted daughter of Do-Kamisso who, in the guise of a buffalo, terrorizes Do because her nephew the King betrayed her. An accomplished *griot* will delight in evoking the image of the Buffalo Woman for his audience as his voice dramatically alternates with his cora. The task is more difficult in the film medium. In *Keïta!* the presence of the Buffalo Woman is simply implied in the reactions of the two brother hunters she pursues, and her eventual appearance is anti-climactic – special effects are in short supply in low-budget African films. Sogolon in turn holds the two hunters at bay, as well as the King of Mandé. *Griots* vary in their account of the consummation of the marriage of the King and Sogolon that was to produce Sundjata, and the reaction of their audiences varies as well. The version that informs the film leaves many contemporary viewers ill at ease. In any case, both the Buffalo Woman and Sogolon, though marginalized, are strong women. Sogolon passes her powers on to her son who will overcome all obstacles and establish the Mali Empire. Strength also characterizes the King's first wife, Sassouma Bérété, who seeks to maintain her son's claim to the throne. And in the film's contemporary story Mabo's mother Sitan, Orange Blossom, prevails in the end.

While the Mandé are peasants, the Do are hunters. The two kingdoms thus represent two major traditions of the Sahel.[10] At the time their traditional religions were becoming amalgamated with Islam. Indeed, the rulers of Mali are said to have been Muslims from before the days of Sundjata. Certainly, a number of Sundjata's successors made the pilgrimage to Mecca. But the *Sundjata* is still imbued with pre-Islamic beliefs. Sundjata will succeed because of the occult powers Sogolon has passed on to him. Not only does the *Sundjata* thrive on supernatural events, it also reverses, as fables are wont to do, established rules and understandings: the younger of the brother hunters shows courage and takes decisive action; the ugly maiden becomes queen; the crippled boy prevails; the second-born will be king.

The performance of a *griot* is usually addressed to a group and elicits the active participation of the audience. *Keïta!* deviates from this pattern with a *griot* who takes on the role of tutor. Djéliba Kouyaté was the *griot* of Mabo's father Boicar Keïta, and his father's father, and he now tells Mabo the *Sundjata* so that he may 'learn the meaning of his name.'[11] We can hear the significance attached to that name when Djéliba salutes Boicar Keïta, at the end of a conversation: '*Keïta!*' Mabo is a schoolboy, and exams are approaching. Thus the stage is set for conflict: what Djéliba tells him about his illustrious ancestor Sundjata is quite different from the imported Western curriculum his teacher has to inculcate in his

7 (cont.) new nation's first President. Fa-Digi Sisòkò's performance in 1968, towards the end of Modibo Keïta's rule, includes several passages praising the President of the Republic and comparing him to Sundjata. If the first passage is rather enigmatic: 'But Son-Jara did not have the wind as shoes,/ To travel far and wide upon' the second is explicit: 'But he did not make airplanes his shoes/For to travel far and wide. (Johnson and Sisòkò, 1992: 43, 54). Modibo Keïta was overthrown in 1968 by Moussa Traoré, a descendant of Tira Maghan Traoré who rebelled against Sundjata Keïta in the thirteenth century.

8 We hear a talking drum announce the birth of Sundjata, its message to be transmitted by other drums across the kingdom. At the court of Do, the *griot* addresses the two hunters with a talking drum – the equivalent of a praise song.

9 The use of cowrie shells in divination and for decoration at the thirteenth-century Mandé court is an anachronism. They are found in the Indian Ocean and were introduced to West African commerce by Portuguese traders after 1515 to become a major currency. Some of the cloth also appears to be of much more recent vintage.

10 Cattle rearing is the third way in which people have managed to survive in the difficult Sahel environment. The three different modes of production have become identified with different ethnic groups. Cheick Oumar Sissoko draws on three such groups to retell the biblical story of the fratricidal conflict between Jacob and Esau, now set in the Sahel, in *Genesis*.

11 Mabô is the name of one of Sotigui Kouyaté's sons: the *griot* is instructing his son's namesake.

pupils. The grandeur of a mythical past, Sundjata's stature enhanced by extraordinary events, confronts the science of evolutionary theory. And the afrocentric history of the *Sundjata* competes with the eurocentric history of Europe's 'discovery' of the world. The conflict is exacerbated as the two educators compete for Mabo's attention.

The confrontation between the teacher and the *griot*, with Mabo watching as the arbiter, articulates the contrast between traditional and contemporary education. It is, of course, a caricature. Any peasant, let alone a *griot*, knows about government, knows that it is powerful and distant. And a generation born long after independence is taught African history in school – it is outside Africa that African history continues to be ignored. But the confrontation carries three important underlying messages. With Western education a European language such as French comes to eclipse African languages. The commitment to a written culture, and teaching based on the written text, entails a loss of the power and beauty of oral communication. And African history is submerged by Western history. Western history is dominant because the West, predominant for several centuries, came to rule much of the world in the nineteenth century. A key element in this predominance has been an extraordinary expansion in Western scholarship since the sixteenth century. Historians in particular have benefitted from the availability of written sources going back to the heyday of Greek civilization. A wealth of scholarship thus buttresses the privileged position Western history continues to enjoy even as the dominant position of the West is increasingly eroded.

As Djéliba tells his tale, he gives us some sense of the art of the *griot*.[12] While he presents himself as unassuming and low-key, he is clearly in charge: he waits for the right moment to state his mission to Mabo's parents; he controls the pace of the story he has to tell and wards off Mabo's impatient questions; he dominates the exchange with the teacher; and he decides when it is time to leave. *Griots* pass on the wisdom of ages: 'No matter how strong you are, you will always find one stronger than you.' Djéliba emphasizes that 'Knowledge is ungraspable, complex.' He keeps reminding Mabo that there are several kinds of truths. 'The same truth can have several versions' is one of several aphorisms making the point. Djéliba thus problematizes his own story. And he presents Mabo with a riddle: 'Do you know why the hunter always beats the lion in stories?' If you turn a critical eye on storytellers, you will soon find the answer: 'It's because it is the hunter who tells the stories. If the lion told his stories, he would occasionally win.'[13] Not only does the lion tell a very different story, but where the hunter blithely affirms 'always,' Djéliba's lion avers a more discriminating 'occasionally.' Djéliba gives this, his last, instruction to Mabo after he has decided to leave. We may take it as a comment on what has just happened. The *griot* who has always had the final word in his stories, has had to cede this privilege to Sitan.

Djéliba's thirteenth-century forebears demonstrate the *griot*'s role as the spokesperson for and the advisor to the high and mighty. When the

12 For viewers conversant with Mandinka there is also the fascination with the elevated form of the language used by the *griot* (Diawara, 2000).

13 Chinua Achebe (2000: 73) tells of a similar proverb: 'Until the lions produce their own historian, the story of the hunt will glorify only the hunter.' African historians, filmmakers, and writers like himself have come to tell the story of the encounter between Africa and Europe, but Western voices still predominate.

Dani Kouyaté directing Sotigui Kouyaté

mysterious hunter comes to visit the King of Mandé, we see the King sitting flanked by the Queen and Doua Kouyaté with his kora. It is the *griot* who responds to the visitor and invites him to divine the future for the King. From time to time the *griot* will turn to the King to see his reaction, and the King will nod his assent. Doua advises the King in private how to make Sogolon submit. In private he does not hesitate to contradict the King, who on his deathbed bows to his *griot*'s advice.[14] As King succeeds King, so *griot* succeeds *griot*: we see Doua's son Balla Fasséké encourage Sundjata and urge him on. Eventually Sundjata will become Keïta, which translates as 'take your heritage.'

The wedding Mabo's parents attend stands in stark contrast to the wedding of Maghan Kon Fatta Konaté and Sogolon. Where in the past everybody joined in the dance, fired on by the drummers, now the drummers have become a spectacle, and only a few guests dance to their rhythms. The *griotte* at the wedding party similarly reflects the different age. *Griots* used to sing the praises of their patrons, and they embellished the history of their patrons and their patrons' ancestors, but here we see their art altogether debased and commercialized. The praises the *griotte* sings for Boicar Keïta as he leaves the party are routine. She will sing

14 Contrary to the Western stereotype of unchanging Africa, the *griot* impresses on the King that laws change, just as Chinua Achebe tells of changes in village custom in *Things Fall Apart*.

Recovering the African Past

The school teacher and Djéliba Kouyaté argue while Mabo Keïta listens

The griots are in the service of everyone. You should know this.

15 With *Guimba the Tyrant* Cheick Oumar Sissoko, like the Kouyatés, recreates the past. He makes it relevant to the present with a story of the abuse of power and the quest for a just society. In this film the king's *griot* is corrupt; he limits himself to singing the ruler's praises. Dani Kouyaté's most recent feature, *Sia – The Dream of the Python*, features a *griot* similarly corrupt, and the role of denouncing the tyrant falls to a madman.

them for others as they go, evoking little emotion but exacting recompense. True *griots* retell history, they inculcate norms, and they will contradict the ruler when he strays from the right path. The Kouyatés, father and son, fulfill 'the meaning of their name' as they convey to us a sense of the rich history of Africa and of the formidable role *griots* played in it.[15]

References and Further Reading

Achebe, Chinua. 1958. *Things Fall Apart*. London: Heinemann.
——. 2000. *Home and Exile*. Oxford/New York: Oxford University Press.
Anonymous. 1995. 'La parole à Kouyaté.' *Ecrans d'Afrique* 13–14: 8–14.
Barlet, Olivier. 2002. 'Universel comme le conte: Entretien avec Dani Kouyaté.' *Africultures* 49: 92–4.
Belcher, Stephen. 1999. *Epic Traditions of Africa*. Bloomington/Indianapolis: Indiana University Press.
Beti, Mongo. 1974. *Remember Ruben*. Paris: Editions 10/18. English translation by Gerald Moore (1980) *Remember Ruben*. Ibadan: New Horn Press; London/Nairobi: Heinemann; Washington, D.C.: Three Continents Press.
Diawara, Manthia. 2000. 'The Iconography of West African Cinema,' in June Givanni (ed.) *Symbolic Narratives/African Cinema: Audiences, Theory and the Moving Image*. London: British Film Institute. 81–9.
Genesis/La Genèse. 1999. Film directed by Cheick Oumar Sissoko, written by Jean-Louis Sagot Duvauroux. Produced by Kora Films (Mali), Balanzan, Centre National de Production Cinématographique du Mali, and Cinéma Public Films (France). Distributed in the U.S. by California Newsreel and Kino International. 102 minutes.

Guimba the Tyrant/Guimba. 1995. Film written and directed by Cheick Oumar Sissoko. Produced by Kora Films (Mali). Distributed in the U.S. by California Newsreel and Kino International. 93 minutes.

Hale, Thomas A. 1990. *Scribe, Griot, and Novelist: Narrative Interpreters of the Songhay Empire.* Gainesville: University of Florida Press.

——. 1998. *Griots and Griottes: Masters of Words and Music.* Bloomington/Indianapolis: Indiana University Press.

Johnson, John William, and Fa-Digi Sisòkò. 1992 (1986). *The Epic of Son-Jara: a West African Tradition.* Second edition, commentary abridged and revised. Bloomington/Indianapolis: Indiana University Press.

Keïta! The Heritage of the Griot/Keïta! l'héritage du griot. 1995. Film written and directed by Dani Kouyaté. Produced by AFIX Productions (France), Les Productions de la Lanterne (France), Sahélis Productions (Burkina Faso), and the Government of Burkina Faso. Distributed in the U.S. by California Newsreel. 94 minutes.

Kourouma, Ahmadou. 1990. *Monnè, outrages et défis.* Paris: Editions du Seuil. English translation by Nidra Poller (1993) *Monnew.* San Francisco: Mercury House.

——. 1998. *En attendant le vote des bêtes sauvages.* Paris: Editions du Seuil.

Kouyaté, Sotigui. 1994. Statement recorded by A.M. *Ecrans d'Afrique* 9/10: 22–3.

Little Senegal. 2001. Film directed by Rachid Bouchareb, written by Olivier Lorelle et Rachid Bouchareb. Produced by 3B Productions (France). 98 minutes.

Names Live Nowhere/Les Noms habitent nulle part. 1994. Film directed by Monique Loreau. Produced by Underworld, RTBF, and Centre de l'Audiovisuel à Bruxelles. Distributed in the U.S. by ArtMattan Productions. 76/59 minutes.

Ngũgĩ wa Thiong'o. 1977. *Petals of Blood.* London/Nairobi/Ibadan/Lusaka: Heinemann; New York: E. P. Dutton.

Niane, D.T. 1960. *Soundjata, ou l'Epopée Mandingue.* Paris: Présence Africaine. English translation by G. D. Pickett (1965) *Sundiata, an Epic of Old Mali.* Harlow, Essex: Longman.

River Niger, Black Mother. 1998. Documentary written and directed by Ola Balogun. Produced by Polystar Productions and Delka Productions. Distributed in the U.S. by Cinema Guild. 43 minutes.

Sia – the Dream of the Python/Sia – le rêve du python. 2001. Film directed by Dani Kouyaté, adapted by Dani Kouyaté from a play by Moussa Diagana. Produced by Les Productions de la Lanterne (France), Sahélis Productions (Burkina Faso), and the Government of Burkina Faso. Distributed in the U.S. by ArtMattan Productions. 96 minutes.

Sotigui Kouyaté, un griot moderne. 1997. Documentary written and directed by Mahamat Saleh Haroun. Produced by La Lanterne (France) and Canal Cholet (Mali). Distributed in France by Médiathèque des Trois Mondes, Paris. Available for viewing at Cinémathèque Afrique, Paris. 58 minutes.

Yeelen (Brightness). 1987. Film written and directed by Souleymane Cissé. Produced by Les Films Cissé (Mali). Distributed in the U.S. by Kino International. 105 minutes.

Engraving, featuring Amílcar Cabral, which was used in a series of postage stamps issued by Guinea-Bissau in 1976 on the third anniversary of his assassination

2 Fighting Colonialism

World War I gave impetus to nationalist demands in some colonies, India the most prominent example, but it was World War II that heralded the end of colonialism. It raised the aspirations of the educated in Asia and Africa. The colonial 'masters' appeared no longer all that imposing after they had limped from defeat to defeat in the early years of the war. The experience was particularly striking for Asians as fellow-Asians humbled the British, French, and Dutch. Where colonial powers were not swept away by the Japanese, they recruited colonial troops to fight their wars in Asia, North Africa, and Europe. These troops were commanded by European officers, but African and Asian soldiers also encountered Europeans of their own station in the army and outside. Those who did return home were no longer habituated to colonial paternalism. And expectations had been raised in the colonies: the colonial powers had imposed heavy demands to supply their stretched war economies, and they had made promises, the most famous of them by Charles de Gaulle at Brazzaville in 1944.

The British emerged victorious but profoundly weakened. France, Belgium, and the Netherlands joined the victors, once liberated from German occupation. But the war had irrevocably shifted power away from them to the two new superpowers, and neither the United States nor the Soviet Union had much sympathy for colonial empires. Nationalist leaders of Indonesia proclaimed their independence in 1945, and the Dutch recognized it after four years of sometimes heavy fighting. Britain let go of its partitioned Indian empire in 1947. The French accepted the cost of eight years of war in Indochina, but after their defeat at Dien Bien Phu in 1954 they granted independence to a Vietnam divided into two for the time being. Still, most Europeans saw independence for the African colonies in the distant future, if they thought about it at all. The process was to accelerate beyond the imagination of all but a very few (see table on page xii).

Faced with mounting nationalist claims for independence, most colonial powers soon concluded that a negotiated transfer of power was preferable to escalating confrontation. Collaboration would allow continued economic and strategic benefits without the political and financial costs of direct control. Decolonization thus was a quite peaceful process in most of Africa South of the Sahara. Britain granted independence to the Sudan (formally an Anglo-Egyptian condominium) in 1956. The

Seek ye first the political kingdom....
(Kwame Nkrumah, quoted by Davidson, 1973: 84)

45

Fighting Colonialism

leadership of Kwame Nkrumah took the Gold Coast to independence in 1957. The British colony was reborn as Ghana, a tribute to the ancient kingdom, though that had been located several hundred miles to the north-west. Nigeria, Africa's most populous country, celebrated independence in 1960. In Kenya, the Mau Mau peasant rebellion could not effectively threaten British rule, even if it took several years of brutal repression to eliminate the guerrilla movement, but it helped persuade Britain to leave power with the African nationalists rather than the settlers when the colony became independent in 1963. In 1966 the British flag was lowered for the last time on the continent, except for developments in Southern Rhodesia to which we will turn in a moment.

France left Indochina and Algeria only after protracted colonial wars, but in Africa South of the Sahara it faced an armed guerrilla movement only in Cameroon, where nationalist demands had been emboldened by the territory's status as a United Nations trust territory. The guerrillas were easily contained, and France ensured the establishment of a government to its liking. Guinea, under the leadership of Sekou Touré, was the only French colony to opt for independence in 1958, but just two years later France granted independence to all but one of its fourteen other colonies South of the Sahara, as well as to the major off-shore colony, Madagascar.

In 1960, in great haste and with virtually no preparation, Belgium granted independence to its huge colony, the Congo. In the ensuing turmoil Patrice Lumumba, the Prime Minister, was arrested and subsequently assassinated. The arrest was carried out by the army led by Joseph Desiré Mobutu, who seized full power in 1965. Belgium's trust territory was divided to establish two independent countries, Burundi and Rwanda, in 1962. Their colonial legacies of ethnic conflict were to be exacerbated to the point of large-scale killings over several decades, culminating in the 1994 genocide in Rwanda.

Italy withdrew from Somalia in 1960 as stipulated by the United Nations. Spain granted independence to its two tiny possessions South of the Sahara, now renamed Equatorial Guinea, in 1968. Only Portugal, once at the forefront of discovery and lucrative trade, the first to establish a major presence on African soil, now one of the poorest countries in Western Europe, ruled by a dictator, was not prepared to let go of its African 'empire': Mozambique, Angola, Guinea-Bissau, Cape Verde, and São Tomé and Príncipe – in order of size of population.

Portugal's refusal to make any concessions to African aspirations and severe repression of any opposition brought forth armed struggle in its three largest colonies. The attack on a prison in Luanda, the capital of Angola, on 4 February 1961, generally attributed to the MPLA, the Movimento Popular de Libertação de Angola, marked the beginning of the armed struggle in the Portuguese colonies. The attack failed in its objective of freeing political prisoners rumored to be scheduled for transfer to Cape Verde or Portugal. Attacks on two other Luanda prisons in the next few days also failed. The attacks, however, served to attract international attention. Subsequently the opposition in Angola was hampered by its division into three liberation movements, supported by different foreign powers and at times at war with each other. Still, the guerrilla movements, to differing degrees, tied down Portuguese troops and imposed a heavy burden on the Portuguese budget. For Angolans the sufferings of colonial war were to be compounded as the divisions among the liberation movements and outside interventions – to which we will return – devastated their country in warfare that continued until 2002.

The military successes of the guerrilla movements in the other two colonies were decisive in bringing independence to all of Portuguese Africa. FRELIMO, the Frente de Libertaçao de Moçambique, operating from bases in Tanzania and Zambia, came to control much of northern Mozambique, closing the Beira railroad and threatening the construction of the Cabora Bassa Dam on the Zambezi. In Guinea-Bissau,[1] PAIGC, the Partido Africano da Independência da Guiné e Cabo Verde, representing both Portuguese Guinea and the Cape Verde Islands, launched the armed struggle for independence from neighboring Guinea in 1963. The movement was led by Amílcar Cabral, the foremost intellectual among African guerrilla leaders. Within ten years PAIGC had achieved more than any other guerrilla movement in Africa: it had established control over most of Guinea-Bissau, and it received recognition from eighty countries within two months when it declared independence in September 1973. In February 1974 António de Spínola, deputy chief of staff of the Portuguese army and former commander-in-chief in Guinea-Bissau, published *Portugal e o futuro*, asserting that Portugal could not win a military victory in Africa. Two months later young officers staged a coup, proclaiming 'Decolonization and Democratization,' and brought down an authoritarian regime that had lasted for 48 years: the impact of the African guerrilla movements on the colonial army had been such as to usher in democracy for Portugal. The new government proceeded to grant independence to all Portuguese colonies.

In the meantime Great Britain had made preparations to grant independence to Southern Rhodesia. This colony had its origins in the invasion of European settlers under the auspices of Cecil Rhodes's British South Africa Company. Only in 1924 did it come under British control as a British Crown colony, self-governed by the settlers who constituted the largest European population in any British colony other than neighboring South Africa. Still, they were a small minority. In 1965, they issued a Unilateral Declaration of Independence (UDI) so as to preempt the universal franchise that independence on British terms would have brought, and to keep political power securely in their hands. Britain protested but was not prepared to use force against its white 'kith and kin,' as some British politicians put it. The United Nations imposed mandatory economic sanctions which were easily circumvented. They increased transaction costs for exports and imports, but they also led to an industrial expansion as imports were replaced by local manufactures. Negotiations between Britain and the settler government remained fruitless. It took a long guerrilla war to bring majority rule in 1980. The

1 The colony was known as Portuguese Guinea. At independence it became identified by its capital Bissau to distinguish it from neighboring Guinea, formerly a French colony.

country was rebaptized Zimbabwe in tribute to the urban civilization that flourished there more than half a millennium ago.

The African national movement in Southern Rhodesia went through a number of structures and names in the late 1950s and early 1960s as it was banned time and again. Eventually it became known as the Zimbabwe African People's Union (ZAPU). Founded in 1961, it was banned in less than a year. In 1963, conflicts over leadership issues led to the breakaway of the Zimbabwe African National Union (ZANU) which in its turn was banned in 1964. Over the years the two movements became identified with the country's Ndebele and Shona people respectively. The beginning of the war of liberation is usually dated to a battle around the settler town of Sinoia, where seven ZANU guerrillas were killed on 28 April 1966.

After FRELIMO had moved across north-western Mozambique to the Rhodesian border, it provided ZANU in 1972 with base areas from which to infiltrate north-eastern Zimbabwe. ZANU now emphasized political education and mobilization among the peasantry. The guerrilla movement drew on memories of earlier resistance to white settlement. The war of liberation came to be known as the second *Chimurenga*, named in tribute to the uprisings against European settlement in 1896–7. The guerrillas called village meetings, the *pungwe*, to exhort the peasants, to have them join in chanting militant slogans, and to sing *chimurenga* songs. Often a system of 'dual power' emerged: the settler state ruled by day, the guerrillas took over at night. The movement thus managed to establish a patchwork of semi-liberated areas and to implant its own administrative structures. The nature of the relationship between the guerrillas and the peasantry is a matter of dispute and presumably varied across the country. Ranger (1985) has argued that the peasants were able to implant their ideas of more land and a better deal for peasants; Kriger (1992) has pointed to tensions as well as collaboration between the two sides.

The war was protracted. The settlers were prepared to make considerable sacrifices to protect their privileges and received crucial outside assistance. The U.N. sanctions were flouted not only by South Africa and the Portuguese while they controlled Mozambique, but by other countries as well. Thus the United States imported chrome from Southern Rhodesia from 1971 to 1977, made no effort to stop investments by U.S. companies or the recruitment of mercenaries – illegal under U.S. law – for the Rhodesian army, and from 1975 supplied aircraft that increased the air force's combat capacity fivefold. The guerrillas were divided by conflict between ZANU and ZAPU, and also by conflicts within these movements. Some of the conflicts escalated into armed clashes. Support from Zambia, Mozambique, Angola, and Tanzania – the 'Frontline States' – surged and ebbed in response to these conflicts and to pressures from Western countries to arrive at a peaceful settlement. After several false starts such a settlement was finally agreed in 1979. In the 1980 elections ZANU, based on the majority Shona and drawing on the administrative structures established during the war, won a solid majority.

Robert Mugabe's first cabinet was based on old-guard politicians and professionals rather than guerrilla leaders. After Joshua Nkomo, the leader of ZAPU, and two other ZAPU ministers were dismissed from the cabinet in 1982, acts of terrorism were committed in rural Ndebele areas. The Zimbabwe National Army, like the Rhodesian army before it, carried out a ruthless 'counterinsurgency' campaign against the 'dissidents' that victimized ordinary peasants.

Mozambique was to pay a heavy price for its support of the liberation struggles in Zimbabwe and South Africa. Southern Rhodesia recruited disaffected Mozambicans and trained them as sabotage units to penetrate Mozambique. They were reinforced by former members of the colonial security forces. In 1980 South Africa took over the recruiting, arming, and funding of what became known as the Resistência Nacional Moçambicana (RENAMO). This guerrilla movement was distinguished by its extreme brutality. More than one million people had died, and about 40 per cent of the population had become refugees by the time a peace accord was signed in 1992.

The two films we are about to examine focus on the two contexts where it took protracted armed struggle to gain independence: Angola where the struggle against Portugal began, and Southern Rhodesia eventually to become Zimbabwe.

References and Further Reading

Cooper, Frederick. 2002. *Africa Since 1940: The Past of the Present*. New Approaches to African History 1. Cambridge/New York/Port Melbourne/Madrid/Cape Town: Cambridge University Press.

Davidson, Basil. 1973. *Black Star: A View of the Life and Times of Kwame Nkrumah*. New York/Washington: Praeger.

Freund, Bill. (1984) 1998. *The Making of Contemporary Africa: the Development of African Society Since 1800*. Second edition. Boulder, CO: Lynne Rienner.

Kriger, Norma J. 1992. *Zimbabwe's Guerrilla War: Peasant Voices*. African Studies 70. Cambridge/New York /Port Chester/Melbourne/Sidney: Cambridge University Press.

Ranger, Terence. 1985. *Peasant Consciousness and Guerrilla War in Zimbabwe: A Comparative Study*. Perspectives on Southern Africa 37. London: James Currey; Berkeley/Los Angeles: University of California Press.

Spínola, António de. 1974. *Portugal e o futuro: análise da conjuntura nacional*. Lisbon: Arcádia. English translation (1974) *Portugal and the Future*. Johannesburg: Perskor Publishers.

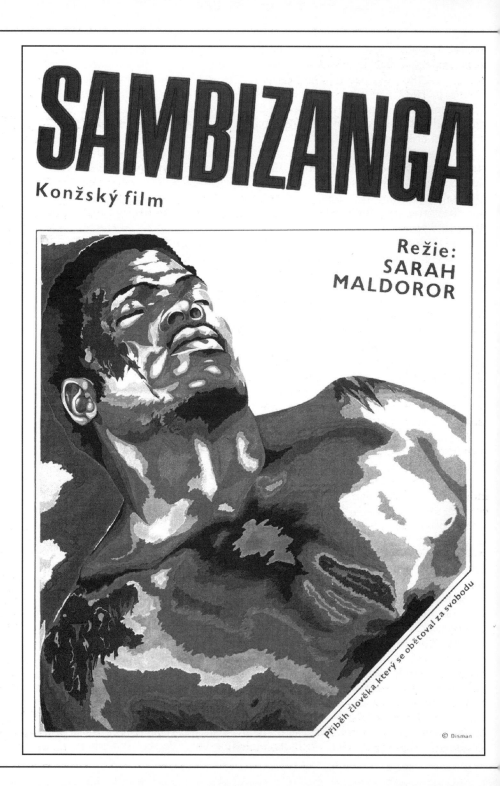

SAMBIZANGA

Konžský film

Režie:
SARAH
MALDOROR

Příběh člověka, který se obětoval za svobodu

© Disman

Sambizanga 1972
The Martyr, His Family, and the Movement

Sambizanga denounces the oppression of Portuguese colonialism in Angola while exalting the emerging resistance that was to establish an effective guerrilla movement. The film shared the Tanit d'Or (the prize takes the form of a gold statuette of Tanit, the Carthaginian goddess) at the 1972 Carthage Film Festival. It is a quality production that has stood the test of time.[1]

Sambizanga follows closely the novel *The Real Life of Domingos Xavier* by José Luandino Vieira. Vieira was born José Vieira Mateus da Graça in Portugal in 1935 to a cobbler. A year later his family emigrated to Luanda, the capital of Angola. In 1959, while working on the construction of a dam, he was arrested by the Polícia Internacional de Defesa do Estado (PIDE), the Portuguese secret police, for political activities and imprisoned for four months (Péju and Girard, 1989). He wrote his short novel while living in Portugal, just after the February 1961 attacks on three Luanda prisons by the MPLA, the Movimento Popular de Libertação de Angola, which marked the beginning of the armed struggle against Portuguese rule in Africa. Vieira completed his novel in November 1961, only days before he was arrested again by the PIDE and sentenced by a military court to 14 years in prison.

Angola had perhaps more European settlers, most of whom had arrived after World War II, than any other colony South of the Sahara. Vieira grew up in in a poor multi-racial neighborhood in Luanda – he might well be the boy playing marbles with Zito near the prison. Vieira indicated his commitment to this setting by changing his name. The anti-colonial struggle also brought together Africans, Europeans, and *mestiços*. The point is well illustrated by the individuals involved with the film and the novel. José Vieira, the European immigrant, had committed himself to Angola. Sarah Maldoror was born in France of a French mother and a father from Guadeloupe.[2] She had married Mário de Andrade, a prominent mestizo leader of the MPLA exile organization, who co-authored the script.[3] Maurice Pons, an established French novelist, was the first author. The novel's epigraph pays homage to Agostinho Neto, the African poet who was to become the first President of independent Angola.

According to Vieira, the novel is substantially based on real events (Chang, 1985). Domingos's arrest by the PIDE at a dam construction site parallels Vieira's own experience. The tailor Mussunda, organizer and ideologue of the resistance, was a historical figure exalted by Agostinho Neto in the very poem that constitutes the novel's epigraph. And Liceu was the nickname of Carlos Aniceto Vieira Dias, the founder and leader of the Ngola Ritmos who valorized traditional Angolan music and the Kimbundu language (Butler, 1989; Andrade, 1971).

I tell the story of a woman, and it could be the story of any woman, in any country, who has taken off in search of her husband. The year is 1960. The political consciousness of the people has not yet been formed. Too bad if that doesn't look 'good.' Too bad if there is no spectacular emergence of consciousness. I have no use for preachy militant films. (Sarah Maldoror, 1973, my translation)

1 This discussion of *Sambizanga* draws on Gugler (1999).

2 Sarah Maldoror's given name was Sarah Ducas. She chose her name after reading *Les Chants de Maldoror*, a nightmarish epic poem replete with grotesque imagery by the nineteenth-century French writer Isidore Ducasse, known as the Comte de Lautréamont (Pfaff, 1988: 205). The artist is portrayed in Anne Laure Folly's documentary, *Sarah Maldoror ou la nostalgie de l'utopie*.

3 On the political role of Mário de Andrade in the Angolan struggle, see Marcum (1969, 1978 *passim*). Andrade also played a major role in promoting Angolan literary voices. *Inter alia* he wrote the introduction to and was the co-translator of the French edition of *The True Life of Domingos Xavier*.

Fighting Colonialism

Three narrative strands are interwoven in the tragic story that is told with pathos in the novel and the film. We witness the martyrdom of Domingos Xavier as he is arrested at the labor camp, taken to prison, tortured, and finally killed. And we follow two journeys of discovery. We are with Maria, his wife, as she travels in search of her husband, carrying their baby on her back. First in Dondo, then in Luanda, 150 miles away, she trudges to administrative offices and police stations. And we follow the efforts of the underground to ascertain the identity of the prisoner, presumably so as to communicate with him and strengthen his resolve, to assist his family, and to warn his contacts who may be in jeopardy.

Novel and film offer composite views of a collective struggle that ranges from popular responses to oppression to the organized fight for independence. In the novel, the solidarity between Domingos and his people is expressed through leitmotifs such as sun, river, rain, and children which serve as cultural conduits among the three narratives. This common thread of irrepressible life makes it an upbeat story, almost luminous, in spite of all the agony (Chang, 1985). The characters are differentiated. A European official is sympathetic to Maria's plight. Some African subalterns in the colonial administration identify with Maria and Domingos; one smuggles a message to Domingos. The oppressed and the militants vary in their understanding of the colonial situation and their commitment to struggle. Maria defines the conflict in racial terms, but Mussunda explains that the conflict is between the rich and the poor. And the story has Silvester, a Portuguese engineer like Vieira himself, working with the resistance.[4] In the novel, when Mussunda announces the death of Domingos at the party organized by the underground, he starts out: 'My fellow Africans....,' but then he sees Silvester, and begins anew:

My fellow Angolans. A brother has come to say that they have killed our comrade. He was called Domingos Xavier and he was a tractor driver. He never harmed anyone, only wanted the good of the people and of his land. I stopped this dance only to say this, not for it to end, for our joy is great: our brother carried himself like a man, he did not tell the secrets of his people, he did not sell himself. We are not going to weep any more for his death because, Domingos Antonio Xavier, you begin today your real life in the hearts of the Angolan people... (p. 84).[5]

The film takes its title from Sambizanga, a poor neighborhood in Luanda from where the first assault on a Luanda prison was launched on 4 February 1961.[6] It follows the novel's story closely in most respects. Some of the changes from the novel to the film reflect the different medium. The action is more tightly organized in the film than in the novel and compressed from five into four days. Thus the film makes do without some of the background information provided by the novel: how Petelo had come to lose a buttock, for example (p. 2); or the arguments among the militants whether to have the dance (p. 78). And the film adds songs: in the very first scene we hear 'Monagambée,' the song of the Angolan rebels.

4 In the 1980 Luanda stage version of *A Vida Verdadeira de Domingos Xavier*, however, the engineer was black (Wolfers, 1982).

5 This and all subsequent references are to the English edition, *The True Life of Domingos Xavier*.

6 Sambizanga, as well as Braga where Vieira grew up, are locally referred to as *museke* for the reddish sand on which such peri-urban settlements arose (Andrade, 1971).

Sarah Maldoror, center, during the shooting

Other changes in the film may be seen to reflect the fact that it was produced a decade after Vieira wrote the novel. Not only is the early 1960s historical context made more explicit in the film's ending, but there is a shift from the novel's emphasis on the victimization that justifies the rebellion that had just begun when Vieira wrote, to the militancy of the struggle that was well under way when Maldoror directed the film. In particular, the film departs from the novel in transforming Domingos: the novel's extremely thin victim, who refuses to betray Sousinha and Silvester, becomes a sturdy militant who heads the underground group at the construction site and distributes the pamphlets from Luanda supplied by Silvester. Maria appears also as a stronger character: in the novel she becomes so discouraged as to abandon her search for Domingos twice, but in the film she presses on without flinching.

Maldoror uses the film medium to great effect. The slow moves and drawn-out takes of the serene idyll of Domingos's family contrast with the quick shots of his arrest taken from several angles. She presents striking images: the long opening scene of back-breaking work in the quarry; the market empty at night and bustling during the day; black and white children playing together in a poor neighborhood. The rapidly flowing river at the beginning and the end of the film suggest the power of the resistance movement. And the scenes of Domingos's arrest, of his interrogations,[7] and of his death among the prisoners confront us powerfully, more dramatically than the text, with his suffering and the brutality of his torturers.[8] Maldoror uses intercutting to move back and forth among the story's three strands, especially between the ordeals of Domingos and Maria. And she repeatedly foreshadows an impending scene by briefly showing its principal character in an earlier shot. Thus the film, unlike the novel, conveys a sense of chronological continuity.[9]

7 After the first brutal interrogation Domingos finds a note in his coffee mug. In the film a voice repeats the Portuguese message as Domingos swallows the torn-up note, but the sub-titled English version fails to provide a translation: 'Courage, *companheiro*! Do not say anything. They do not know anything. Courage! Timoteo.'

8 Domingos's martyrdom was the *leitmotif* in the promotion of *Sambizanga*, as in the Czech poster reproduced here.

9 For an analysis of the narrative structure of *Sambizanga*, see Larouche (1991).

Fighting Colonialism

Neighbors comfort Maria after the arrest of Domingos, one cradling Maria's baby

Sambizanga, like the novel, spends somewhat more time with the underground than with Domingos, more time with Domingos than with Maria. Still, the images of Maria's quest to find Domingos, of her despair when she has learned of his death, and of the women comforting her have an emotional impact that parallels the wrenching experience of Domingos's martyrdom. This impact is reinforced by two songs. A mourning song speaks of the road and of love during Maria's long march, and then once more during her bus ride to Luanda. The same female voice repeats the prisoners' song lamenting the death of Domingos twice, the last time as we watch Maria in despair. If Vieira told the story of an unknown soldier in the struggle for liberation, Maldoror presents the ballad of an unknown soldier and his wife.

The director's gender may explain her success in translating a few short sentences in the novel into beautiful scenes of women comforting Maria and her baby after her husband has been taken away, and when she comes to stay with friends in Luanda after she has learnt of Domingos's death – at that time, the women tenderly consoling her stand in stark contrast to the men playing cards. And perhaps a director from the diaspora was particularly well placed to make her viewers discover the beauty of Africa and its people. The camera lyrically presents the countryside; it magnificently portrays Domingos and Maria; it lingers lovingly on the faces of the women surrounding Maria.

Presumably the writer and the director both had foreign audiences in mind. The novel is unsparing in its account of colonial brutality, and it would seem unlikely that Vieira expected the authorities to allow *The Real Life of Domingos Xavier* to appear in print. His early stories were published in an edition of a few hundred copies by overseas students in Lisbon in 1960, but another collection of short stories, described as anti-racist and presenting a modest challenge to colonial values, had been confiscated by the colonial authorities at the Luanda printer in 1957 (Wolfers, 1982). Various clandestine copies of *The Real Life of Domingos Xavier* circulated in the 1960s, but regular publication came only after the overthrow of the Portuguese dictatorship in 1974. Russian (1970) and French (1971) translations published during the war served to mobilize public opinion in Europe. After the war they were followed by translations into English, German, Norwegian, Spanish, and Swedish (Butler, 1989; Wolfers, 1982). Likewise the film, made during the war, was not intended to be shown in Angola, or anywhere the Portuguese regime held sway, but to mobilize foreign opinion in support of the struggle against the last remaining colonial power in Africa. Hence some of the actors could be left to speak their different vernaculars (Hennebelle, 1973). Vieira and Maldoror were quite successful in reaching their intended audiences as evidenced by the translations of the novel and the numerous reviews when the film was first released.[10] And they created works of art that continue to grip readers and viewers alike.

José Luandino Vieira served a prison term while Maurice Pons and Mário de Andrade wrote the screenplay and while Sarah Maldoror directed the film. The director who produces a film without any input from the novel's author might be expected to take great liberties. But Maldoror remained true to the text while bringing to *Sambizanga* a woman's perspective and her discovery of the beauty of Africa and of Africans. Together with Ousmane Sembène, she had trained with Sergei Gerassimov and Mark Donskoy at the Gorki Studio in Moscow in 1961–2 (Pfaff, 1988: 206). By the time she directed *Sambizanga*, she had gained a good deal of experience filming in Africa. She had assisted Gillo Pontecorvo during the filming of the seminal documentary-style *Battle of Algiers*. She had directed *Monagambée*, which is also based on writing by Luandino Vieira, in this case a short story. And she had produced a full-length feature film in black and white with the guerrillas in Guinea-Bissau, *Des Fusils pour Banta* (*Guns for Banta*), which was, however, never released (Hennebelle, 1973).

Maldoror worked with amateurs, except for the French actor Jacques Poitrenaud who took on the repugnant role of the torturer (Larouche, 1991). Her choices were inspired. Domingos Oliveira, an Angolan exile recruited off a tractor in the Congo, effectively conveys the stoic endurance of Domingos. Elisa Andrade, an economist from Cape Verde who had already played a part in *Monagambée*, beautifully expresses the full range of Maria's emotions from loving mother and wife to anger, stoicism, and desperation in her search for Domingos. Maldoror had to make do without much of the literary language Vieira had created to reflect the popular creole of Luanda, but she introduced songs to good effect.[11]

Sambizanga was shot in Congo-Brazzaville. It was sponsored by the Congolese Government which provided accommodation, transport, and various other kinds of support, by the Agence de Coopération Culturelle et Technique of France (the NATO ally of Portugal!), and by the MPLA. The Centre National du Cinéma Français offered an advance of 380,000 francs, then about $70,000. Production costs approached $100,000

10 For a summary of critical comment on *Sambizanga*, see Pfaff (1988: 212–13).

11 Vieira sought to create a literary language that reflects the popular language of Luanda, a variation of Portuguese that had its distinct rules established in a tradition that reaches back to the 19th century (Péju and Girard, 1989). Creolized Kimbundu-Portuguese speech pervades not only the voices of the characters but is also used by the narrator. This incorporation involves vocabulary as well as sentence construction. The shared creolized discourse underscores the narrative's collective vision. Vieira developed this transformational practice further in his subsequent writing (Butler, 1989, 1991; Peres, 1997: 37–46).

(Pfaff, 1988, 207). Maldoror shot the film in only seven weeks, but was able to see rushes developed in Paris (Hennebelle, 1973). A generation later, *Sambizanga* retains its emotional poignancy and aesthetic quality.

References and Further Reading

Andrade, Mário de. 1971. 'Nouveau langage dans l'imaginaire angolais.' Introduction to Luandino Vieira, *La vrai vie de Domingos Xavier* suivi de *Le complet de Mateus*. Paris: Présence Africaine. 7–18.

The Battle of Algiers. 1966. Film written by Franco Solinas, directed by Gillo Pontecorvo. Produced by Magna (Algeria and Italy). Distributed in the U.S. by International Historic Films. 123 minutes.

Butler, Phyllis Reisman. 1989. 'Colonial Resistance and Contemporary Angolan Narrative: *A Vida Verdadeira de Domingos Xavier* and *Vidas Novas*.' *Modern Fiction Studies* 35: 47–54.

——. 1991. 'Writing a National Literature: The Case of José Luandino Vieira.' *Toward Socio-Criticism: Selected Proceedings of the Conference 'Luso–Brazilian Literatures, A Socio-Critical Approach,'* edited by Roberto Reis. Tempe, Arizona: Center for Latin American Studies, Arizona State University. 135–42.

Chang, Linda Stockton. 1985. 'Identity Behind Bars: Political Prisoner Protagonists of Luandino Vieira.' *Journal of the Society of Contemporary Hispanic and Lusophone Revolutionary Literatures* 1: 391–405.

Ducasse, Isidore (a.k.a. the Comte de Lautréamont). 1868. *Les Chants de Maldoror*.

Gugler, Josef. 1999. 'African Writing Projected onto the Screen: *Sambizanga*, *Xala*, and *Kongi's Harvest*.' *African Studies Review* 42 (1): 79–104.

Hennebelle, Monique. 1973. ''Sambizanga': un film de Sarah Maldoror sur les débuts de la guerre de libération en Angola.' *Afrique Littéraire et Artistique* 28: 78–87.

Larouche, Michel. 1991. 'Le temps que l'on met à marcher.' *Films d'Afrique,* edited by Michel Larouche. Montréal: Guernica. 21–39.

Maldoror, Sarah. 1973. Statement in an article ''Sambizanga' de Sarah Maldoror: Le temps que l'on met à marcher' signed M.E., *Le Monde*, 27 April, page 15. An alternative English rendering is provided in 'It Takes Time to March,' *Women and Film* 1 (5 and 6): 72–3, 1974.

Marcum, John A. 1969, 1978. *The Angolan Revolution. Volume I: The Anatomy of an Explosion (1950–1962). Volume II: Exile Politics and Guerrilla Warfare (1962–1976)*. Cambridge, MA/London: M.I.T. Press.

Monagambée. 1969. Film directed by Sarah Maldoror, written by Serge Michel. Produced by the Congress of National Organizations in the Portuguese Colonies (Algeria). 18 minutes.

Péju, Marcel and Patrick Girard. 1989. 'José Luandino Vieira: 'Nous avons perdu le contact avec les autres littératures.'' *Jeune Afrique* 1479, 10 May.

Peres, Phyllis. 1997. *Transculturation and Resistance in Lusophone African Narrative*. Gainesville: University Press of Florida.

Pfaff, Françoise. 1988. *Twenty–Five Black African Filmmakers: a Critical Study, with Filmography and Bio-bibliography*. New York: Greenwood Press.

Sambizanga. 1972. Film directed by Sarah Maldoror, written by Maurice Pons and Mário de Andrade. Produced by MPLA and People's Republic of the Congo. Distributed in the U.S. by New Yorker Films. 102 minutes.

Sarah Maldoror ou la nostalgie de l'utopie. 1998. Documentary written and directed by Anne Laure Folly. Produced by Amanou Productions (France). Available for viewing at Cinémathèque Afrique, Paris. 26 minutes.

Vieira, José Luandino. 1960. *A Cidade e a Infância*. Lisbon: Casa dos Estudantes do Império.

——. 1974. *A Vida Verdadeira de Domingos Xavier*. Lisbon: Edições 70. English translation by Michael Wolfers (1978) *The Real Life of Domingos Xavier*. London: Heinemann. Also staged as a play.

Wolfers, Michael. 1982. 'José Luandino Vieira.' *Index on Censorship* 11.1: 35–6.

Flame 1996
A Twofold Struggle

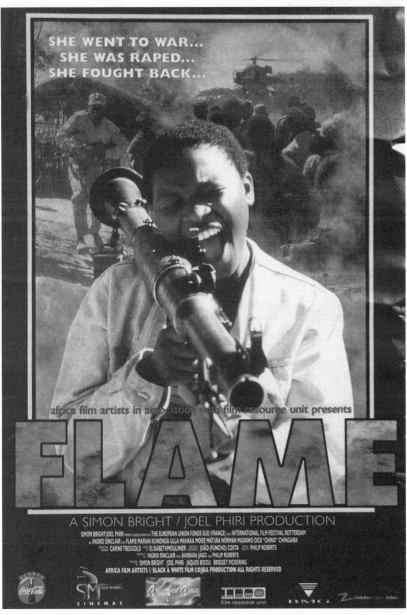

In order not to fall into the traps of the clichés of stories or legends that are told today about the presence of women in the war, I based the film solely on true stories that had really been experienced. (Ingrid Sinclair in an interview with Speciale, 1996: 14)

Fighting Colonialism

Flame distinguishes itself from other accounts of guerrilla warfare by having two young women as the chief protagonists. At the same time, the film offers a comprehensive view of the guerrilla experience. We come to understand how two adolescent girls are motivated to join the armed struggle in 1975. We accompany their arduous trek across the border to reach a guerrilla camp. The village girls Florence and Nyasha become the guerrillas Flame and Liberty. We watch the training of women recruits, desultory at first. We follow Flame and Liberty as they return across the border to fight in Southern Rhodesia. We applaud when Flame blows up an army landrover, the moment caught in the first poster. We experience the horrors of an aerial attack on their camp. We share the exultation of Flame and Liberty at victory in 1979 – and their disappointment at what Zimbabwe has become.

Florence lives with her parents in the village, but the situation of Nyasha is rather unusual: we are told that she has no family. After the war she never returns to the village. Her pursuit of education separated her from her friend: the movement sent her to college, and she succeeded in pursuing an urban career after the war. The village girl Nyasha who had adopted the *nom de guerre* Liberty has liberated herself, she has realized her ambition – and become a solitary professional. When the two friends meet in 1995, sixteen years after Liberty announced to Flame that the war was over, they are separated by a class barrier. It falls to the articulate professional to narrate the story from the 1995 present.

Flame bears comparison with Shimmer Chinodya's novel *Harvest of Thorns*, the most detailed and persuasive account of the guerrilla experience anywhere.[1] Benjamin Tichafa, Chinodya's protagonist, is different from Florence and Nyasha in that he comes from an urban background and is a couple of years older and better educated when at age 17 he joins the guerrillas in 1977. But in other respects the parallels between film and novel are striking, all the more so as Sinclair (2001) had not read the novel at the time. Both stories are situated in the last few years of the war for Zimbabwe. Mixed motives propel the three adolescents to enlist in the struggle for liberation. After a dangerous journey they manage to cross the border and join the guerrillas, but at first they are under suspicion of being spies. Benjamin, like Flame, experiences a devastating aerial attack on the camp that kills the girl he loves, then fights with his unit in Southern Rhodesia. Both Flame and Benjamin encounter lone enemy soldiers, presumably Selous Scouts, government forces who masqueraded as guerrillas. Benjamin's emotional involvement with Ropa largely mirrors Flame's infatuation with Danger. Benjamin shares with Flame the disillusionment of a victory that rewarded only a few. The guerrilla experience has not become a badge of honor: Benjamin is fired by a white foreman because he is an ex-guerrilla, Danger is fired because he is 'too cheeky.'

Neither film nor novel acknowledges the conflict, leading to armed clashes at times, between the two guerrilla movements, the Zimbabwe African National Union (ZANU), based in Mozambique, and the Zimbabwe African People's Union (ZAPU), based in Zambia. In *Flame* we

1 Shimmer Chinodya is three years older than his protagonist. Still, the quality of his account is such that I took it for granted that it had to be informed by his own experiences and was greatly surprised when he told me that he had never been with the guerrilla movement, that his writing was based on what he had learned from neighbors and from David Lan's *Guns and Rain*. For a discussion of *Harvest of Thorns* that relates the literary techniques employed by Chinodya to the changing historical context of the life of Benjamin and his parents, see Veit-Wild (1992: 321–9). Her volume provides a comprehensive account of the literature of Zimbabwe, relating it to the encounter with the West, the war of liberation, and the disillusionment of the 1980s.

Pepetela's *Mayombe*, set in Angola, is the other lasting literary monument to the armed struggle for African liberation. A penetrating account of guerrilla warfare written by a guerrilla commander who was to become Minister of Education in independent Angola, it is distinguished by its portrayal of individual guerrillas from a wide range of backgrounds. Their commitment to the struggle is based on a variety of personal experiences rather than a common ideology, and they offer, in the fashion of Kurosawa's *Rashomon*, divergent interpretations of the narrated events.

are told that Florence and Nyasha crossed into Mozambique. We can infer that Benjamin went there as well and that all three joined units linked to ZANU. Unlike the novel, *Flame* barely touches on two key issues in guerrilla warfare: the commitment of leaders and followers, and the relationship between the guerrilla and the peasantry. When the villagers bring food to the guerrillas, their meeting is a pale reflection of the *pungwe* so well narrated in *Harvest of Thorns*. And the episode when Flame confronts the shopkeeper who had denounced her father is rather unlikely. Her going off on her own to avenge the betrayal of her father may appeal to viewers, but runs counter to the discipline inculcated during her training. Furthermore, guerrilla units usually operated away from the home areas of members who might be recognized, their relatives victimized.[2]

Chinodya and Sinclair both problematize the guerrilla experience, but they do it in very different ways. *Harvest of Thorns* tells of conflicts among the men of Benjamin's unit, and between the guerrillas and the peasants, but these relationships are unproblematic in *Flame*. Instead, Sinclair focuses on the discrimination women recruits experience, on their sexual exploitation, and on handicaps that continue to confront the former women fighters after their victory. The difference in perspective is dramatized by the contrast in the first sexual experience of Benjamin and Flame, after first loves that were never consummated. It is Tashataka who initiates casual sex with Benjamin, but Flame is raped by Che, the very commander who emphasizes the importance of motivation in the training of new recruits.

Flame and Liberty are involved in a twofold struggle: against the Rhodesian army and against the male domination of the rebel army and the sexual advances of fellow soldiers.[3] *Flame* presents shy village girls who become strong women. And it exposes the abuse of power by men. But it takes a conciliatory stance: Flame eventually forgives Che, who has raped her, and comes to live with him. This may be shocking to many viewers, but the film makes Flame's decision plausible. Che's contrition is genuine; she feels sympathy for his solitude, which echoes her own despair – she has just learnt that her father has been killed. And they are living in exceptional times: Flame is about to leave for the front and may never come back. As Che puts it: 'War changes everything, you know. Sometimes we forget that we are human beings.'[4]

In the later stages of the war, perhaps ten per cent of the guerrillas fighting in Southern Rhodesia were women (Kriger, 1992: 191–2). But as we watch the Heroes Day parade on television towards the end of *Flame*, we do not see a single woman among the assembled brass, nor among the troops marching by. Guerrillas had been integrated into the armed forces of Zimbabwe, but women could no longer bear arms, and the army had them serve as clerical workers and cooks. Some women, such as Liberty, and many more men, had found a better life in town. But, as *Flame* illustrates, the bulk of the peasantry remained impoverished – Flame comes to town to try and find the resources to support her children and her mother in the village. The land holdings of the

2 Barnes (1995) presents accounts by four ex-guerrillas. They touch on their motivation in joining the guerrilla movement, the injuries all four sustained, and the captivity of two, but the main emphasis is on their postwar experiences. For interviews with women ex-combatants, see Nhongo-Simbanegavi (2000), Weiss (1986), and Zimbabwe Women Writers (2000).

3 Both struggles are touched on in *Those Whom Death Refused*, Flora Gomes's film on the guerrilla war in Guinea-Bissau and its aftermath.

4 An interpretation that rape may not be such a serious matter in their cultural context has to contend with Liberty's comment, 'Something had broken inside her, she was afraid. Months passed before she regained her strength.'

Liberty and Flame, devastated by loss after their camp has been attacked by jet planes, pose for a foreign journalist[5]

5 A still of this scene, but showing only Flame, is featured on the second poster issued when *Flame* was selected to be presented at the Cannes Film Festival.

6 Access to land has been the central issue ever since European settlers seized African lands by force of arms in the late nineteenth century. But little land was redistributed during the first two decades of independence. Only in 2000 did the government pursue the issue more actively. At first it abetted the seizure of white-owned farmland by supposed war veterans. Then in 2002 the government ordered the eviction of white landowners without compensation. These measures were tainted by the fact that they appeared as the last desperate acts of the increasingly unpopular regime of Robert Mugabe to cling to the power he has held since 1980. Given the importance of these commercial farms to Zimbabwe's economy, the consequences of the interruption of their production have been dire.

7 Mbuya Nehanda was a famous woman leader in the first *Chimurenga*; 'the people in the mountains' refers to the guerrillas. This and another song written during the war by Dick Chingaira Makoni, a.k.a. Comrade Chinx, are reproduced in the original Shona and in English in the press booklet for *Flame*.

European settlers remained largely intact until very recently.[6] And government policies neglected and exploited the peasantry, a common pattern in post-independence Africa that we will address in Chapter 5.

Flame and *Harvest of Thorns* were released many years after the war had dislodged the settler regime. They did not serve to mobilize support for the struggle, but stand as monuments to the guerrillas. They tell of extreme sacrifices to denounce the betrayal of the victory and to challenge the present. Zimbabwe, born in fire and blood, is far different from the vision that inspired the guerrillas. As Liberty puts it at the beginning of *Flame*, 'life did not match our expectations.' Flame leads a guerrilla unit towards the end of the war, but some years later she hoes a barren field with a baby on her back. One of the *chimurenga* songs inspiring the guerrillas in *Flame*, 'Tinofa Tichienda', translates:

We will die on our way to Zimbabwe
until we finally reach Zimbabwe
until we finally cross the Zambezi

Nehanda bless the people of Zimbabwe
Nehanda bless the people of the mountains.[7]

It belongs to a distant past.

The guerrillas engendered a new nation, but the character of the new society was shaped by others. The aspirations for justice, social equality,

Ingrid Sinclair, during the shooting

and the emancipation of women remain to be realized.[8] Film and novel call for a better future, but neither offers a prescription for how to get there. Instead both turn away from the political arena to focus on the domestic. Flame abandons her husband Danger, who has descended into alcoholism and domestic violence – the ex-guerrilla has the strength to thus emancipate herself. Benjamin commits himself to his young wife and their new-born son. It is left to the viewers and readers to reflect on the sacrifices made by the guerrillas, and to take up their battle cry: 'Pamberi ne chimurenga!', 'Forward with the struggle!'

Sinclair, who had trained at the Bristol Film-Makers Co-op, worked for British television before coming to Zimbabwe in 1985 (Sinclair, 2002; Speciale, 1996). Her outsider status offered the advantage that she was not identified with either of the guerrilla movements in conflict during and after the war. Sinclair initially conceived of *Flame* as a documentary. The film starts out as a brief documentary of the *chimurenga*, the uprisings against European settlement in 1896–7, but then Sinclair shifts to fiction because none of the seven women on whose experiences the film is based dared discuss sexual abuse on camera. The film's present, Flame coming to town to find Liberty, constitutes a framing story around the principal story that begins twenty years earlier with two village girls.

The production of *Flame* was constrained by a budget that had to be reduced from $1.2 million to $800,000 (Barlet, n.d.). Still, we are treated to beautiful photography and a fine soundtrack that combines choral music with the *chimurenga* songs that were popular during the war. And

8 Zakes Mda's play *We Shall Sing For the Fatherland* similarly tells of guerrillas who do not partake of the fruits of victory. Set in South Africa, the play was performed and published while the white minority government was still firmly in power.

foreigners do not have to struggle with subtitles: just about the entire dialogue is in English, with only the occasional greeting or song conveying the local setting. This, of course, does not reflect the pattern of language use in Zimbabwe today, and is altogether implausible in the context of a peasant family such as Florence's.

Most of the actors had some professional experience. Marian Kunonga, in the role of Florence/Flame, is a professional actress but had never been in front of a camera. Ulla Mahaka had some experience filming; her transformation from 15-year-old village girl to urban professional 20 years later is remarkable (Zimmemedia, n.d.). Sinclair trained them in workshops before the shooting started, focusing on the emotional contents of the scenes rather than on the dialogue (Snyman, 1996). Still, events are rarely dramatized by a display of emotions, even as *Flame* presents viewers with poignant scenes – the death of a woman guerrilla we have just come to know, Flame and Liberty being made to pose for a foreign journalist while they are visiting the casualties of an air raid at a hospital, Flame being handed Che's gun and promoted to detachment commander, a commander exalting the women's contribution to the struggle. It falls to Nyasha, the narrator, to comment on the impact of such events. We may wonder whether Sinclair's background in documentary film led her to take this appoach in her first feature film or whether she was constrained by the limitations of her actors. More likely she accurately conveyed the stoicism of soldiers, whether they be men or women – the village girl Florence did cry when her father was arrested.

The government had given its support to the project. However, the War Veterans Association of Zimbabwe turned hostile during the production and began a campaign against the film in the national media. Accusations that the film was pornographic prompted the police to seize the negatives during editing (Speciale, 1996). The negatives were returned after a few days, but the media campaign continued. When *Flame* was released, it was reported to have broken box office records. The film elicited heated discussions. They concerned the film's account of sexual abuse, rather than its charge that all too many of those who had sacrificed in the war of liberation had been left behind once the war was won.

References and Further Reading

Barlet, Olivier. n.d. 'Interview avec Joël Phiri.' http://www/africultures.com/cineastes_africains/producteurs/joelphiri.htm.

Barnes, Teresa A. 1995. 'The Heroes' Struggle: Life after the Liberation War for Four Ex-Combatants in Zimbabwe.' *Soldiers in Zimbabwe's Liberation War*, edited by Ngwabi Bhebe and Terence Ranger. London: James Currey; Portsmouth, NH: Heinemann; Harare: University of Zimbabwe Publications. 118–38.

Chingaira Makoni, Dick, n.d. (1996). 'Tinofa Tichienda' and 'Maruza,' in press booklet 'Flame'.

Chinodya, Shimmer. 1989. *Harvest of Thorns*. Harare: Baobab Books. African Writers Series. Oxford/Portsmouth, NH/Ibadan/Nairobi/Gabarone: Heinemann.

Flame. 1996. Film directed by Ingrid Sinclair, written by Ingrid Sinclair with Barbara Jago and Philip Roberts. Produced by Black and White Film (Zimbabwe), JBA Production (France), and Onland Productions (Namibia). Distributed in the U.S. by California Newsreel, in Africa by Media for Development International. 85 minutes.

Kriger, Norma J. 1992. *Zimbabwe's Guerrilla War: Peasant Voices*. African Studies Series 70. Cambridge: Cambridge University Press.

Lan, David. 1985. *Guns and Rain: Guerrillas and Spirit Mediums in Zimbabwe*. Harare: Zimbabwe Publishing House; London: James Currey; Berkeley: University of California Press.

Mda, Zakes. 1980. *We Shall Sing for the Fatherland and Other Plays*. Ravan Playscripts 6. Johannesburg: Ravan Press.

Nhongo-Simbanegavi, Josephine. 2000. *For Better or Worse? Women and Zanla in Zimbabwe's Liberation Struggle*. Harare: Weaver Press.

Pepetela (Artur Carlos Maurício Pestana dos Santos). 1979. *Mayombe*. Lisbon: Edições 70. English translation by Michael Wolfers (1983) *Mayombe*. Harare: Zimbabwe Publishing House. African Writers Series. London/Ibadan/Nairobi: Heinemann.

Ranger, Terence. 1998. 'Zimbabwe and the Long Search for Independence.' *History of Central Africa: the Contemporary Years*, edited by David Birmingham and Phyllis Martin. London/New York: Longman. 202–29.

Rashomon. 1951. Film written and directed by Akira Kurosawa. Produced by Daiei (Japan). Distributed in the U.S. by Cowboy Pictures and Criterion Film. 83 minutes.

Sinclair, Ingrid. 2001, 2002. Personal communications.

Snyman, Wilhelm. 1996. 'Calm Woman Behind 'Flame'.' *Cape Times*, 7 June.

Speciale, Alessandra. 1996. 'Since You Can Do It, Go Ahead.' *Ecrans d'Afrique* 16: 13–17.

Stoneman, Colin, and Lionel Cliffe. 1989. *Zimbabwe: Politics, Economics and Society*. Marxist Regimes. London/New York: Pinter.

Those Whom Death Refused/Mortu Nega. 1988. Film directed by Flora Gomes. Guinea-Bissau. Distributed in the U.S. by California Newsreel. 93 minutes.

Veit-Wild, Flora. 1992. *Teachers, Preachers, Non-Believers: a Social History of Zimbabwean Literature*. New Perspectives on African Literature 6. London/Melbourne/Munich/New York: Hans Zell Publishers.

Weiss, Ruth. 1986. *The Women of Zimbabwe*. London: Kesho Publishers; Harare: Nehanda Publishers.

Zimbabwe Women Writers. 2000. *Women of Resilience*. Harare: Zimbabwe Women Writers.

Zimmemedia. n.d. http://www.zimmemedia.com/flame/.

*Nelson Mandela votes in South
Africa's first election with universal
suffrage, 1994*

3 The Struggle for Majority Rule in South Africa

In 1652 the Dutch East India Company established a permanent base at Cape Town to supply its ships plying the trade with Asia. Europeans began to settle at the Cape, farming and trading cattle and sheep with the local Khoikhoi. As their numbers grew, they established their own herds and moved ever further inland, displacing the Khoikhoi by force of arms. Nearer the Cape, European settlers established plantations worked by slaves from Mozambique, Madagascar, and Asia. By the end of the eighteenth century about 25,000 Europeans had settled at the Cape. They became known as Afrikaners, their language, derived from Dutch, as Afrikaans. They were also referred to as *Boers*, which translates as 'peasants.'

In 1806 the Cape came under British rule. To escape from it the first parties of Afrikaners initiated the Great Trek in 1834. Eventually some ten thousand established themselves in two independent republics, the Transvaal and the Orange Free State. With the advantage of firearms they defeated various African peoples and took over their land. In Natal, an advance party of trekkers was massacred by King Dingaan and his followers in 1838, but subsequently the Zulu army was decisively defeated. However, the British intervened in their turn and annexed Natal in 1843.

South African history was set on a new course by the emergence of fabulous prospects for mining. The discovery of diamonds at Kimberley in 1867, and the rush of fortune-seekers it engendered, propelled the British to annex the area in 1871, and the Transvaal republic in 1877. The Zulu defeated the British at Isandhlwana in 1879, but eventually they and other African states were brought under British control. The discovery of huge gold deposits on the Witwatersrand in 1886 gave fresh impetus to British expansion. The British had restored the Transvaal republic to a form of independence in 1881, but now the stakes had been greatly raised. The Anglo-Boer War (1899–1902) was to become the most costly episode in the Scramble for Africa. The British had to field 300,000 men to prevail. They countered the Boers' strategy of guerrilla warfare by interning their families in concentration camps, burning their fields, and looting and destroying their homesteads. Perhaps ten per cent of the Afrikaners in the republics, especially children, perished as a result of these policies.

The Union of South Africa was established as a self-governing British

We of the A.N.C. had always stood for a non-racial democracy, and we shrank from any action which might drive the races further apart than they already were. But the hard facts were that fifty years of non-violence had brought the African people nothing but more and more repressive legislation, and fewer and fewer rights.... At the beginning of June, 1961, after a long and anxious assessment of the South African situation, I, and some colleagues, came to the conclusion that as violence in this country was inevitable, it would be unrealistic and wrong for African leaders to continue preaching peace and non-violence at a time when the Government met our peaceful demands with force. (Nelson Mandela, at the Rivonia Trial in 1964, Karis and Gerhart, 1977: 776–7)

The Struggle for Majority Rule in South Africa

dominion in 1910. Its constitution consolidated political power in the hands of whites, 21 per cent of the population according to the 1911 census. Only in the Cape Province could Africans and other 'non-whites' continue to vote according to the existing property qualifications, and even this minor concession was to be whittled away subsequently: by 1956 only whites could sit in parliament, while by 1970 the electorate was exclusively white – even though by that time the proportion of whites in the population had shrunk to 17 per cent. The deputations, associations, and protests of the spokesmen of the African middle class had been entirely ignored in the negotiations leading to Union. In 1912 Africans established the South African Native National Congress, the oldest African nationalist party. It was to become the African National Congress, South Africa's foremost political force. But at this time it had no leverage. The Europeans lost no time in pressing their advantage. In 1913 the Native Land Act was passed. It reserved about eight per cent of the land for Africans, who made up two thirds of the population. European farmers thus gained access to land, while competition from African farmers was reduced. Africans, dispossessed of their land and their cattle, were turned into proletarians: they were forced to provide cheap labor for the mines, for the emerging industry, for the European farmers, and for domestic service.

Some African workers accumulated considerable experience, but they earned only a small fraction of the wages of white workers with similar skills. They thus posed a serious competitive threat to white workers. However, the militancy of white mine workers, in particular the bloody Rand Revolt of 1922, and the white franchise ensured that white workers were protected: the color bar was enshrined in law for various categories of jobs in the 1920s. If the job color bar served the interests of white workers, employers took advantage of the exploitation color bar: the movement of Africans was strictly controlled under the pass laws, they were not allowed to unionize or strike, and racism was pervasive. In the mining industry, the gap between the cash wages of white and African workers was never less than eleven to one after 1920, or ten to one when allowance is made for the food the companies supplied to the African workers. Furthermore, by 1939 white miners were entitled to paid leave and pensions, which African workers did not receive, and far larger disability payments than those of Africans (Thompson, 2001: 167).

World War II brought a boom to South Africa, and its manufacturing industry expanded greatly. The conflict with fascism spurred international declarations denouncing racism, and the imperial powers relinquished their possessions in Asia soon after the war. More militant leaders came to the fore among Africans, 'coloureds,' meaning people of mixed origin, and Indians. Some industrialists demanded a relaxation of segregationist practices. And the government began to consider reforms. They were rejected by about 60 per cent of Afrikaners and 20 per cent of English-speakers in the 1948 elections. The National Party gained a majority of seats in Parliament, even as it failed to obtain a majority of votes, and formed the government (Beinart, 1994: 133). It set out to give reality to its election slogan of *apartheid* or apartness. All 'non-white' South Africans were required to carry identification labeling them according to race, and all Africans had to have their passes endorsed by the police to live anywhere outside the 'reserves.' The Bantu Education Act ensured that Africans would receive distinctly inferior education. The Immorality Act made sexual intercourse between whites and 'non-whites' a crime. Whites and 'non-whites' were to use separate public facilities and amenities. The Group Areas Act further segregated the racial groups in urban areas, and forced large numbers of 'non-whites' to relocate. Soweto,[1] the biggest of many new black settlements, became home to 400,000 people.

In 1949 the African National Congress (ANC) responded by committing itself to militant resistance. Links with 'coloured' and Indian leaders were strengthened, and the Defiance Campaign organized by ANC President-General Albert Luthuli attracted wide support. In 1955, the Congress of the People brought together 3,000 delegates from all racial groups. Meeting in an open space for two days, they debated and passed the clauses of the Freedom Charter one by one. In addition to affirming a list of basic rights and freedoms, they demanded the redistribution of land and the nationalization of mining, banking, and industrial monopolies. The Charter was to endure as the basic policy statement of the ANC. A faction rejecting the multi-racial approach of the ANC formed the Pan-Africanist Congress (PAC) in 1959, but the ANC continued to be the major anti-*apartheid* force.

The Sharpeville Massacre was a turning point for the anti-*apartheid* movement. On 21 March 1960, during a pass-burning campaign organized by the PAC, police at the Sharpeville police station opened fire, killing 67 Africans and wounding many more. Most had been shot in the back. Sharpeville was bloody testimony to the cost of civil disobedience campaigns that had failed to wring any concessions from the *apartheid* regime. By the end of 1960 much of Africa had become independent, but Africans in South Africa, the most educated, most urbanized, and most Westernized on the continent, remained a subject people.

Virtually the entire opposition had to go underground as both the ANC and the PAC were banned. That same year Albert Luthuli was awarded the Nobel Peace Prize, but the die had been cast. Both the ANC and the PAC committed themselves to a policy of armed struggle in 1961. The South African security apparatus, bolstered by increasingly repressive legislation and resorting to torture, effectively suppressed the opposition. Within a few years most of the leadership of the ANC, its allies, and the PAC had been arrested and sentenced to long prison terms, usually on the notorious Robben Island off Cape Town. The state appeared unassailable even as militants managed to carry out sporadic acts of sabotage. Over the years the land reserved for Africans had been increased to 13 per cent of the surface of South Africa. Now elections were held and governments established in ten 'homelands,' most of them scattered into several fragments separated by 'white' land. Supposedly they were becoming independent. All Africans were assigned membership in a

1 Soweto stands for South-Western Townships – of Johannesburg, that is.

The Struggle for Majority Rule in South Africa

'homeland,' even though many had never set foot there. In any case, only a small minority could find a livelihood in what critics came to refer to as the Bantustans.

The early 1970s brought a series of strikes by African workers, but it was school children who were to give new impetus to the struggle. The Black Consciousness Movement drew on the U.S. Civil Rights and Black Power movements to challenge the hegemony of the *apartheid* state. 'Black,' borrowed from the U.S., specifically included 'coloured' and Indians while rejecting *apartheid*'s negative 'non-whites.' The movement found wide resonance among students. When the government attempted to enforce the use of Afrikaans on a par with English as the medium of instruction in secondary schools, the students organized large-scale demonstrations for 16 June 1976. The demonstration at Orlando West Junior Secondary School, Soweto, started out peacefully, but after the police had fired into the crowd, killing two and injuring several more, rioting broke out in Soweto and spread across the country. The government response was brutal. According to the very conservative official estimates, 575 had been killed, including 134 under age 18, by February 1977. Later that year Steve Biko, political leader of the students and intellectual leader of the Black Consciousness Movement, was savagely tortured and killed by the police.

Precisely because the cost was so heavy, what came to be known as the Soweto Uprising strengthened the opposition in three major ways. The ANC was able to emerge from the underground and re-establish a public presence in the African townships. Large numbers of students went into exile, and many joined the ANC's military wing, Umkhonto we Sizwe (MK) or Spear of the Nation. And foreign opinion turned increasingly against the *apartheid* regime.

In the early 1980s the government initiated some reforms. They amounted to little, and they came too late. When 'coloureds' and Indians were offered a narrowly circumscribed form of political participation, while Africans continued to be entirely excluded from the official political process, most refused to participate. Instead, in 1983, a thousand delegates of all races, representing 575 organizations – trade unions, sports clubs, community groups, women's associations, and youth organizations – established the United Democratic Front to coordinate opposition.

In 1990, after four decades in power, the National Party abruptly changed course and opened the road to majority rule: the government lifted the ban on the ANC, the PAC, and the Communist Party, and released the political prisoners, Nelson Mandela the most prominent. When the government called a referendum in 1992, 69 per cent of the white electorate approved continued negotiations for democratic reform. The turnabout, and the peaceful transition that followed, came as a surprise to most observers. In hindsight, major developments in three areas appear to have forced the hand of the government and its white constituency: the struggle within South Africa, the withdrawal of foreign investors, and the hostility of neighboring states.

The struggle within South Africa intensified in the 1980s. The infiltration of guerrillas became more effective and acts of sabotage multiplied. African trade unions, legalized since 1979, were gaining in strength, and the Congress of South African Trade Unions (COSATU) went beyond strikes to confront the state. Students boycotted schools. Consumers boycotted white stores. Government control over the African townships became increasingly tenuous. Tenants in public housing refused to pay rent. A few township councillors and larger numbers of black policemen and suspected government informers were killed; others lost their homes and businesses. Many councillors resigned their offices. Youths barricaded the streets and attacked the police with stones and molotov cocktails. The funerals of those shot by the police became the occasion for mass demonstrations, some gathering tens of thousands. The coffins would be draped with the green, black, and gold colors of the ANC. They would be accompanied by youths wearing uniforms, brandishing wooden guns, performing a militant jive known as the *toyi-toyi*, and chanting their defiance in ANC songs. These demonstrations commonly ended with another violent clash with the police or army and new victims. Even in rural areas the government faced increasing resistance.

In the 1960s a boom had been fueled by foreign investors who, after the initial shock waves from Sharpeville, poured more funds into South African industry and the Johannesburg stock exchange than into the rest of the continent put together (Freund, 1998: 298). Now, however, foreign investors perceived that turmoil in South Africa jeopardized their investments; they faced protests and boycotts from anti-*apartheid* organizations at home; and they were increasingly constrained by the imposition of economic sanctions. As ever more countries adopted sanctions, the US government remained committed to 'constructive engagement.' But public opinion was aroused by television pictures of brutal repression in the townships, and the US Congress passed legislation imposing comprehensive economic sanctions over President Ronald Reagan's veto in 1985. South Africa had become isolated on the international scene, and its economy was paying a heavy price.

In 1975 South Africa's Portuguese allies withdrew from Angola and Mozambique. South Africa sought to prevent the establishment of unfriendly regimes by supporting opposition groups more amenable to its interests. In Mozambique, South Africa took over the sponsorship of the RENAMO guerrilla movement that had been established by the Rhodesian minority regime. After Mozambique and South Africa had agreed in 1984 to end all support for the ANC and RENAMO respectively, South Africa continued to support RENAMO. The murderous war was to last until 1992.

As the Portuguese prepared to hand over power in Angola, the South African Defence Force (SADF) invaded in support of UNITA, the União Nacional para a Independência Total de Angola. Their march on Luanda, the capital of Angola, was checked by the MPLA and Cuban troops. The intervention, and undercover US aid, plunged Angola into a devastating civil war which came to an end only in 2002. The war served South African interests by destabilizing Angola and facilitating its continued hold over South West Africa. South Africa had rejected United Nations demands that it grant independence to the former German colony, entrusted to South Africa after World War I. Since 1964 it had been embroiled in guerrilla war with the South West African Peoples' Organization (SWAPO). Now South African involvement in Angola served to harass SWAPO bases there.

In 1980 South Africa lost its last ally in the region. After a long guerrilla war Africans took control of Zimbabwe. South Africa had become an isolated bastion of white domination. At various times South African commandos raided or carried out undercover operations against every one of its neighbors, and further afield as far as Zambia and Tanzania – forays that came at the cost of reinforcing the isolation of the last white rulers on African soil. In 1988 the South African Defence Force (SADF) failed in its attack on Cuito Cuanavale, where the Angolan government had set up an air-defense installation to keep South African aircraft from supplying UNITA. The SADF incurred substantial losses, in part because it had lost air superiority: the arms embargo imposed by the United Nations made it dependent on planes produced in South Africa, and they could no longer match the Soviet planes piloted by Angolans and Cubans. The South African government concluded that it could not afford to pursue the war. The end of the Cold War facilitated negotiations that led South Africa to retreat from Angola as well as South West Africa, which became independent as Namibia in 1990.

Commentators vary in the weight they attach to these developments within South Africa, in the region, and in the wider international arena. In any case, peace was finally within reach in southern Africa, even if the civil war South Africa had fostered in Angola was to continue for years to come. In 1994, the first elections on a universal franchise were held in South Africa. The ANC won 63 per cent of the vote. Nelson Mandela became President of South Africa to confront the momentous task of redressing the inequities entrenched by more than three centuries of white domination, even as the country faced widespread unemployment. The new national anthem started out with *Nkosi Sikelel' i Afrika*, the African hymn adopted by the ANC long ago.

We will examine three films set in South Africa under *apartheid*, from a Hollywood film that foregrounds white characters, to a film focusing on the struggle of Africans that was surreptitiously produced in South African under *apartheid*, to a post-*apartheid* film that explores the profound effect of *apartheid* on the African community. But before we move to these films which denounce *apartheid* in their different ways, we will discuss *The Gods Must Be Crazy*, a hugely successful South African film which, along with slapstick comedy, conveyed the world view of *apartheid*.

References and Further Reading

Beinart, William. 1994. *Twentieth-Century South Africa*. Oxford/New York: Oxford University Press.

Freund, Bill. (1984) 1998. *The Making of Contemporary Africa: The Development of African Society Since 1800*. Second edition. Boulder, CO: Lynne Rienner.

Karis, Thomas, and Gail M. Gerhart. 1977. *Challenge and Violence, 1953–1964. From Protest to Challenge: A Documentary History of African Politics in South Africa, 1882–1964*, volume 3. Stanford: Hoover Institution Press.

Mandela, Nelson. 1994. *Long Walk to Freedom: The Autobiography of Nelson Mandela*. Boston/New York/Toronto/London: Little, Brown.

Thompson, Leonard. (1990) 2001. *A History of South Africa*. Third edition. New Haven/London: Yale University Press.

The Gods Must Be Crazy 1980
The World According to *Apartheid*

The Gods Must Be Crazy was produced, written, directed, filmed, and edited by Jamie Uys, a well-established South African filmmaker. It is a very funny movie which tells of an African Garden of Eden. Voice-over of !Kung[1] and Tswana dialogue and a dubbed English version of the Afrikaans original make it more accessible than most African films. It has been a huge success. On its release in South Africa, *The Gods Must Be Crazy* shattered every box office record. The film had its greatest success in Japan, where it was the highest-grossing movie in 1982. In France, it won the Grand Prize at the Chamrousse Festival dedicated to film comedies in 1982 and became the top box office success in 1983. In the U.S., after a false start in 1982, it was released afresh in 1984, moved from art houses to commercial theaters, and became the biggest foreign box-office hit in movie history. A major television network continues to show it, and most video stores carry it. The film's triumph inspired a sequel, the less accomplished *The Gods Must Be Crazy II*, as well as three Hong Kong feature films.

Slapstick and broad humor are so persuasive that many Western viewers fail to perceive the underlying ideology. *The Gods Must Be Crazy* pokes fun at the tyranny of the clock over 'civilized man,' recalling Charlie Chaplin's *Modern Times*.[2] And Andrew Steyn, the bumbling Afrikaner scientist, is good for many laughs. But as we encounter Africans, we are initiated into the world view of *apartheid*. The film introduces us to four kinds of Africans: traditional Africans who are happy and content until modern society intrudes; good Africans who are grateful for the help of

I asked him through an interpreter if he would like to work for us, but they have no word for 'work' so he didn't understand. Then I just asked if he would like to come with us, and he immediately said O.K.
(Jamie Uys, speaking of N!xau, in an interview with Maslin, 1984)

1 ! serves to indicate one of the click sounds that distinguish some languages in southern Africa.

2 We can easily recognize that 'civilized man' lives in Johannesburg, the multi-million metropolis. We get glimpses of Europeans and a few Africans comfortable with each other in the street, factory, office, and restaurant.

The Struggle for Majority Rule in South Africa

white people; incompetent Africans who run their own governments; and bad Africans who have been led astray by evil foreigners.

!Xi, the 'traditional' African, is the film's chief protagonist. He is not an individualized character, but rather the representative of the 'bushmen,' to use the derogatory term employed in the film. The film starts out as a documentary about the 'bushmen.' We are told that they live in the Kalahari Desert which 'is devoid of people, except the little people. Pretty, dainty, small, graceful, the bushmen.... They must be the most contented people in the world.... No crime, no punishment, no violence, no laws, no police, no judges, no rulers or bosses.' It takes a Coca Cola bottle, dropped from an airplane – the ultimate symbol of Western superiority, to shatter the happy life of people who do not know money and are not used to walls. And we listen to their voices, which go 'click,' 'click,' 'click.' !Kung does use click sounds, but the film overlaid some of the dialogue with extra clicks, thus enhancing its exoticism (Volkman, 1988). The !Kung, however, do not get much of a voice. Most of the time the narrator speaks for !Xi and his family. Only in a few instances are !Xi's thoughts or words translated.

The Gods Must Be Crazy

!Xi and his family according to The Gods Must Be Crazy

The !Kung have seen their land encroached upon by European settlers for centuries. And they happen to have been the subject of a great deal of anthropological research as well as a series of documentaries produced by John Marshall between 1951 and 1978. Marshall drew on his documentaries and the work of a leading researcher, Marjorie Shostak, to produce *N!ai, the Story of a !Kung Woman*. Contrary to Uys's tale, Marshall shows traditional !Kung life to have been characterized by severe hardships. The hunt was difficult: it might take four men five days to track down a giraffe. Early marriage – !Nai was married at age 8 to a 13-year-old boy – was traumatic for girls who wanted to stay with their mothers. Sexual conflicts and jealousies were rampant. Childbirth was extremely dangerous, the death of children common, and the men who tried to help and cure went into life-threatening trances. By the time Uys made his film the !Kung had experienced profound changes.

Uys claimed reality for his fictions by fictionalizing the production of the film. The stories he told reviewers varied. According to one account, he had spent three months criss-crossing the Kalahari Desert looking for the right man to play !Xi. He took photographs of every likely face, then 'we marked the longitude and latitude, so that we could find them again.' In Botswana he finally found N!Xau who in his whole life had seen only one other white man, a missionary. When Uys asked him, through his interpreter, if he would come and work with him, N!Xau 'didn't understand, because they have no word for work.' Every three or four weeks, N!Xau would be flown back to his home in the bush, 'so he wouldn't suffer culture shock,' said Uys. N!Xau had no use for money. Uys found that the money given him 'had blown away' – just as in the movie (Klemesrud, 1985: 15).

N!ai, the Story of a !Kung Woman, Marshall's documentary, reveals the fictional character of Uys's account. It shows the filming of *The Gods Must*

The Struggle for Majority Rule in South Africa

3 The documentary's account of the camp is a searing indictment of the South African authorities.

4 In Japan the film was released as *Bush Man* and advertising focused on N!Xau. The poster feaures N!Xau with a child against a background of a diverse array of animals, a snow-capped mountain such as could not be found anywhere near the film's setting, and the skyscrapers of a distant city. The film program was nearly entirely devoted to the 'Miracle World' of the 'Bush Man,' including comments on the body, tools, and loincloth of a drawing of N!Xau. Numerous photos are dedicated to the San, several to animals and the landscape, a few to Thompson, Steyn and Mpudi. No Africans other than the San are to be seen. N!Xau reprised his role as the 'Bush Man' in three Hong Kong features, Billy Chan's *Crazy Safari*, Wellson Chin's *Crazy Hong Kong*, and Dick Cho Kin Nam's *The Gods Must Be Funny*. The films refer to his character as N!Xau or Nixau, the credits identify him as Lik So. N!Xau is probably the only black African actor to have held the lead role in so many films. The former cook's performance is truly remarkable – and the image of Africa he represents continues to hold wide appeal overseas. N!xau died of tuberculosis in 2003, the circumstances of his life little changed. He lived near Tshumkwi, and his visible 'wealth consisted of 21 cattle, 11 sheep, two horses, two bicycles, two spades, two rakes, and five axes' according to *The Namibian*.

5 Uys's work as a consultant for *Crazy Safari* may have reinforced his reluctance to acknowledge the fictions he had created around the production of his films.

6 Botswana's relationship with South Africa was uneasy. On one hand, Botswana, unlike Zimbabwe, was not seen as a threat to the *apartheid* regime. On the other, South Africa repeatedly attacked South African refugees, supposedly guerrillas, in Botswana.

Be Crazy with N!ai playing !Xi's wife in the hut. We are at the Tshumkwi camp the South African authorities have established in the north-eastern corner of what was still South West Africa. The !Kung live on food hand-outs, and tuberculosis is rampant. N!ai's first child and only son died as an adult at Tshumkwi.[3] The South African Defence Force offers a way out of the miserable camp life: it is recruiting !Kung for its war against SWAPO, the guerrilla forces fighting for the independence of what was to become Namibia. As for N!Xau Kganna, he had never been the hunter Uys depicted. He grew up as a herd boy on a Herero farm in Botswana. In 1976 he moved to Namibia to work as a cook in the Tshumkwi school where Uys found him. N!Xau knew the uses of money very well, but he was paid a mere pittance: 2,000 Rand, then about $1,700, for *The Gods Must Be Crazy*, which made a fortune – the film cost $5 million and earned $90 million in its first four years. Even after these record earnings, and after N!Xau had become a national hero in Japan,[4] he had to settle for 5,000 Rand and a monthly retainer of 200 Rand for the lead role in the sequel *The Gods Must Be Crazy II* (Tomaselli, 1992; Klemesrud, 1985). When Uys was interviewed for the documentary *In Darkest Hollywood* a decade later, he was still not prepared to own up to the truth, and it was left to John Marshall and N!Xau to contradict him.[5]

The arrival of Kate Thompson, a South African of British descent, provides us with a glimpse of the good Africans to be found in Botswana.[6] She has come to teach Africans – a few years after hundreds of students had died in South Africa protesting the inferior education imposed on them; she recalls Karen Blixen providing schooling for the children of her workers in *Out of Africa*. Lo and behold, the entire village rises to chant the praises of the good lady. Also in Botswana, a border guard and police officers appear with the forces of good in several scenes. Trouble is, they are invariably surpassed by events. It takes a white man to subdue the forces of evil.

Incompetent Africans run Harare. Here and elsewhere *The Gods Must Be Crazy* mixes up the geography of southern Africa.[7] But for those who know that Harare is the capital of Zimbabwe, the reference to that country is obvious. We see a cabinet meeting devoted to spending money. The irruption of guerrillas serves to suggests the instability of African government, and the comic vagaries of the army's pursuit of the guerrillas demonstrate that African armies are not to be taken seriously.[8] This way of characterizing neighboring Zimbabwe was particularly pertinent to the concerns of white South Africans. Zimbabwe became independent in 1980, the very year *The Gods Must Be Crazy* was released, and South Africa lost the buffer of a fellow minority regime.

Guerrillas are, of course, the bad Africans. If the white minority regime in Zimbabwe had to accept majority rule after a protracted guerrilla war, *The Gods Must Be Crazy* offers reassurance to the hold-outs in the South African white *laager*. Its guerrillas are dangerous and destructive all right, but they are also indolent and bumbling.[9] In the end even Kate Thompson gets to disarm one of them. Their leader Sam Boga articulates what the film is showing us about African guerrillas: 'Why do

I have to work with amateurs?' He in turn serves to confirm the *apartheid* credo that Africans would be happy with the white dispensation were it not for evil foreigners fomenting discontent and making trouble. While his first name recalls Sam Nujoma, the leader of SWAPO, his Latin looks and his beard à la Castro reminded South African viewers of the Cuban troops that had come to support the MPLA when South Africa invaded Angola as Portuguese colonial rule came to an end.[10] As for Zimbabwe, it was subject to subversion instigated by South Africa and incursions by the South African army rather than any guerrillas led by foreigners.

The Gods Must Be Crazy introduces viewers to one more distinction. Mpudi, the mechanic from Botswana, would be considered 'coloured' in South Africa. As he banters with Steyn, we begin to wonder whether Uys is prepared to admit him to 'civilized' society. Indeed, even if Mpudi feels for the San, he is just as patronizing as the narrator: 'They are the sweetest little buggers.' But then we are reminded of the great difference that separates 'civilized' whites from all the other 'races': Mpudi, it turns out, has seven wives. That Steyn should have been ignorant of Mpudi's family and life conveys, as in *Out of Africa*, the social distance between the races. Eventually we learn that Mpudi had to flee into the Kalahari Desert and nearly died because he slapped a British colonial officer who had insulted his father. Uys readily condemns colonialism – while perpetuating the myths of *apartheid*: an ordered world, with whites on top, a world where Africans are content but for the interference of outsiders.

The South African poster for *The Gods Must Be Crazy* reproduces key elements in the film's discourse and promotion. It features a Coca Cola bottle about to impact like a missile. In the foreground is !Xi in a pose of anguish, behind him four photos: Uys at the camera, in his outfit as the reverend he plays in the film, trades on recognition of the director in South Africa; Steyn carrying Thompson across the stream conveys the love interest; !Xi and the monkey are presented as part of nature; and Boga holding a gun to Thompson's head is the bad guy. The text also draws on the director's reputation: 'Jamie Uys ... delighted you with *Beautiful People*, convulsed you with *Funny People*, now you'll go crackers with *The Gods Must Be Crazy*.'[11] Outside South Africa *The Gods Must Be Crazy* was promoted as a slapstick comedy. Posters everywhere were composed of caricatures of various comic scenes. They usually featured the two white protagonists, sometimes !Xi. And there would invariably be an animal – a monkey, a rhino – representing the nature angle.

In the U.S. *The Gods Must Be Crazy* was released by Jensen-Farley Pictures, a small distributor, in 1982. It was promoted as a sexy slapstick comedy. The poster presents a rich variation on the slapstick posters used elsewhere. It has a Cola bottle disgorging, like a cornucopia, gaudily distorted characters from the film, among them the Botswana border guard clad in a slip and holding a spear. Its affirmation 'At last, a comedy everyone can laugh with!' sounds preemptive. The film did poorly in half a dozen test cities, and the distributor soon went out of business. After its enthusiastic reception in Japan and Europe Twentieth Century-Fox

The Gods Must Be Crazy

7 Other inventions are rather odd as well: the turbans worn by the Tswana villagers, adults and children alike, the Zulu chants and Venda hymns they sing (Davis, 1996: 92). Perhaps the turbans were meant to make them more exotic, while the Zulu chants and Venda hymns would remind white South African audiences of 'happy Africans' in their midst. But what to make of that most implausible shot of !Xi, the head of the kinship group, kneeling before a young woman to take leave?

8 The scene in which a captured guerrilla is persuaded to indicate the hideout of his comrades by the pretense of being dropped from a helicopter is very funny – until we recall the Vietnam War practice of the U.S. and its South Vietnamese allies who interrogated and killed prisoners that way.

9 The Battle of the Banana Plantation is one of the most hilarious scenes in *The Gods Must Be Crazy*. The supposedly funny association between guerrillas and bananas may be traced to the derogatory reference to Central American republics as banana republics in U.S. parlance – a disdain that fails to acknowledge that the region's banana plantations were exploited by major U.S. corporations, and that concern for these corporate interests prompted the U.S. to topple governments in the region, most notoriously the regime of Jacobo Arbenz Guzmán, democratically elected in Guatemala in 1951. Woody Allen's *Bananas* exploited the association between Latin American guerrillas and bananas, and reinforced it in its turn.

10 In *The Gods Must Be Crazy II*, a Cuban soldier is just as incompetent as his African adversary. Both soldiers are taken prisoner by a white woman, a corporate lawyer from New York, no less. The film was released in 1989, one year after Angolan government troops and their Cuban allies halted an attack by the South African Defence Force on Cuito Cuanavale and inflicted heavy losses. The defeat presaged South Africa's retreat from Angola as well as what has since become Namibia.

launched it afresh in 1984, first in art houses, then in commercial theaters. It became the biggest foreign box-office hit in U.S. movie history. Now the film was accompanied by a serene poster that conveyed the sense of a wide open landscape in which eleven people more or less representative of characters in the film, dispersed on the film's monumental title partly reversed against the sky, are lost. It promised 'An Epic Comedy ... of Absurd Proportions.'

Outside South Africa *The Gods Must Be Crazy* was released as a 'Botswana' production. Still, it sparked protests, especially in Europe, less so in the U.S. They did not impede the film's smashing success. Japanese and Western audiences were drawn to the story of an African Eden. Production of a film as blatantly condescending and patronizing towards African-Americans, making them the object of outright ridicule, was no longer conceivable. But 'just good fun' could still be had at the expense of Africans, whether 'traditional,' 'good,' 'incompetent,' or 'bad.' For many critics the ironic take on Western 'civilization' served to camouflage the *apartheid* ideology conveyed by *The Gods Must Be Crazy*. If the ideology represented reality for the director, it is disconcerting to see how effectively it was passed on and taken for granted. The *apartheid* regime, for its part, fully appreciated that *The Gods Must Be Crazy* was the most effective promotion ever of its ideology. Uys had produced films for three decades, but it was after the success of this film that he received the highest South African civil decoration in 1983. The citation read in part: 'And most especially for having given the example ... of faith in the future of our country and our people' (Tomaselli, 1986: 26, my translation from the article's French).

Only a couple of films produced in South Africa offered positive images of Africans while *apartheid* lasted. Zoltan Korda's *Cry, the Beloved Country* is the best known. It is based on the eponymous novel by Alan Paton, the most widely read South African novel ever. It is the story of a black country minister and a wealthy white farmer who find common ground in the deaths of their sons. The novel was written at a time when there was a genuine prospect for significant improvements in race relations in South Africa following the changes wrought by World War II. The government of the day considered reforms, but it was narrowly defeated in the 1948 elections that brought the National Party and its repressive policies to power. By the time the film was released in 1951, the liberal hope of black and white coming together had turned out a chimera. As for the social analysis of *Cry, the Beloved Country*, it had been flawed from the beginning: the notion that Africans belong in the countryside – the Eden of *The Gods Must Be Crazy* – and that the city is destructive, failed to acknowledge that Africans had worked in the mines, in industry, and in domestic service for generations, and that Africans were well-established in the cities.[12]

When *Cry, the Beloved Country* was remade under the direction of Darrell James Roodt in 1995, street scenes did suggest a pulsating metropolis, even if the city spelt doom for all but one of the members of Stephen Kumalo's family that had ventured there. Most striking is the shift in the

11 The poster is reproduced in Gugler (2004).

12 *Jim Comes to Jo'burg*, created by Donald Swanson and Eric Rutherford, who had come from Britain to work on another film, holds the distinction of becoming in 1949 the first feature film dominated by African actors. The Hollywood-style comedy was important in revealing a large pool of African entertainers to the all-white South African film establishment, and its success led to the production of a number of similar entertainment films (Davis, 1996: 21–31).

Can Themba, Bloke Modisane, Miriam Makeba, and Lewis Nkosi in a shebeen in Come Back, Africa

perspective on political protest. In 1951, Kumalo's brother John appeared as a godless agitator; now Kumalo's fellow priest and guide Msimangu allows that John has some truth on his side and that perhaps God is also on his side. And we hear Msimangu's sobering reflection, found in the novel but omitted from the 1951 film: 'I have this great fear in my heart that one day, when the white man turns to loving, he will find that we have turned to hate.' Now we see police brutality, and we witness a bus boycott the two priests are persuaded to honor. And with *apartheid* gone, this hopeful tale of reconciliation has some plausibility.

In 1959 Lionel Rogosin, an independent U.S. filmmaker, went to South Africa to depict conditions of life under *apartheid.* He managed to connect with leading African intellectuals, and Bloke Modisane and Lewis Nkosi joined him in writing the script for the clandestine production of *Come Back, Africa.* They conveyed, as no other film had ever done before, the reality of Africans who were at home in the city. Bloke Modisane, Lewis Nkosi, and Can Themba engage in spirited discussion in a shebeen, an illegal bar. Along the way they denounce *Cry, the Beloved Country.* At one point Miriam Makeba joins in, singing and dancing. It is her first appearance on screen, but Rogosin launched her towards international stardom (Makeba, 1987: 66–83). As her fame spread, hers became a powerful voice in the anti-*apartheid* struggle on the stage, in press conferences, and at the United Nations. *Come Back, Africa* was banned in South Africa until 1988. It remains a moving evocation of Sophiatown.[13] One of the few multi-racial neighborhoods in Johannesburg where Africans

13 Daniel Riesenfeld and Peter Davis have Lionel Rogosin and Lewis Nkosi comment on footage from the production of *Come Back, Africa* in their documentary *In Darkest Hollywood.*

The Struggle for Majority Rule in South Africa

could own houses, it had become the center of African cultural and intellectual life in the 1940s (Coplan, 1985: 143–82; Nixon, 1994: 11–41). Sophiatown was demolished under the Group Areas Act in the 1950s. In its place a white neighborhood was built. 'Triomf' it was called, which translates as 'Triumph.'

When the anti-*apartheid* struggle took a militant turn in the 1960s, this was reflected in South African literature well before being expressed on the screen. From amongst the oppressed Alex La Guma became perhaps the most distinguished novelist. His *In the Fog of the Season's End* dramatically portrays clandestine activity against the racist regime in the early 1960s underground, where he had been active himself. And it strikingly conveys the commitment of the ANC to a common front embracing all the races that the *apartheid* regime distinguished so painstakingly. *Survival,* by Workshop '71, took the new militancy beyond the stage as the actors turned on their white audiences in the course of the play. *Woza Albert!* by Percy Mtwa, Mbongeni Ngema, and Barney Simon, was a wildly funny exposure of the bigotry of an oppressive regime that claimed to be Christian. The play had audiences roaring with laughter across the racial divide in South Africa and abroad. A filmed performance, directed by David Thompson, was a similar success. It complemented the sketches with footage on conditions in South Africa and on the genesis and reception of the play, and it featured excerpts from an interview with Albert Luthuli. Ngema went on to create a musical, *Sarafina!* that toured for several years in Europe and North America to become one of the most effective vehicles spreading the anti-*apartheid* message. It was produced as a film in South Africa in the waning days of *apartheid*. Directed by Darrell James Roodt, it featured well-established South African actors: Leleti Khumalo, the musical's lead, and John Kani, Miriam Makeba, and Mbongeni Ngema in supporting roles, as well as Whoopie Goldberg, the popular U.S. actor. Throughout the years, a number of documentaries served to denounce *apartheid* abroad: Nana Mahomo's *Last Grave at Dimbaza,* clandestinely filmed in South Africa and smuggled out, the most effective.[14]

14 It took courage to appear in documentaries denouncing *apartheid*. Some people who came forward to bear witness to the brutality of the South African security forces were subsequently killed, their assassins never found (Gavshon, 1989).

References and Further Reading

Bananas. 1971. Film written and directed by Woody Allen. Produced by United Artists (USA). 82 minutes.

Come Back, Africa. 1959. Film directed by Lionel Rogosin, written by Lionel Rogosin with Lewis Nkosi and William (Bloke) Modisane. Produced by Lionel Rogosin (USA). Distributed in North America by Villon Films. 83 minutes.

Coplan, David. 1985. *In Township Tonight! South Africa's Black City Music and Theatre*. London/New York: Longman.

Crazy Hong Kong. 1993. Film directed by Wellson Chin, written by Edwin Kong and Lawrence Lau. Produced by Edko Classics Films (Hong Kong) and Golden Flare Films (Hong Kong). 91 minutes.

Crazy Safari. 1991. Film directed by Billy Chan, written by Barry Wong. Produced by Win's Movie Production & We (Hong Kong) and Samico Films Production (Hong Kong). Distributed by Media Asia

Distribution. 96 minutes.

Cry, the Beloved Country. 1951. Film directed by Zoltan Korda, written by Alan Paton. Produced by Zoltan Korda (Britain). 111 minutes.

Cry, the Beloved Country. 1995. Film directed by Darrell James Roodt, written by Ronald Harwood. Produced by Anant Singh (South Africa). Distributed in the U.S. by Swank Motion Pictures. 109 minutes.

Davis, Peter. 1996. *In Darkest Hollywood: Exploring the Jungles of Cinema's South Africa.* Johannesburg: Ravan Press; Athens: Ohio University Press.

Gavshon, Harriet. 1989. '"Bearing Witness": Ten Years Towards an Opposition Film Movement in South Africa.' *Radical History Review* 46/7: 331–45.

The Gods Must Be Crazy. 1980. Film written and directed by Jamie Uys. Produced by New Realm, Mimosa, and C.A.T. Film (South Africa). 108 minutes.

The Gods Must Be Crazy II. 1989. Film written and directed by Jamie Uys. Produced by Boet Troskie (South Africa). Distributed in the U.S. by Swank Motion Pictures. 90 minutes.

The Gods Must Be Funny in China. 1994. Film directed by Dick Cho Kin Nam, written by Keith Wong, Lam Kee To, and Lam Chiu Wing. Produced by China Film Co-Production (Hong Kong). Distributed by Tung Loong Films Limited and Hong Kong Film Entertainment Production. 95 minutes.

Gordon, Robert J. (1992) *The Bushmen Myth: the Making of a Namibian Underclass.* Boulder, CO/San Francisco/Oxford: Westview Press.

Gugler, Josef. 2004. 'Fiction, Fact, and the Responsibility of the Critic: *Camp de Thiaroye, Yaaba,* and *The Gods Must Be Crazy.' Focus on African Film,* edited by Françoise Pfaff. Bloomington, IN: Indiana University Press.

In Darkest Hollywood: Cinema and Apartheid. 1993. Documentary written, filmed, and edited by Daniel Riesenfeld and Peter Davis. Produced by Nightingale (USA) and Villon (USA). Distributed by Villon Films. 112 minutes.

Jim Comes to Jo'burg/African Jim. 1949. Film directed by Donald Swanson. Produced by Warrior Films (South Africa). Distributed in North America by Villon Films. 58 minutes.

Klemesrud, Judy. 1985. ''The Gods Must Be Crazy' – A Truly International Hit.' *New York Times* 28 April, section 2, pages 15 and 18.

La Guma, Alex. 1972. *In the Fog of the Season's End.* African Writers Series. London/Ibadan/Nairobi/ Lusaka: Heinemann.

Last Grave at Dimbaza. 1973. Documentary directed by Nana Mahomo. Morena Films (South Africa). 55 minutes.

Makeba, Miriam, with James Hall. 1987. *Makeba: My Story.* New York/Scarborough: NAL Books.

Maslin, Janet. 1984. 'A Bushman and the Clash of Cultures.' *New York Times,* 6 July, section 3, page 8.

Modern Times. 1936. Film written and directed by Charlie Chaplin. Produced by Chaplin (USA). Distributed in the U.S. by Kino International. 87 minutes.

Mtwa, Percy, Mbongeni Ngema, and Barney Simon. 1983 (first produced in 1981). *Woza Albert!* London: Methuen. Reprinted 1986 in Duma Ndlovu (ed.) *Woza Afrika! An Anthology of South African Plays.* New York: Braziller. 3–53.

N!ai, the Story of a !Kung Woman. 1979. Documentary directed by John Marshall. Distributed in the U.S. by Documentary Educational Resources. 59 minutes.

Ngema, Mbongeni. Unpublished (first produced in 1987). *Sarafina!*

Nixon, Rob. 1994. *Homelands, Harlem and Hollywood: South African Culture and the World Beyond.* New York/London: Routledge.

Out of Africa, see pages 23–8.

Paton, Alan. 1948. *Cry, the Beloved Country: a Story of Comfort in Desolation.* London: Jonathan Cape; New York: C. Scribner's Sons.

Sarafina! 1992. Film directed by Darrell James Roodt, written by William Nicholson and Mbongeni Ngema, songs and lyrics by Mbongeni Ngema and Hugh Masekela. Produced by Anant Singh (South Africa). Distributed in the U.S. by Swank Motion Pictures. 98 minutes.

Shostak, Marjorie. 1983. *Nisa: The Life and Words of a !Kung Woman.* New York: Vintage.

Tomaselli, Keyan. 1986. 'Le rôle de la Jamie Uys Film dans la culture afrikaner.' *CinémAction* 39: 24–33.

———. 1992. 'The Cinema of Jamie Uys: From Bushveld to 'Bushmen'.' Johan Blignaut and Martin Botha (eds) *Movies–Moguls–Mavericks: South African Cinema 1979–1991.* Cape Town: Showdata. 191–231.

———, Alan Williams, Lynette Steenveld, and Ruth Tomaselli. 1986. *Myth, Race and Power: South Africans Imaged on Film and TV.* Bellville, South Africa: Anthropos.

Volkman, Toby Alice. 1988, 'Out of South Africa: *The Gods Must Be Crazy.*' Larry Gross *et al.* (eds) *Image Ethics: The Moral Rights of Subjects in Photographs, Film, and Television.* Communication and Society. New York/Oxford: Oxford University Press. 236–47.

Workshop '71. 1981 (first produced in 1976). *Survival.* In *South African People's Plays. Ons phola hi.* London/Ibadan/Nairobi: Heinemann. 125–71.

Woza Albert! 1982. Film directed by David Thompson. Produced by the British Broadcasting Corporation. Distributed in the U.S. by California Newsreel. 55 minutes.

A Dry White Season 1989
A White Awakening

As a black film-maker, my first responsibility was to make a film about the situation in South Africa. But I wanted to make it from the black point of view. It was impossible, because the people who have got the money here to make films, they are not interested in films with black leads. So I had to look for a solution to circumvent this problem. So I started to look, you know, to read books about South Africa, written by South African writers, and I found that one from André Brink which actually gave me the opportunity to deal with black characters and white characters. (Euzhan Palcy, quoted by Davis, 1996: 109)

It took the major Western studios until the mid-1980s to address the anti-*apartheid* struggle. Television images of police brutality in South Africa had spread awareness of the repressive nature of the white minority regime, rekindled memories of the Civil Rights Movement in the U.S., and finally led the U.S. to join the international boycott of South Africa. Two years later, in 1987, Hollywood released its first anti-*apartheid* movie, *Cry Freedom.* Ostensibly about Steve Biko, the distinguished leader of the Black Consciousness Movement tortured and killed in police custody, the film is in the main about the tribulations of Donald Woods, his white biographer. The following year brought *A World Apart* from Britain. Based on the autobiographical script of Shawn Slovo, the daughter of Ruth First and Joe Slovo, prominent white leaders in the struggle, the film emphasized the heavy price the family, and 13-year old Shawn in particular, had to pay for the parents' political commitment. *A Dry White Season* was released in 1989. These films arrived just in time as the confrontations in South Africa disappeared from television screens: the South African government, under the State of Emergency, denied television crews access to such events in 1987. But they came rather late to have much of a political impact: the white minority regime was to change course abruptly in early 1990. And public interest was limited. None of these films was a success at the box office. *A Dry White Season*, which cost on the order of $10 million, took in just over one million in its initial run in the U.S. (Collins, 1989; Shipman, 1990).

Euzhan Palcy directing Marlon Brando

A Dry White Season was different from the two earlier films in two important respects. For the first time Hollywood recruited a black person to direct a film about *apartheid*. The first black woman to direct any film in Hollywood, she chose to base hers on a novel about the suffering and courage of ordinary people. Palcy, born and raised in Martinique, had obtained a degree in French Literature at the Sorbonne before training as a filmmaker at the Ecole de Cinéma Louis Lumière, also in France. By the time she embarked on *A Dry White Season*, she had already taken a novel to the screen. *Sugar Cane Alley*, based on Joseph Zobel's autobiographical novel of growing up in poverty in Martinique in the 1930s, had been a success. Palcy was committed to making a film about *apartheid* and started out in 1984 with a scenario that adopted the perspective of a little girl in Soweto (Ferenczi, 1989). But her efforts to find producers in France failed. Hollywood was interested in her, but the studios were not prepared to have black leads. Black African characters, played by unfamiliar actors, were unlikely to reach the large market Hollywood productions aim for. Palcy settled for the novel of a white author with an Afrikaner as the principal protagonist. Given the constraints, it was an inspired choice.[1]

André Brink, the author of the novel, is an Afrikaner himself, one of the descendants of the early settlers who were most committed to *apartheid* policies. He has described how seeing *Come Back, Africa* transformed his outlook on blacks. The film, of course, had not been shown on South African screens; Brink saw it while he was a student in Paris. Later, in an interview, he recalled how 'it came to me as a revelation, just this rediscovery of the most important of all things, that we are all human' (Davis, 1996: 56). In the 1970s the recurrent reports of Africans who had died in detention, supposed suicides, propelled him to write *A Dry White Season*. Brink articulated both this compulsion and the need to reach for a better future in his speech accepting the Martin Luther King Memorial Prize in Britain in 1980:

> In *A Dry White Season* I have tried to accept that responsibility that one owns to one's society and one's time; it was conceived in anguish and written in pain and rage, but not in hate. Even if one's conscience drives one to a position of *J'accuse*, it can be valid as a literary experience only if it derives not from the sterility of a merely negative attitude but from an all-consuming belief that man can be rescued from his blindness and follies; and that the world can be a more just and a more free place to live in than it is. If one is driven to say 'No' it should transcend the immediacy of denial to become an affirmation of something more just, more true, and more compassionate than whatever one has been allowed to experience in the past.[2] (Brink, 1983: 204)

Brink shows another Afrikaner's awakening to the horrors of a regime solidly supported by most Afrikaners. His protagonist Ben du Toit, a white man privileged by the racist regime, an Afrikaner at that, becomes aware how his world is maintained by the brutal repression of the Other, a repression carried out by his own people, in his name, and commits himself to oppose his own community.[3] Brink himself shared the experiences of his protagonist of having become a traitor to his fellow Afrikaners and a subversive to government. His mail was opened and his phone tapped; he became the subject of police surveillance and searches; his writing was confiscated and his publications banned; he, his family, and even his fans became the targets of threats (Brink, 1983: 246–7).[4]

Brink took a passage from Mongane Wally Serote's poem 'For Don M – Banned' as his epigraph. The concluding lines, 'it is a dry white season – but seasons come to pass,' have an obvious political resonance. But for Ben du Toit, to start with, it is a childhood trauma that constituted a dry white season. In the Great Drought of 1933, when he was nine or ten years old, he and his father had to trek with their sheep in search of pasture. The drought closed in on them; there was no way out. They

1 The poster that accompanied the film on its U.S. release clearly demonstrates the marketing strategy: it features pictures of Donald Sutherland, Sarah Sarandon, and Marlon Brando, and further lists Janet Suzman, Jurgen Prochnow, and Zakes Mokae, in that order. Subsequently advertising was modified. In a later poster a naked African sitting on his buttocks conveys the oppression of *apartheid*. The poster for the video, reproduced here, complements this image with pictures, from left to right, of Sutherland, Sarandon, Brando, and Mokae. The French film poster is similar, but it features Mokae first, followed by Sutherland and Brando. The Australian, British, and German posters replaced Zakes Mokae, in the role of the subversive Stanley, with Winston Ntshona's Gordon, the victim.

2 On the impact of existentialism on white South African dissident writers such as Brink, see Peck (1997: 121-37).

3 Neither the English version of the novel nor the film convey that three generations of Afrikaners are most unlikely to use English rather than Afrikaans at home. The film does introduce Afrikaans accents and forms of address.

4 When Levinson refers to Ben as Mr Coetzee (p. 43), Brink pays tribute to J. M. Coetzee, his fellow Afrikaner writer against *apartheid*.

The Struggle for Majority Rule in South Africa

were left with the white skeletons of their herd (pp. 30–1). But now the image takes on new significance for Ben as he finds himself 'on the edge of yet another dry white season, perhaps worse than the one I knew as a child' (p. 163). The story begins in the South African winter of 1976, shortly before Jonathan, the son of Gordon and Emily Ngubene, is arrested at the beginning of the Soweto Uprising and dies in custody.[5] It ends in the South African autumn of 1977:

> The pale autumn days growing ever more wintry. The leaves falling, the trees barer, drier. All sap invisible, unbelievable. All softness, tenderness, all femininity, all gentle humanity, compassion, burnt away. Dry, dry, and colourless. An inhospitable autumn. (p. 286)

In Soweto, the children's militancy, their repudiation of their elders' passivity, had created a wide generation gap. In the du Toit family, Ben's gradual awakening, his hesitant steps which eventually lead to a firm commitment that justice be done, bring separation and betrayal. As Melanie Bruwer tells Ben:

> This country doesn't allow me to indulge myself.… It isn't possible to live a private life if you want to live with your conscience. It tears open everything that's intimate and personal. (p. 246)

Melanie's father Phil Bruwer, a retired professor of Philosophy, contrasts the present with other historical periods when a whole civilization seemed to be moving in the same gear and in the same direction, when people found themselves in complete harmony with society and did not need to make their own decisions. At this time in South Africa, history has not yet settled on a firm new course, and individuals are on their own, they have to find their own definitions (pp. 221–2). Ben certainly feels utterly isolated. And, indeed, he has been separated from his family; and even while his son Johan understands his position and supports him, Ben finds his eagerness to 'help' an embarrassment (p. 299). He is alienated to the point where he asks himself whether he has gone mad. He becomes paranoid; at one time he even wonders whether Melanie spies on him. He has discovered that premises and basic conditions he had taken for granted simply do not exist. Where he had expected something solid there turns out to be nothing. Ben has come to reject the Afrikaner view of South Africa, but he has not established an alternative understanding of his times. Melanie and Phil provide comfort and some orientation. They have always been critical of the *apartheid* regime. Phil characterizes it:

> it's a matter of power. Naked power. That's what brought them there and keeps them there. And power has a way of becoming an end in itself ... once a flick of your wrist can decide the fate of others – you need a very active conscience to start acting against your own interests. And a conscience doesn't stand up to much heat or cold, it's a delicate sort of plant. (p. 244)

Ben's conscience turns out to be a plant that grows slowly but then withstands all the heat. And he comes to understand that the people of Soweto have to define their real needs and discover for themselves their integrity and affirm their own dignity (p. 304). He remains an outsider

5 Mbulelo Vizikhungo Mzamane's three-part story, *The Children of Soweto*. conveys a sense of the excitement and the horrors of the Soweto Uprising.

to the world of Stanley, the African cab driver. Jonathan's brother Robert utterly rejects him. Neither the African National Congress and its multi-racial vision, nor Steve Biko and the Black Consciousness Movement, are ever mentioned. While Ben commits himself to the pursuit of justice, he does not join the struggle for a different South Africa. He carries his burden alone, supported by Phil's reassurance:

> There are only two kinds of madness one should guard against.... One is the belief that we can do everything. The other is the belief that we can do nothing. (p. 244)

The film was shot in Zimbabwe and London. But Palcy recruited well-known South African artists to perform the music: the renowned Hugh Masekela for the lead score, the famous South African group Ladysmith Black Mambazo for most of the songs, the cast of the extraordinarily successful musical *Sarafina!* for additional vocals. And she chose to have South African rather than African-American actors. They came secretly and returned to South Africa, thus risking their lives, except for Zakes Mokae who was already living in exile. For the lead roles Palcy assembled a distinguished cast, who agreed to work for much less than their usual fees (Bouzet, 1989).[6] Donald Sutherland lived up to his formidable reputation by conveying, in his performance as Ben du Toit, a good deal of what the novel articulates as the reflections of this tormented man. Zakes Mokae, the distinguished South African actor, gives full weight to formidable Stanley Makhaya, whose subversive activities we can only guess at.[7] The most famous of them all, Marlon Brando, after eight years away from the cameras, offered his act as the lawyer for $4,000 union wages, rewrote his part, charged that MGM had reneged on its initial agreement to donate the $11 million that what would have been his regular fee to an anti-*apartheid* organization, and complained bitterly that MGM had cut his eviction from the court (Grassin, 1989; Kolocotroni and Taxidou, 1992; Stouvenot, 1989). The film conflates the two separate roles of solicitor dealing with the client and barrister representing the case in court, characteristic of the British-derived South African system of legal representation: the novel's Levinson and de Villiers merge into Ian McKenzie. But then, who would want to forego the joy of watching Marlon Brando's laconic comment as he counsels Ben: 'Justice and the law are distant cousins, and in South Africa, right now, they are not on speaking terms,' or his subversive wit in the court room, the relief, transient though it is, from the continual victimization of those who dare to protest?[8]

The actors' appearance, their expressions, and their actions replace much that is difficult to transfer from the novel to the screen: the discourse of Phil, Ben's long reflections, and the narrator's descriptions of Ben and Susan. If we thus lose psychological depth and political comment, Palcy shows us what the novel only touches on, confronts us more powerfully than the written word can ever do with the horrors of repression. The du Toit family's suburban idyll contrasts with the violence of the police and army, the lifeless bloodied bodies of the victims, and the horrors of torture – scenes so vivid that some viewers find them hard to

6 The accents of some sound wrong to South African audiences, even (or especially) when they endeavored to imitate South African speech.

7 Mokae's brother, like Stanley's brother in the novel, was hanged for common crimes.

8 Marlon Brando's performance risks distracting from an important distinction Ian McKenzie makes. Courts continued to follow the law in *apartheid* South Africa – for example, all the accused were acquitted in the Treason Trial that had begun with the arrest of 156 participants in the Congress of the People that had adopted the Freedom Charter in 1955. The source of injustice was legislation that became ever more discriminatory and repressive.

take.[9] And we get to hear the students singing *Nkosi Sikelel' i Afrika*.

Palcy pared the story to its essential elements by omitting much detail. The du Toits have fewer children. Ben confronts only two Special Branch officers. He does not seek help from members of his family, from his pastor, from a government minister. Ben is not solicited by Henry Maphuna and other victims. There are fewer attacks on Ben, nor is he subject to a phone tap and mail inspection. Ben does not get emotionally involved with Melanie. There is no detainee who, once released, reports that he had been made to sign his affidavit, like Tsabalala, under torture. Grace Nkosi does not appear at the inquest to tell how she was tortured in detention. And the film drops the framing story of the narrator writing the story from the papers his friend Ben had left with him – a framing that had been rather problematic as the story moved seamlessly between the narrator's and Ben's prose.

If none of these omissions make much difference to the thrust of the story, other changes definitely do. The film's message is blunter, the characters are less differentiated. The film simplifies the story by omitting elements that produced a more complex, liberal understanding: the crimes committed by Stanley's brother, Henry Maphuna's brutal revenge on the man who had raped his sister, blind violence in Soweto that nearly kills Melanie and Ben, Melanie's traumatic experiences in independent Africa. Where in the novel a gang of *tsotsis*, hooligans, attack a group of older men at a beerhall, in the film they are young militants trying to close down the beerhalls and mobilize support. Between the novel and the film several characters become more firmly committed. Levinson, the professional and conman, a Clark Gable *redivivus* in the novel, becomes Marlon Brando, resigned yet fighting regardless. Emily does not seek solace from Ben after the inquest; rather, he goes to hug her. And she does not kill herself – but then her suicide in the novel was not all that plausible to start with, since she still had three children to look after. Rather, she is beaten up and dies of a heart attack when she resists deportation to Zululand, her 'homeland.' Johan is transformed from a loyal son whose eagerness to 'help' is an embarrassment to his father to an accomplice who thwarts his sister's betrayal.

Palcy increases the distance of race between Ben and Stanley. In the novel they get quite close at times, to the point where Stanley echoes Humphrey Bogart's classic line in *Casablanca*: 'Lanie, you wait. I got a feeling you and I are going a long way together' (p. 182). We never see such camaraderie in the film, even if Ben eventually graduates Stanley from the ironic 'lanie,' a term akin to 'whitey,' to 'man.' In the novel Ben draws on their similar childhood experiences to establish common ground with Stanley, but in the film Stanley curtly reminds him of the overriding differences that separate the life experiences of an African from those of a white man in South Africa. The ingrained racist assumptions are overturned: the African knows best, and he is in charge. Instead of coming personally close to Ben, Stanley establishes a paternal relationship with Johan. When Johan has accomplished a crucial mission, Stanley hugs him: 'Well done, little *lanie*.'

9 Euzhan Palcy visited South Africa on a 6-day visa obtained under false pretenses and went to Soweto hiding under a blanket in a car, like Ben. She saw people who had been tortured by their interrogators, a child whose arms had been broken, a 14-year-old whose finger nails had been torn out (Rousseau, 1989). The photographs Ian McKenzie shows in court as he challenges Captain Stolz were supplied by Amnesty International (Stouvenot, 1990).

Ben, the undertaker, and Stanley at the casket of Gordon Ngubene

Palcy empowered Stanley, her principal black protagonist. At the end, he no longer disappears but acts decisively. She thus created a different, dramatic ending for the film. The novel had left the reader with questions: What future for the narrator-writer? What will happen to the documents collected at such enormous cost in suffering? Where has Stanley gone? Is Melanie carrying Ben's child? In the film Captain Stolz[10] pays for his evil deeds; and the documents.... I will let you find out for yourself.

Some of the changes Palcy made as she interpreted Brink's novel for the screen can be seen as responses to the requirements and opportunities of the different medium: paring the story to its essential elements, dropping lengthy discourse and reflection. But with her choice of elements, her modifications in characters and changes in events, the director from the African diaspora created a different, more militant story, unencumbered by the ambivalence of Brink's liberal approach. In her reading, the chasm between the races in South Africa could no longer be bridged even by those few whites who were sympathetic to the oppressed.[11]

The shifts in perspective presumably reflect Palcy's views on militancy and race. They allowed her to transcend to some extent the constraint imposed by Hollywood's insistence on a white lead. She dropped longing and sex, key ingredients of virtually any Hollywood production, however violent, 'because I didn't want to shift the focus of the film' (McKenna, 1989: 35). In other respects the changes Palcy wrought brought the film closer to conventional Hollywood formulas: a more manichean world than in Brink's novel, a conclusive ending instead of an ongoing story, a triumph of sorts. As Brink, who had no hand in the script, put it, the film's ending is 'a bit too glib' (Davis, 1996: 111).[12] But then, the film addressed a different audience in more than one respect. If it is generally

10 In German Stolz means 'Pride,' and Palcy reinforced the connection with fascism by casting a well-known German actor, Jürgen Prochnow, in the role.

11 If Dr Hassiem served as a reminder of the collaboration of Asians in the anti-*apartheid* struggle, Palcy reinforced the point by introducing the Asian woman passing Melanie's papers on to Stanley.

12 Kolocotroni and Taxidou (1992) argue that the film's ending presents the moral of the story and constitutes a realistic political choice. I am inclined to see the actions of both Stolz and Stanley that last night, as presented by the film, in terms of emotion rather than political calculus.

Palcy, Brink, and Mokae comment on *A Dry White Season* in the documentary *In Darkest Hollywood*.

The Struggle for Majority Rule in South Africa

13 The film conflates the beginning of the Uprising on 16 June, the marching students being unexpectedly stopped by police bullets, with the large-scale killings that started the following day after riots had broken out and Prime Minister John Vorster had vowed that law and order would be maintained at all cost.

14 Brink wrote Afrikaans and English versions of his novel, both published the same year. He had done this before, and he had commented on how the English and Afrikaans versions of his novels had come to differ (Brink, 1983: 113-15).

15 After his publisher demanded drastic cuts and revisions, Brink resorted to publication by subscription. A printing of 3,000 copies of the novel was thus distributed before the censors could act and ban it. The ban was lifted a couple of years later (Cope, 1982: 136, 141).

the case that most movie goers do not read serious novels, in this case the intended audiences of the novel and the film were different altogether. The film was addressed to audiences outside South Africa who needed to be made aware of the stark contrast in living conditions between white and black in South Africa, who no longer remembered, twelve years after the Soweto Uprising, how young the children were and how brutal the repression, and who would not be concerned if the film took some liberties with period details.[13] Whereas Brink intended to reach his countrymen, and especially his fellow Afrikaners,[14] even if he may well have anticipated, as it came to pass, that the novel would be banned in South Africa initially.[15] When the novel's narrator puts down the novel's last paragraph, we hear the author – and recognize the final sentence, uttered all too readily by many Germans after the holocaust:

> Perhaps all one can really hope for, all I am entitled to, is no more than this: to write it down. To report what I know. So that it will not be possible for any man ever to say again: *I knew nothing about it*. (p. 316, italics in original)

Susan, in the film, confronts Ben trenchantly: 'But you don't think the blacks would do the same to us, and worse, if they had half a chance?' After the ANC got 63 per cent of the vote in the first elections with a universal franchise in 1994, and Nelson Mandela became President of South Africa, the Truth and Reconciliation Commission gave the historic answer that was heard around the world: 'Confess your crimes, and you may go free.'

References and Further Reading

Biko, Steve. 1978. *I Write What I Like: a Selection of His Writings*. Edited by Aelred Stubbs C.R. London/ Ibadan/Nairobi: Heinemann.

Brink, André. 1979. *A Dry White Season*. London: W. H. Allen; New York: William Morrow.

——. 1979. *'n Droë Wit Seisoen*. Johannesburg: Taurus.

——. 1983. *Mapmakers: Writing in a State of Siege*. London: Faber and Faber. Also published as *Writing in a State of Siege: Essays on Politics and Literature*. New York: Summit Books.

Brooks, Alan, and Jeremy Brickhill. 1980. *Whirlwind before the Storm: The Origins and Development of the Uprising in Soweto and the Rest of South Africa from June to December 1976*. London: International Defence and Aid Fund for South Africa.

Bouzet, Ange-Dominique. 1989. 'Un réalisatrice noire française et une furie de productrice juive-américaine.' *Libération*, 11–12 November, pages 34–5.

Casablanca. 1942. Film directed by Michael Curtiz. Produced by Metro Goldwyn Mayer (USA). Distributed in the U.S. by Swank Motion Pictures. 102 minutes.

Collins, Glenn. 1989. 'A Black Director Views Apartheid.' *New York Times*, 25 September, section C, page 12.

Come Back, Africa. 1959. Film directed by Lionel Rogosin, written by Lionel Rogosin with Lewis Nkosi and William (Bloke) Modisane. Produced by Lionel Rogosin (USA). Distributed in North America by Villon Films. 83 minutes.

Cope, Jack. 1982. *The Adversary Within: Dissident Writers in Afrikaans.* Cape Town: David Philip; Atlantic Highlands, N.J.: Humanities Press; London: Rex Collings.

Cry Freedom. 1987. Film directed by Richard Attenborough, written by John Briley. Produced by Warner Brothers (USA) and Marble Arch Productions (Britain). Distributed in the U.S. by Swank Motion Pictures. 157 minutes.

Davis, Peter. 1996. *In Darkest Hollywood: Exploring the Jungles of Cinema's South Africa.* Johannesburg: Ravan Press; Athens, OH: Ohio University Press.

A Dry White Season. 1989. Film directed by Euzhan Palcy, written by Colin Welland and Euzhan Palcy. Produced by Metro Goldwyn Mayer (USA) in association with Star Partners II (Britain). Distributed in the U.S. by Swank Motion Pictures. 106 min.

Ferenczi, Aurélien. 1989. 'La fée, l'apartheid et Brando.' *Le Quotidien de Paris,* 8 November 1989, page 24.

First, Ruth. 1965. *117 Days: An Account of Confinement and Interrogation Under the South African Ninety-Day Detention Law.* New York: Stein and Day; Harmondsworth, Middlesex: Penguin Books.

Grassin, Sophie. 1989. 'Un saison en enfer.' *L'Express,* 3 November 1989, page 157.

Herbstein, Denis. 1978. *White Man We Want to Talk to You.* Harmondsworth/New York: Penguin.

In Darkest Hollywood: Cinema and Apartheid. 1993. Documentary written, filmed, and edited by Daniel Riesenfeld and Peter Davis. Produced by Nightingale (USA) and Villon (USA). Distributed by Villon Films. 112 minutes.

Jolly, Rosemary Jane. 1996. *Colonization, Violence, and Narration in White South African Writing: André Brink, Breyten Breytenbach, and J. M. Coetzee.* Johannesburg: Witwatersrand University Press; Athens: Ohio University Press.

Kane-Berman, John. 1978. *Soweto: Black Revolt, White Reaction.* Johannesburg: Ravan Press.

Kolocotroni, Vassiliki, and Olga Taxidou. 1992. '*A Dry White Season:* The Personal and the Political.' John Orr and Colin Nicholson (eds) *Cinema and Fiction: New Modes of Adapting, 1950–1990.* Edinburgh: Edinburgh University Press. 39–53.

McKenna, Kristine. 1989. 'Tough, Passionate, Persuasive: Euzhan Palcy Battled for Five Years to Put Her Vision of Apartheid on the Screen, and Then Lured Marlon Brando Back to Work – for Free,' *American Film* 14 (10): 32–8.

Mzamane, Mbulelo Vizikhungo. 1982. *The Children of Soweto: A Trilogy.* Johannesburg: Ravan Press; Harlow, Essex: Longman; Athens, OH: Ohio University Press.

Peck, Richard. 1997. *A Morbid Fascination: White Prose and Politics in Apartheid South Africa.* Contributions to the Study of World Literature 78. Westport, CT/London: Greenwood Press.

Rousseau. Nita. 1989. 'Hollywood lave plus blanc.' *Le Nouvel Observateur,* 2 November 1989, page 160.

Shipman, David. 1990. 'Quarterly Film Review,' *Contemporary Review,* July, 45–8.

Slovo, Joe. 1995. *Slovo: the Unfinished Autobiography.* Johannesburg: Ravan Press; London: Hodder and Stoughton; Melbourne/New York: Ocean Press.

Stouvenot, Michèle. 'Brando, séduit retrouve le goût de jouer'. *Le Journal du Dimanche,* 5 November 1989.

Sugar Cane Alley/Rue Cases Nègres. 1983. Film written and directed by Euzhan Palcy. Produced by NEF Diffusion, Orca, and Su Ma Fa (France). Distributed in the U.S. by New Yorker Films. 106 minutes.

A World Apart. 1988. Film directed by Chris Menges, written by Shawn Slovo. Produced by Palace, British Screen, Atlantic, and Working Title (Britain). 114 minutes.

Zobel, Joseph. *La Rue Cases-Nègres.* English translation by Keith Q. Warner (1980) *Black Shack Alley.* Washington: Three Continents Press; London: Heinemann.

LIFE AND DEATH ON THE STREETS OF SOWETO

BANNED IN S. AFRICA

"A TERRIFIC MOVIE...
EVEN MORE REMARKABLE
THAN *CRY FREEDOM*
AND *A WORLD APART*."

Derek Malcolm, The Guardian

MAPANTSULA

15

HAVERBEAM AND DAVID HANNAY PRESENT A MAX MONTOCCHIO PRODUCTION OF A FILM BY OLIVER SCHMITZ AND THOMAS MOGOTLANE
WITH THOMAS MOGOTLANE, THEMBI MTSHALI, MARCEL VAN HEERDEN, DOLLY RATHEBE, PETER SEPHUMA, EUGENE MAJOLA DIRECTOR OF PHOTOGRAPHY BOB STEWART
EDITOR MARK BAARD ART DIRECTOR ROBYN HOFMEYR MUSIC BY THE OUENS EXECUTIVE PRODUCERS DAVID HANNAY AND KEITH ROSENBAUM PRODUCED BY MAX MONTOCCHIO DIRECTED BY OLIVER SCHMITZ
FEATURING THE HIT SINGLE "EVERYTHING MUST CHANGE"

Mapantsula 1988
Black Resistance to White Oppression

Mapantsula is the first militant anti-*apartheid* feature film to be produced in South Africa. It was filmed in its entirety in Soweto and Johannesburg at the height of government repression under the third State of Emergency. Oliver Schmitz and Thomas Mogotlane (1991: 23) had submitted a dummy script of 'a nice, clean harmonious little gangster movie set anywhere in the world' to their sponsors – who were taking advantage of the generous tax breaks the government provided to encourage film production: the *apartheid* state subsidized the production of *Mapantsula*. The South African laboratory, however, appeared to have caught on: the negative was badly scratched; and the police arrived at the editing rooms, demanding a copy of the film. In spite of these and other obstacles Schmitz and Mogotlane managed to produce a film that was endorsed by the African National Congress and was embraced by part of the cultural establishment: in 1989 *Mapantsula* won South Africa's AA Life/M-Net Vita Awards for best film, best script, best original music score, best sound, best actor, and best supporting actress, sharing the award for best direction.[1]

In some respects *Mapantsula* is indeed a gangster movie. Panic, the principal protagonist, is a *pantsula*, a Zulu term for a street tough, a rebellious underworld figure popular in South African fiction and urban folklore. '*Mapantsula*' (the plural form) refers to an exaggerated way of talking, dressing, and swaggering originally derived from Hollywood gangster movies of the 1940s and, more recently, from disco dancing and fashions copied from *Esquire* (Tomaselli, 1991).[2] As Michael Wilmington (1989) puts it, Johannes Themba Mzolo, a.k.a. Panic, appears as a sociopathic charmer who gets away with a lot because of his quick smile, fast knife, and the outrageous things he does with absolute self-confidence: within a dangerous, repressive society he seems to be free. He most certainly does not panic; presumably he inspires panic. An accomplished pickpocket, he rifles through his victim's wallet at leisure, switchblade between his teeth, silently daring his victim to challenge him; fast as lightning he takes a broken bottle to the throat of the fellow crook who has attacked him with a switchblade at the bar; deftly he puts his knife into a victim who fights back. He has been imprisoned for burglary, a second time for breaking into a factory, armed robbery, and assaulting a white man, and a third time for burglary.

Mapantsula, however, is anything but a regular gangster movie.[3] Contrary to the dummy script, it takes its South African setting seriously. Panic operates in a context of collective struggle. In 1985–6 protests are escalating. Students are boycotting school. Soweto is in the middle of a bitter rent strike by the public housing tenants.[4] Protesters are shot,

I was feeling that it was a story important to tell from this black perspective, regardless of whether the filmmaker is black or white.
(Oliver Schmitz in an interview, Schmitz and Mogotlane, 1991: 24)

1 Schmitz and Mogotlane (1991: 17–50), in an interview with Jeremy Nathan, give a detailed account of the remarkable story of the production and distribution of *Mapantsula*. They also comment on their film in the documentary *In Darkest Hollywood*.

2 The film in turn draws on stylistic elements of *film noir*.

3 In the movie theater scene we catch glimpses of Ronnie Isaacs's *One More Shot*, common South African *kung fu* fare in Zulu.

4 Mbongeni Ngema wrote and directed a play on the rent strike that was subsequently filmed. Play and film take for their title the popular slogan we hear at the town meeting: '*Asinamali!*' i.e. 'No money!' (to pay the rent).

vs Tsotsi

Funeral march

arrested, tortured, and killed in prison. Militant funeral marches for the martyrs lead to fresh confrontations and more victims. At the beginning of the film we first hear the rhythmic chanting at a protest march, then see a short *toyi-toyi* sequence:[5]

> Eitah! Tah! Tah! Tah-tah! (Hey man! man! man! man-man!)
> Eitah! Tah! Tah! Tah-tah!
> Naziya! Ziya, ziya-ziya! (There they [the police] are! They are! They are–they are!)
> Pull up your gun, ready to shoot!
> Pull up your gun, ready to shoot!
> Aim the Boer, the farmer!
> Aim the Boer, the farmer!
> Kill the Boer, kill a man!
> Kill the Boer, kill a man!
> Shayizandla macomrades! (Clap your hands comrades!)
> Shayizandla macomrades!
> Eitah! Tah! Tah! Tah-tah!

5 The term *toyi-toyi* apparently originated with South African guerrillas in Zimbabwe as a term for the physical exercise of jogging on the spot. In South African protest marches it conveyed the notion of confident military exertion while moving forward.

At the end of the film we come to witness more of this protest march and now also hear:

> Mshaye nge AK! Nge AK! (Shoot them with an AK[47]! With an AK!)
> Nelson Mandela, ngu-baba wethu! (is our father!)

U-Botha lona, voetsek! Voetsek-voetsek! (Botha [the President of South Africa]
   get lost! Get lost! Get lost!)
Oliver Tambo [the ANC leader in exile], ngu-baba wethu!
Joe Slovo [the leader of the ANC's military wing], ubaba wethu![6]

In the midst of these upheavals, Panic pursues a self-centered life. He has rejected regular work and makes money as a thug. When imprisoned previously, he got himself released early by informing for the police. His only interest in the rent strike is opportunistic: he takes it as an argument not to pay his landlady, Ma Modise. But Panic changes as he is rejected by Pat, as a diviner tells him of the ancestors' truth that you always reap what you sow, as he meets the trade unionist Duma, as Ma Modise's son Sam dies in police captivity, as he accompanies Ma Modise on a protest march, as she is shot and he is arrested, as he shares a prison cell with militant prisoners. In the end Panic risks death by refusing to sign a statement that would criminalize Duma by implicating him in terrorist activities.[7] When the video was eventually released in South Africa, the sleeve conveyed the process of Panic's transformation: Panic the criminal, stolen wallet and knife in hand, stands out, but scenes of protest intrude on him.

True to his past, Panic has not joined anything or anybody; he remains an isolated individual, his ordeal all the more excruciating. Dandridge-Perry (1990) relates him to the anti-hero, a well-established character in South African lore and literature, the trickster whose escapades represent resistance to and rebellion against the system that has formed him. Panic's victims are usually white, and he refers to them as *lanies*, a term more akin to 'whiteys' than the subtitles' 'yuppies.' Duma, in contrast, may be seen to stand for the alternative way of dealing with *apartheid*, for struggle that is collective, organized, strategic, and patient – we see him wearing T-shirts of several of the organizations that had come together as the United Democratic Front in 1983. Ma Modise and Panic's girlfriend Pat resemble Duma in their quiet strength. At first we see them operating within the constraints imposed on them by white racism, but then they are propelled into protest: Ma Modise against the police who killed her son, Pat against the employer who dismissed her summarily.[8]

The film starts out with children playing in the middle of the road. Their play is abruptly interrupted by a police landrover screeching around the corner. In it Panic and other men and women are being taken to prison. With Panic the audience hears the chant of a protest march and gets a glimpse of it – only towards the end of the film will we realize the crucial importance of that event in the transformation of Panic. The action of the film covers perhaps five days in the prison. Flashbacks take us, in more or less chronological order, to the events of the preceding nine days or so. At first, they appear as Panic's flashbacks, but then it becomes clear that they include events Panic did not witness.

Most of the scenes that are not part of the recollections of Panic center

6 The chant has been transcribed and translated by Sicelo Makapela and Josef Gugler. We have omitted the chorus which repeats some of the elements. In the script the chant is different in content and less repetitive in form (Schmitz and Mogotlane, 1991: 53, 135–6).

7 Panic is ordered to sign a statement that 'Duma assaulted two soldiers, in an attempt to kill them, before running off. On the same night he fled to Botswana taking four youths with him to receive military training.' The script has a different statement (Schmitz and Mogotlane, 1991: 138–9).

8 Ma Modise is played by Dolly Rathebe who received the AA Life/ M-Net Vita Award for best supporting actress. She had sung the female lead role in *Jim Comes to Jo'burg* in 1949 and become a star (Davis, 1996: 25-33, 117). Those who remember her from those days will savor the irony in her riposte to Panic: 'If I was twenty years younger ... if I was twenty years younger, I'd steer clear of you!'

Thembi Mtshali, who took on the role of Pat, had grown up in the countryside with her grandparents, looking after their cattle. Her parents had her join them in Durban when she was 15 so she could continue school. She became pregnant, dropped out of school, and took a job as a nanny. Starting out with a group performing at Natal University, she eventually earned international acclaim in musicals, living in New York for a while. Mtshali had just begun to work at the famous Market Theatre in Johannesburg when she was recruited for *Mapantsula*. She was 36 years old but managed to portray the much younger character of Pat convincingly (Ellerson, 2000: 193–7).

The Struggle for Majority Rule in South Africa

on Pat: her treatment by the 'madam' who employs her; the town meeting in which township dwellers, chanting and dancing the *toyi-toyi*, confront the mayor and his deputy, Africans both, with angry shouts of '*Amandla!*' ('Power!' – to the people); Pat's meetings with Duma. Panic's relationship with Pat is complex. He scrounges off her and makes her lose her job through his reckless behavior. But he cares sufficiently about her to rebuke Dingaan for letting on about their criminal activities.[9] For her benefit he fabricates a story about returning a handbag to a white woman and getting a reward. And when Pat leaves him, he sets out in pursuit. Mogotlane's portrayal of Panic convincingly conveys the transformation of a complex character.

Using English, Zulu, Soto, Afrikaans, and *tsotsitaal*, the slang of the street toughs, *Mapantsula* conveys actual language use in a country that now has eleven official languages. In this context the choice of language has political implications, and people switch between languages according to context. Panic speaks Afrikaans, the language of power, when he is acting the big tough in the township. But he hides his knowledge of Afrikaans from his interrogator, whether to be able to listen in on exchanges between police officers or out of a sense of rebellion. Then, when he desperately tries to plead with his interrogator, he falls into Afrikaans, the language of choice to ingratiate oneself with white police officers, predominantly recruited among Afrikaners.[10]

Mapantsula has for principal character a street tough in a modern metropolis, an individualistic character, boasting a life style derived from Hollywood. If *Yaaba* portrayed a village that time forgot, we are now in Africa's most industrialized country where mining and industry were established over a century ago. Large numbers of Africans have worked in the mines, factories, and cities for generations. In spite of the ruthless efforts of the *apartheid* state, many are urbanites without any rural connection. And they have experienced Western influences for a long time: Christian missionaries proselytizing and educating, Hollywood movies,[11] African-American music, the African-American struggle that inspired the Black Consciousness Movement led by Steve Biko.

Mapantsula and *A Dry White Season* resemble each other in a number of ways: both are set in Johannesburg and Soweto, both tell of ordinary people, both denounce *apartheid*. But it's a long way from Johannesburg to Hollywood. There black director Palcy had to settle for a script with a white man as its principal protagonist, in South Africa white director Schmitz could produce a film set among Africans. *A Dry White Season* dramatizes by contrasting scenes of the du Toits' suburban existence with destruction in Soweto, by showing police shooting down school children, and by giving glimpses of gruesome torture. *Mapantsula* first and foremost addresses South Africans who know all about the extent of repression under *apartheid*. Much of the film is taken up with scenes of everyday life; we are simply told that Sam has died in police custody; Panic is not subjected to the kind of horrendous torture we witnessed in *A Dry White Season*; we see small but well-kept houses in Soweto. But if *Mapantsula* is less dramatic, the racial divide is total: the only sympathetic whites are to be found

9 In naming Panic's sidekick Dingaan, the film pays tribute to the Zulu king of that name, a prominent leader in the struggle against the invasion of white settlers in the nineteenth century.

10 The language issue – the government's decision to enforce the use of Afrikaans on a par with English as the medium of instruction – triggered the Soweto Uprising of 1976. Ten years later the burnt-out school in *Mapantsula* – with an Afrikaans text on the blackboard – reminds us of the continuing turmoil.

11 *In Darkest Hollywood* comments on the impact of Hollywood on black South Africans.

outside the story: Schmitz and the white actors and technicians who agreed to produce an anti-*apartheid* film under the very eyes of the *apartheid* regime during a State of Emergency. Thembi Mtshali reminisced:

Oliver Schmitz, Juliet Mazamisa, and Thomas Mogotlane during the shooting

> I did not act in that movie. I just became myself; I just did what I did when I was a nanny. It was funny, because the woman who played the role of my madam is a very nice person. We worked together at the Market Theater. She found it very difficult to be harsh. They tried to push her saying, 'You have to be harsh to be in this role.' After the take she would come and say, 'You know, I did not mean to do that.' I would say to her, ' Please, come on, we are acting here!' (Ellerson, 2000: 199)

Neither Schmitz nor Mogotlane had formal training in filmmaking. And their experience with film was limited. Schmitz had worked as an editor and participated in workshops and amateur groups. Mogotlane, an experienced stage and screen actor, had written two plays and contributed to a film script.[12] They opted for natural acting, and the script changed quite a lot in the process. Their budget was limited to 2 million Rand, then about $1 million (Schmitz and Mogotlane 1991:

12 Schmitz went on to make *Hijack Stories*. An action film with wild car chases, it touches lightly on the context of South Africa after *apartheid:* the frustration of black South Africans who continue to live in poverty while watching white affluence, and the gap that separates them from the black middle class that has moved into the formerly 'whites only' neighborhoods. *Hijack Stories* is dedicated to Mogotlane who died in 1994 at age 40.

The Struggle for Majority Rule in South Africa

13 The music has been released on cassette, CD, and LP.

14 Outside South Africa *Mapantsula* was promoted in terms of both its political message and the gangster story. Thus the British poster reproduced here shows people demonstrating and advertises that the film had been banned in South Africa, but it foregrounds Panic in 'gangster' pose and an altogether misleading headline 'Life and Death on the Streets of Soweto.'

15 On the varied responses of South African students to *Mapantsula*, see Tomaselli (1995).

19–22, 26, 33). The film pulsates with the urban beat of 'Township Jive,' the original music by The Ouens ('The Guys'),[13] and *Mapantsula* has been compared to Perry Henzell's *The Harder They Come*, the film set in Jamaica that brought Reggae star Jimmy Cliff to the screen. The two novice filmmakers managed, with limited resources, to surreptitiously produce a powerful film.

On its release in 1988 *Mapantsula* was promptly banned by the South African censors.[14] Subsequently it gained only very limited release with cuts imposed. However, pirated video copies were distributed widely across the country and beyond, reaching prisoners on Robben Island and MK soldiers in Zambia (Schmitz and Mogotlane, 1991: 47). By all accounts, the film was a success with those Africans who got a chance to see it. Schmitz and Mogotlane (1991:39) tell of a screening at a workshop for workers when the whole audience marched out of the hall, dancing and singing.[15] It remains sufficiently popular in South Africa to have been released on DVD, a distinction none of the other African films featured here has gained so far.

Slabbert 1985
Pinnock 1985

References and Further Reading

Asinamali: Nothing to Lose. 1986. Directed by Ross Devenish. Produced by Portobello (Britain), 66 minutes.

Dandridge-Perry, Cheryl. 1990. 'Mapantsula.' *African Arts* 32: 88–9.

Davis, Peter. 1996. *In Darkest Hollywood: Exploring the Jungles of Cinema's South Africa*. Johannesburg: Ravan Press; Athens, OH: Ohio University Press.

A Dry White Season, see pages 80–9.

Ellerson, Beti. 2000. *Sisters of the Screen: Women of Africa on Film, Video, and Television*. Trenton, NJ/ Asmara: Africa World Press.

The Harder They Come. 1972. Film directed by Perry Henzell, written by Perry Henzell and Trevor D. Rhone. Jamaica. Distributed in the U.S. by Criterion Film. 93 minutes.

Hijack Stories. 2000. Film directed by Oliver Schmitz, written by Oliver Schmitz and Lesego Rampolokeng. Produced by Schlemmer Film (Germany), Septième Production (France), and Xenos Pictures (Britain). Distributed in South Africa by Ster Kinekor. 91 minutes.

In Darkest Hollywood: Cinema and Apartheid. 1993. Documentary written, filmed, and edited by Daniel Riesenfeld and Peter Davis. Produced by Nightingale (USA) and Villon (USA). Distributed by Villon Films. 112 minutes.

Jim Comes to Jo'burg/African Jim. 1949. Film directed by Donald Swanson. Produced by Warrior Films (South Africa). Distributed in North America by Villon Films. 58 minutes.

Mapantsula. 1988. Film directed by Oliver Schmitz, written by Oliver Schmitz and Thomas Mogotlane. Produced by One Look Productions (South Africa), David Hannay Productions (Australia) and Haverbeam (Britain). Distributed in the U.S. by California Newsreel. 104 minutes.

Ngema, Mbongeni. 1986. *Asinamali!* In Duma Ndlovu (ed.) *Woza Afrika! An Anthology of South African Plays*. New York: George Braziller. 177–224.

——. Unpublished (first produced in1987). *Sarafina!*

One More Shot. 1984. Film written and directed by Ronnie Isaacs. Produced by AIM Productions (South Africa).

The Ouens. n.d. *Mapantsula – The Music*. Cassette, CD, and LP.

Schmitz, Oliver, and Thomas Mogotlane. 1991. *Mapantsula: The Book*. Fordsburg, South Africa: COSAW.

Tomaselli, Keyan G. 1991. 'Popular Communication in South Africa: 'Mapantsula' and Its Context of Struggle.' *South African Theatre Journal* 5 (1): 46–60.

——. 1995. 'Some Theoretical Perspectives on African Cinema: Culture, Identity and Diaspora.' Panafrican Federation of Film Makers (ed.) *Africa and the Centenary of Cinema*. Paris/Dakar: Présence Africaine. 105–34.

Wilmington, Michael. 1989. 'Mapantsula.' *Los Angeles Times*, 23 November, Calendar, page 4.

Yaaba, see pages 29–36.

Fools 1997
Ordinary People Under *Apartheid*

Fools, even more so than *Mapantsula*, follows the precepts of the Black Consciousness Movement in being African-centered. Virtually the entire action takes place in an African township. Europeans representative of the oppression of *apartheid* make only two brief irruptions. The film is set in 1989, but it was produced in the mid-1990s, after South Africa's first elections on a universal franchise had brought the African National Congress to power, its leader Nelson Mandela to the presidency. *Fools* moves beyond the manichean stance characteristic of much politically engaged art. If *Mapantsula* depicted African resolve in the face of white oppression, *Fools* presents a range of responses among men of three generations, and most of their responses are flawed. In distinct contrast, most of the women – like the women in *Mapantsula* – impress us with their strength, even if their roles are less prominent, defined more by the domestic than the public sphere.

Fools is based on the eponymous novella by Njabulo Ndebele, part of a collection that in 1984 won the prestigious Noma Award for the year's outstanding book published in Africa. The novella is set in 1966, a time when all internal resistance to the *apartheid* regime had been crushed. It is situated in Charterston, the African township of Nigel where Ndebele grew up. Charterston is only 33 miles from Johannesburg, but we learn that it had never seen African protest.

The story is told by Zamani Duma, a 55-year old schoolteacher. He has, in his own words, degenerated; he seems so resilient, so understanding, and so compassionate, because all these traits offer refuge to his growing inability to assert himself (pp. 199, 157). When he first came to

Fools... first of all seeks to get out of the traditional black/white chasm. I wanted to consider Africans together, as a ... holistic people, trapped like animals in the apartheid system, whether in their daily lives or behind prison bars. Trapped psychologically and materially all the way to the will to resist apartheid. Like the film's principal character, Zamani, who tried to fight apartheid in the 1970s. But for him as for the others, time has passed and he has lost hope and consequently all humanity. Apartheid made him what it wanted him to be: an animal that in turn would apply beastly methods to his own people. (Ramadan Suleman, 1997, my translation)

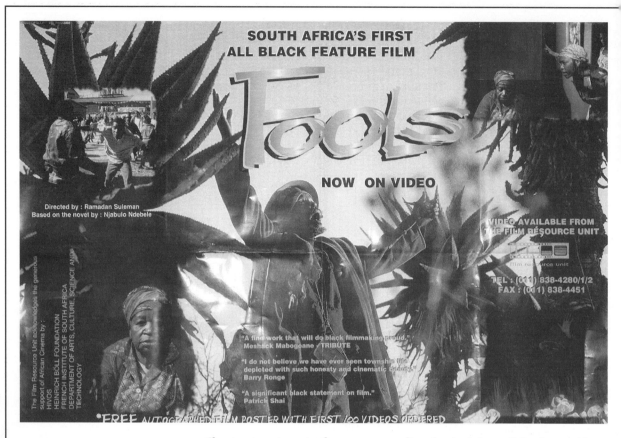

Charterston, twenty-three years earlier, he had been full of new ideas. Eager to change the township and put some life into it, he had started the boy scout movement. When the All Saints Church recruited him as treasurer, he had embezzled church funds: he despised the church and Christians, and he wanted to ruin it and bring it down to the poverty that it preached – so he tells us. But Zamani did not have the moral courage to stand exposure. He let the priest protect him, agreed to marry his daughter, and paid moral ransom: his father-in-law ran his life and his house. The marriage remained childless. Zamani took to women and drink. And the *apartheid* regime's violence became his own. He brutally beat his pupils. Then, three years ago, he raped one of his former students, Mimi Vuthela, who bore his child. Fired by the school board, he was reinstated because of the shortage of teachers.

The novella starts out with a chance encounter between Zamani and Mimi's brother Zani, who is returning from Swaziland where he has just completed high school.[1] Zani has been away many years, but he recognizes the teacher who raped his sister and insults him. If he towers over the teacher in these early scenes, and some later ones, we gradually come to see his immaturity, to appreciate the experience of Zamani. Their names hint at the contrast: Zani means 'come' in Zulu, Zamani 'let's try.'

1 Swaziland was then a British protectorate where Africans could get an education superior to that available to them in South Africa after the closure of the mission schools in 1955 and the establishment of a system of inferior education for Africans.

That very afternoon Zani insults a fellow who stood him drinks in a bar and gets himself knifed. When Zamani happens on the scene, he implores the teacher to take him home. Zamani, so meek and dejected until now, surprises us with his courage: he takes Zani to the home whose daughter he violated. There he encounters three distinct responses that leave the reader uncertain which to embrace. Busi, Mimi's older sister, insults Zamani and threatens him physically; Mimi tries to restrain her, while remaining silent; their mother Ma Buthelezi reminds everybody that the teacher took care of Zani and insists that he be treated as a guest.

Zani is an angry young man. One source of his anger may well be that he has no father; he carries his mother's name. He has returned to Charterston to bring, in his own words, light where there has been darkness, light that is destined to spread to the whole country (p. 164). Even before their confrontation, Zamani describes him in terms of stark contrasts:

> within the space of twenty-five minutes I had seen his restlessness, his impatience, his arrogance, his humiliation and agony, his helplessness, his joyfulness, and his amazing recovery through aggression and intimidation. (p. 163)

Zani starts a campaign to boycott the forthcoming celebrations of the Day of the Convenant, 16 December, the day in 1838 when Afrikaners killed thousands of followers of the Zulu King Dingaan. But all his efforts are futile. His leaflets calling for the boycott rapidly disappear. He is refused access to the high school. Zamani's 10-year-old pupils do not understand Zani's bookish lecture. When he appears on the street with a placard, the police destroy it and beat him up. And his exhortations to the revelers arriving for the day's picnic, not to celebrate the victory of their oppressors, fall on deaf ears.

The self-assurance of four women provides a stark contrast to the two men. Matriarchal Ma Buthelezi upholds traditional norms of hospitality for the man who raped her daughter. Mimi explains to her brother the turmoil of the man who raped her. Nosipho, when she finally finds out about the role of her father in her marriage, takes the initiative towards reconciliation with Zamani, who had wantonly abused her. And Ntozakhe's love and support for Zani stand in stark contrast to his immature conflict over their relationship. The strength of these women resides in how they handle their domestic relationships. At work, however, Nosipho, the registered nurse, is frustrated like Zamani: institutions controlled by Europeans deal in authoritarian fashion with African patients, just as they mete out inferior education to African students.

Only at the very end of the novella does a European come to play a significant role. Zani responds to an Afrikaner's insult with an insult – and flees when the Afrikaner charges him with a whip. It is Zamani who stands his ground and lets himself be whipped; he laughs at the Afrikaner who ends up weeping:

> The blows stopped; and I knew I had crushed him. I had crushed him with the sheer force of my presence. I was there, and would be there to the end of time:

a perpetual symbol of his failure to have a world without me. And he walked away to his car, a man without a shadow. The sun couldn't see him. And the sound of his car when he drove away seemed so irrelevant. There he went: a member of a people whose sole gift to the world has been the perfection of hate. And because there was nothing much more in them, they will forever destroy, consuming us and themselves in a great fire. But the people of the north will come down and settle the land again, as they have done for thousands of years. (p. 276)

We have come to sympathize with Zamani's frustrations; we may be prepared to understand his depravation; we now witness, perhaps, his redemption.[2] His victory is psychic, he vanquishes his own corruption and he brings the Afrikaner to his knees, but Ndebele gives it political meaning: whites will have to come to terms with the African majority in South Africa – or they will perish together, and Africans will come from the north to take their place.

When the young, impetuous Zani appears as the spokesperson for the author's complex position we may be surprised, but we have become familiar with the wide range of his emotions, and at this juncture he is confiding in Nosipho:

> too much obsession with removing oppression in the political dimension, soon becomes in itself a form of oppression. Especially if everybody is expected to demonstrate his concern somehow. And then mostly all it calls for is that you thrust an angry fist into the air. Somewhere along the line, I feel, the varied richness of life is lost sight of and so is the fact that every aspect of life, if it can be creatively indulged in, is the weapon of life itself against the greatest tyranny. (p. 236)

Ndebele wrote in the early 1980s, after the Soweto Uprising which had cost more than a thousand lives. In spite of these sacrifices, the *apartheid* regime remained firmly entrenched. If the Soweto Uprising opened up a large generational gap, Ndebele appears to side with the cautious parents. Soon, however, young militants like Zani would make many townships ungovernable and put pressure on employers that compelled them to make concessions to African demands. Their actions would play a major role in persuading elements in the National Party to seek an accommodation by the end of the decade.

Njabulo Ndebele resembles Zani in that he was born in 1948 and completed high school in Swaziland. Ndebele's differentiated stance may be related to the fact that he went to college in Lesotho, another former British protectorate, and stayed on to teach first in high school, then at the university. He was thus removed from the daily oppressions of *apartheid*. At the same time his position was quite different from those exiled overseas: if they were intent on mobilizing foreign opinion against the *apartheid* regime, he lived in a small country surrounded by South Africa, a country which did not dare oppose its mighty neighbor; he could easily stay in contact with people in South Africa – he was to become President of the Congress of South African Writers; and he presumably taught a good number of students from there who remained similarly close to home. In a paper presented in the year following the

2 This interpretation is at odds with Suleman's who does not believe that Zamani can find redemption (Barlet, 1997).

publication of *Fools* he argued for moving beyond the 'spectacular representation' of protest literature:[3]

Ramadan Suleman directing Robin Smith

> we must contend with the fact that even under the most oppressive of conditions, people are always trying and struggling to maintain a semblance of normal social order. They will attempt to apply tradition and custom to manage their day-to-day family problems: they will resort to socially acquired behaviour patterns to eke out a means of subsistence. They apply systems of values they know. Often those values will undergo changes under certain pressing conditions. The transformation of those values constitutes the essential drama in the lives of ordinary people.
>
> ... the ordinary daily lives of people should be the direct focus of political interest because they constitute the *very contents* of the struggle, for the struggle involves people not abstractions. If it is a new society we seek to bring about in South Africa then that newness will be based on direct concern with the way people actually live. That means a range of complex ethical issues.... These kinds of concerns are destined to find their way into our literature, making it more complex and richer. (Ndebele, [1985] 1994: 55, 57; italics in original).

Many judged Ndebele's differentiated stance an impediment to the

3 On the intense debate that ensued, especially after Albie Sachs, the prominent ANC leader, had taken a similar position in 1989, see Pechey (1994). Athol Fugard's play *Boesman and Lena*, like *Fools*, does not dwell on *apartheid's* oppression but rather explores its consequences for ordinary people, how personal relationships are degraded and victims become victimizers. Ross Devenish directed a film adaptation in 1973, John Berry another in 2000.

single-minded struggle required to overcome *apartheid*, but the uncompromising honesty of *Fools* is altogether appropriate in the post-*apartheid* era when Suleman produced the film. The director appears to share Ndebele's orientation (Worsdale, 1998). He drew on the novel for the epitaph of his film:

> The sound of victims laughing at victims,
> and when victims spit at victims,
> should they not be called fools? (p. 278)

Suleman comes from a small African Muslim community in Durban. After studying at the Centre for Research and Training in African Theatre in Johannesburg, he became active in alternative theater. He was one of the founders of the Dhlomo Theatre in Johannesburg in 1983, the first African theater in South Africa, as was Bhekizizwe Peterson, the co-author of the script. After the theater was closed for political reasons, Suleman went into exile. In France he worked with Med Hondo and Souleymane Cissé before proceeding to train at the National Film and Television School in Britain. *Fools* is his first full-length feature film, indeed the first feature film from South Africa directed by an African. Shot in Soweto on a budget of 4 million Rand, then less than $1 million, *Fools* features a number of accomplished actors. The film is enhanced by the fine musical score of Ray Phiri who recorded and performed with Paul Simon. It earned the Silver Leopard at the Locarno International Festival.

The film presents a major difficulty for viewers not familiar with the novella. Only almost halfway into the film do they learn of the rape when Zamani relives it as he stands with Zani in front of Mimi's home. Without that information viewers cannot understand that Zani, in the train, is rehearsing what Mimi wrote about being raped. They are left bewildered by Busi shouting after the elders who have just visited her home, presumably to announce that they are going to have Zamani resume teaching. The elders' visit to his home and the ensuing confrontation between Zamani and Nosipho remains enigmatic. Zani's unprovoked and intensely personal rage at Zamani, as he denounces the political failure of 'you and your generation,' is puzzling. And the significance of Zamani's friends asking him whether he really wants to take Zani home is lost.

The film compresses time. While Mimi has a two-year old child by Zamani in the novel, the rape is set in the recent past in the film and her pregnancy comes to an abrupt end.[4] Major elements of the novella were lost in the transposition to the screen. The relationship between Zani and his girlfriend Ntozakhe remains less developed, even though the film starts out with a gratuitous sex scene. We miss the two letters that convey so much about Zamani's past and Ntozakhe's maturity. Most importantly, Zamani no longer shares his innermost thoughts and feelings with us. Still, Patrick Shai, an experienced actor, succeeds in a memorable portrayal of the troubled character of Zamani. And the film imparts the turmoil that ensues from his rape of the student he had nurtured, by showing Zamani in a demented state twice. Immediately

4 It would appear that she had a miscarriage, but according to Suleman it is supposed to be an abortion (Ukadike, 2002: 294).

Zamani defies his aggressor with laughter

after the rape he addresses the chicken Mimi gave him: 'Why can't you love me?' and strangles it – the action dramatized with the blood splattered on Zamani's face. And after the confrontation at Ma Buthelezi's he runs home and sees himself surrounded by a grass fire and the madman prancing around.

While the novel was written in English, with only a couple of Afrikaans words thrown in, subtitles allow the film to strikingly convey the strategic use the residents of Charterston make of the several languages at their disposal: Zamani talks with his wife in English, uses a mixture of English and Afrikaans with his cronies, argues with the principal in English, and teaches in Afrikaans. The women speak Zulu with each other. The principal seeks to assuage the rage of the white bully in Afrikaans, the language of submission, even as he is insulted in English. The street gang use *tsotsitaal*, the street slang we encountered in *Mapantsula*.

The film is set in December 1989, a generation after the novella. The National Party is still in power, but the *apartheid* state is under siege. Now Zamani's final stand, confronting the Afrikaner, elicits a response from the partying crowd, even in tranquil Charterston: the people who ran away from the whip-wielding Afrikaner in 1966 return to surround him in 1989 when he attacks Zamani. And we see Zani's girlfriend Ntozakhe picking up a stone, suggesting a quite different ending. Indeed Suleman has related how he and his friend Bhekizizwe Peterson, through several drafts of the script they co-wrote, considered Zamani defending himself and the Afrikaner dying in a hail of stones. But they eventually concluded that Ndebele's was the more powerful image: Zamani's pain

The Struggle for Majority Rule in South Africa

symbolizing 350 years of suffering endured by Black South Africans, and the white man left to live and, hopefully, regret his deeds (Ukadike, 2002: 295).

The different political context shows in other ways as well. We see the political graffiti. While a choir chants 'I will follow Jesus' at the train station, a man passes through singing 'I will follow Mandela.' Now a group of young men shout 'Amandla!' in the streets – and after the victory of the African National Congress the film can acknowledge that some such young men were little more than thugs in political clothes, 'using politics as an alibi for delinquence' as Suleman put it (Bouzet, 1997, my translation). At the same time it is altogether implausible that Zani should not be able to link up with genuine local opposition at this stage in the struggle.

The film goes further than the novella in showing how some collaborators of Zamani's generation embraced Afrikaner ideology: the school principal lovingly installs the picture of the new president to join the row of pictures of the white South African leaders of the last half century hanging on his office wall, while humming to himself an Afrikaner song that includes the lines 'we the Boers, victorious over the English...' And we now see Zamani's cronies who reject 'colonialism' but are content to pursue their pleasures. Ma Buthelezi and the elders who demand that Zamani return to school represent a third generation: they are dignified, enjoy a measure of authority in the community, and manage as best they can. If one of the elders uses a beautiful metaphor derived from the rural experience, Ma Buthelezi appears to be running a shebeen. Suleman dedicated his film 'to our mothers and families.'

Mapantsula was released in 1988, at the height of the struggle against the *apartheid* regime, to sustain the militant, to mobilize the uncommitted. *Fools* reminds us of the suffering under *apartheid*.[6] But in 1997, after the struggle has been won, it is first and foremost an exhortation for South Africans to examine the failures and the guilt of the past:

> Fools is addressed to blacks as well as whites. So that blacks may see themselves as a community all the way to their most extreme contradictions, and that whites may no longer pretend that they did not know how destructive apartheid has been. (Suleman, 1997, my translation)

Such a critical stance is rarely popular. Suleman found it difficult to secure funding from producers who thought he was too critical of Africans (Bottéon, 1997). Two years after its release, the box office receipts of *Fools* in South Africa came to less than 2 per cent of those of *The Gods Must Be Crazy*. And in the U.S. this challenging film has not yet found a distributor.

A minor figure in the novella, a man who daily asks for forgiveness for an evil deed his neighbors no longer clearly remember, takes on a more prominent role in the film and appears at the center of the South African poster. He is recast in the film as a madman, a victim of World War II – reminding us of the sacrifices Africans made in support of the colonial powers in that war, and of promises broken. The film opens with the

5 We may take it that in December 1989 the school principal is not aware that the new President, Frederik Willem de Klerk, is about to initiate the process that will lead to majority rule in 1994.

6 Mickey Madoda Dube's searing *A Walk in the Night*, while based on Alex La Guma's eponymous novella of the early 1960s, is set in post-*apartheid* South Africa. The visually stunning film dramatically conveys the profound emotional impact of racism on Mikey Adonis, the 'coloured' protagonist. It focuses more narrowly than the novel on Mikey while adding complexity to his relationship with 'Uncle' Doughty, his poor white neighbor. Produced for South African television, *A Walk in the Night* surprises by making the white foreman even more obnoxious and the white police officer even more brutal and murderous than they are in the novella – at a time when the African National Congress is established in power.

7 Peterson and Suleman went so far as to give the best lines to the least attractive characters. The principal confronting Zani: 'Do I have to hear a fart to know its foul smell?' Zamani's crony commenting on Zani's arrest: 'He will have Lenin coming out of his right ear meeting Nkrumah coming out of his left ear.' The Boer reprimanding the principal: 'People who use a toilet must aim well.'

homeless madman, he connects the various episodes, and he is there at the end. He enunciates the dominant element in South African discourse since the African National Congress came to power: for his fellow South Africans of all races – the wall next to his makeshift hut shows masks white and black – he chants to the heavens: 'Forgive them, God, they know not what they do.'[7]

References and Further Reading

Bartlet, Oliver. 1997. 'Entretien: Ramadan Suleman,' *Africultures* 1: 52–4.

Boesman and Lena. 1973. Film adapted from Athol Fugard's eponymous play and directed by Ross Devenish. Distributed in the U.S. by New Yorker Films. 102 minutes.

Boesman and Lena. 2000. Film adapted from Athol Fugard's eponymous play and directed by John Berry. Produced by Pathé Image (France) and Primedia Pictures (South Africa). Distributed in the U.S. by Kino International. 84 minutes.

Bottéon, Christophe. 1997. 'Interview: Ramadan Suleman.' *Cinéma* 590: 21–2.

Bouzet, Ange-Dominique. 1997. ''L'apartheid nous a marqués de l'intérieur': Ramadan Suleman, 43 ans, analyse les défaites d'une génération.' *Libération,* 3 September, page 2.

Fools. 1997. Film directed by Ramadan Suleman, written by Bhekizizwe Peterson and Ramadan Suleman. Produced by JBA Production (France), Natives at Large (South Africa), Ebano Multi-Media (Mozambique), Framework International (Zimbabwe), M-Net Africa (South Africa), and Périphérie Production (France). Distributed in South Africa by Film Resource Unit, in France by Cinéma Public Films. 90 minutes.

Fugard, Athol. 1973 (first produced in 1969). *Boesman and Lena*. Oxford: Oxford University Press.

The Gods Must Be Crazy, see pages 71–80.

La Guma, Alex. 1962. *A Walk in the Night*. Ibadan: Mbari Publications; London: Heinemann; Evanston, IL: Northwestern University Press.

Mapantsula, see pages 91–7.

Maughan Brown, David. 1994. 'Politics and Value in South African Literature: Some Thoughts on Recent Interventions by Albie Sachs and Njabulo Ndebele.' *Literary Theory and African Literature/Théorie littéraire et littérature africaine*, edited by Josef Gugler, Hans-Jürgen Lüsebrink, and Jürgen Martini. Beiträge zur Afrikaforschung 3. Münster/Hamburg: LIT. 143–61.

Ndebele, Njabulo S. 1983. *Fools and Other Stories*. Johannesburg: Ravan Press; London: Readers International. All references are to the 1993 Readers International edition.

——. (1985) 1994. 'The Rediscovery of the Ordinary: Some New Writings in South Africa.' *Journal of Southern African Studies* 12: 143–57. Reprinted in Njabulo S. Ndebele, *South African Literature and Culture: Rediscovery of the Ordinary*. Manchester/New York: Manchester University Press. 41–59.

Nkosi, Lewis. 1996. 'Njabulo Ndebele.' In Bernth Lindfors and Reinhard Sander (eds) *Twentieth-Century Caribbean and Black African Writers, Third Series*. Detroit/Washington/London: Gale Research. 227–34.

Pechey, Graham. 1994. 'Introduction by Graham Pechey.' In Njabulo S. Ndebele, *South African Literature and Culture: Rediscovery of the Ordinary*. Manchester/New York: Manchester University Press. 1–16.

Suleman, Ramadan. 1997. Interview in press booklet 'Fools: un film de ramadan suleman.'

Ukadike, Nwachukwu Frank. 2002. *Questioning African Cinema: Conversations with Filmmakers*. Minneapolis/London: University of Minnesota Press.

A Walk in the Night/'nagstappie. 1998. Film directed by Mickey Madoda Dube, written by Mickey Madoda Dube, Mandla Langa, and Molefi Moleli. Produced by Interface Productions (South Africa). Distributed in the U.S. by California Newsreel. 78 minutes.

Worsdale, Andrew. 1998. 'Tales of Township Life.' *Mail and Guardian,* 21 May.

Ghana's Silver Jubilee

25 YEARS

1957–1982

Lt.-GEN. ANKRAH:- 1966–1968
"We will only have ourselves to blame if we allow ourselves to be swayed by mere empty words."
29/12/67.

FLT.-LT. J. J. RAWLINGS (AFRC):- 1979 (3 Months)
"It is no exaggeration to say that unity is difficult to attain when so many are hungry and angry while others have lived in relative abundance." 9/2/79.

Lt.-GEN. AKWASI AMANKWA AFRIFAH:- 1968–1969
"The sole criterion for those holding or not holding public office must be the judgement of the people."
12/11/68.

OSAGYEFO DR. KWAME NKRUMAH:- 1957–1966
"In the modern world, independence also means interdependence." 6/3/57.

PRESIDENT HILLA LIMANN:- 1979–1981
"We must not allow ourselves to be cheated out of our birthright again; enough is enough." 1/12/79.

DR. K. A. BUSIA:- 1969–1972
"The views of the opposition in every society must be respected at all times." 5/12/69.

IGNATIUS KUTU ACHEAMPONG:- 1972–1978
"Fighting for political power is very easy but fighting for our economic independence is very difficult." 13/6/74.

GEN. F. W. K. AKUFFO:- 1978–1979
"We believe that our common ethnic and cultural and historical bonds are so deep-rooted that we must live in peace."

FLT.-LT. J. J. RAWLINGS:- (PNDC):- 1981
"Personalities will not count; Rawlings is not important, but the country Ghana." 8/3/82.

106

4 Betrayals of Independence

Most of Africa became independent well over a generation ago. At last count, there were 48 countries in Africa South of the Sahara, including the island states off the subcontinent's coast. The colonies carved out of Africa by the imperial powers in nearly every case comprised people of diverse cultures. Colonial rule imparted a new diversity to Africa, as the colonial powers pursued different policies and imported their languages and cultures. The extent of European settlement in turn differentially affected colonial policies. And since independence African countries have moved along distinct trajectories. The foreign relations of African countries, especially their relation with the former colonial power and their position during the Cold War, varied, and often shifted over time. A number of countries were ravaged by civil wars, which continued for several decades in some cases. In part because of different colonial and post-colonial histories, in part because resource endowments vary greatly across the subcontinent, there is a considerable range in income levels and living conditions. Great economic, political, and cultural diversity thus characterize the more than 700 million people who live across Africa South of the Sahara, a land mass slightly more than three times the size of the 48 contiguous states of the United States. Any generalizations about the subcontinent have to be tempered by an awareness of this diversity (see table on page xii).

During the struggle for independence, Kwame Nkrumah had proclaimed: 'Seek ye first the political kingdom.' Once Africans had gained that kingdom, it turned out that it brought little improvement for most of them. The advent of independence had been accompanied by great expectations. After the exactions of colonial rule, Africa was about to enter a golden age. As the flags of the colonial powers were lowered, enthusiastic crowds chanted the new national anthems. They were to be bitterly disappointed.

The turbulent history of Ghana is not unusual. The calendar illustration preceding this chapter appears to promote all the men who ruled Ghana in its first 25 years of independence, even if Kwame Nkrumah holds pride of place. And indeed, nearly all of them came to power amid applause. But usually their regimes were short-lived and ended amongst widespread disaffection. Nkrumah had gained the political kingdom from the colonial power all right, but his policies led to economic decline, corruption spread in party and government, and his

A man who has just come in from the rain and dried his body and put on dry clothes is more reluctant to go out again than another who has been indoors all the time. The trouble with our new nation ... was that none of us had been indoors long enough to be able to say 'To hell with it'. We had all been in the rain together until yesterday. Then a handful of us — the smart and the lucky and hardly ever the best — had scrambled for the one shelter our former rulers left, and had taken it over and barricaded themselves in. And from within they sought to persuade the rest through numerous loudspeakers, that the first phase of the struggle had been won and that the next phase — the extension of our house — was even more important and called for new and original tactics; it required that all argument should cease and the whole people speak with one voice and that any more dissent and argument outside the door of the shelter would subvert and bring down the whole house. (The narrator in Chinua Achebe's novel A Man of the People, pp. 34–5)

Betrayals of Independence

regime became repressive in the face of mounting opposition. The fruits of independence remained elusive for most Ghanaians. Nine years after independence the charismatic leader of the independence movement was deposed in a military coup to popular acclaim. The next fifteen years were to see two more elected civilian governments brought to an abrupt end by military coups, and military rule in turn twice changing hands through military intervention. In other countries rulers managed to cling to power for decades, their regimes characterized by ever more flagrant corruption and increasingly severe repression of dissent.

The political and economic performance of most African countries has been dismal. Nearly everywhere the democratic institutions bequeathed to the new nations at independence soon became mere trappings, if they were not discarded altogether. Rulers entrenched themselves *de jure* or *de facto* in one-party states which turned oppressive and corrupt. Most of them were dislodged by coups which brought to power military men, who proved themselves just as corrupt and even more authoritarian. Many countries endured a series of military coups. By the 1980s, the disastrous consequences were there for all to see:

> Bloated public administrations operate inefficiently, erratically and sometimes dishonestly, partly as a result of the many officials who are appointed and promoted on the basis of nepotistic, factional, and personal ties. Corruption creates administrative bottlenecks. The economic infrastructure deteriorates or operates irregularly. Breakdowns in the administration of justice and political instability foster uncertainty as to the sanctity of private property and contracts. Heavy-handed regulation of civil society by suspicious autocrats discourages autonomous, grassroots initiatives and provokes people to flee into the unregulated informal sector, into illegal activities like smuggling, or even into exile. Ambitious individuals seek to make their fortunes through parasitical manipulation of the government's regulatory and spending powers. Risk-taking entrepreneurial activities are seldom the quickest and easiest road to wealth. Manipulating state offices, contracts, regulations, licensed monopolies, access to foreign exchange and other underpriced goods and services is far more lucrative. (Sandbrook, 1993: 17)

In this context economic growth was slow while the population grew rapidly. *Per capita* income, after growing at a respectable rate in the early independence period, dropped continually from the late 1970s onwards. Today it is little higher than at independence. The promise of independence has been betrayed.

The trappings of the colonial powers had been cast aside, but they often continued to wield considerable influence. The French in particular played a major role in the affairs of nearly all their former colonies. They extended their involvement to the three other francophone countries in Africa South of the Sahara – the former Belgian colonies of Congo (Kinshasa), Burundi, and Rwanda – and more recently to formerly Spanish Equatorial Guinea. Foreign diplomats channeled aid and weighed in on political and economic decisions, powerful foreign corporations pursued their interests, foreign advisors steered bureaucracies, and foreign troops intervened in conflicts. Critics coined the label 'neo-colonialism' to signify that, because of such foreign involvement, supposedly independent African countries continued to be subject to outside control.

The authoritarianism characteristic of most African governments until recently may be explained in terms of the colonial heritage, internal divisions, the absence of centers of power other than the military, and the often problematic role of foreign governments and corporations. At independence the new states inherited the authoritarian institutions of colonial administration. And in all but a few small countries most people identified with, and single-mindedly promoted, regions rather than the nation. These regional allegiances were usually cast in terms of language and cultural heritage. In fact, such ethnic identities, and the oppositions they entailed, usually had been articulated only recently in political and economic competitions in the urban context, often actively encouraged by the divide and rule policies of the colonial powers – if the term 'tribe' acquired pejorative connotations in the colonial era, the concept of 'tribalism' is quite misleading anyhow. In a few cases, divisions arose from confrontations between Muslims and Christians which were regionally based as well. Because of these deep divisions, political parties tended to follow 'the territorial principle' and were regionally based. The one-party state promised to bring divisions to an end and establish national unity – and it assured the rulers of the day that they would stay in power indefinitely: presidents for life proliferated across the continent. Authoritarian rule met only limited opposition in a context where peasants constituted the great majority of the population, urban workers were a small minority, the middle class was small, and commercial interests were dependent on governments which controlled much of the economy in various ways. Patronage and coercion ensured that effective civilian opposition was rarely mounted. Popular protests were virtually always quickly suppressed. At times, the army, rather than follow orders to shoot, would turn on abusive rulers and establish military rule.

The corruption of politics allowed a few to enrich themselves, while living conditions for much of the population deteriorated. Income inequalities increased dramatically. A number of regimes proclaimed themselves 'socialist,' but they failed to fulfil their promises. For some it was just a label to align themselves with the Soviet Union. Others did initiate egalitarian policies, but they foundered in economic decline and mismanagement. Many countries committed themselves to improve the condition of women, but such progress as was made usually remained quite circumscribed. Thus women have had much less access to education than men (see table on page xii). And nearly everywhere, the peasantry suffered from neglect or even outright exploitation – the next chapter is consecrated to its condition.

Civil wars devastated a number of African countries. In Angola, Mozambique, and the Sudan they continued for decades. In the 1990s the human toll rose to levels without precedent in African history – except for the ravages in the Congo Free State, the personal property of King Léopold II that was to become the Belgian Congo. More than half a million people were killed in the genocide in Rwanda in 1994. An

Betrayals of Independence

estimated two million people died as a consequence of the civil war that ensued in the Congo (Kinshasa). The Western powers had supported factions in the ethnic conflict in Rwanda and propped up the Mobutu dictatorship in the Congo for decades, but now they stood aside. In the Balkans they had intervened eventually. Africa, however, was seen differently. In Somalia a few casualties had led the U.S. to cut short its engagement. Now political leaders were not prepared to rally domestic opinion to the need for intervention in Rwanda. Instead they played down the enormity of what was happening. Small Belgian and U.N. contingents in Rwanda were withdrawn during the genocide rather than being reinforced and given authority to stop the massacres. Subsequently no effort was made to disarm the Rwandan refugees in the Congo.

The last decade brought major political progress throughout much of Africa South of the Sahara. A new era was ushered in 1990. The 'Velvet Revolution' in Benin turned a national conference into a civilian coup that stripped the dictator of effective power, established a transitional government, and prepared the way for multi-party elections. In South Africa, Nelson Mandela was released from prison, the opposition parties were 'unbanned,' and negotiations towards enfranchising the majority began. Pressures for democratic change increased dramatically across the subcontinent. A wave of revolutions swept through the region as long-suffering people took to the streets, and trade unions, which had been muzzled for decades, asserted a public role. Many regimes were forced to change their ways, if they did not collapse altogether. Since 1990 most African countries have held multi-party elections. And most Africans came to enjoy a level of freedom of expression they had not known for decades. In 1999, one of the very few military regimes still to be found handed over power to a democratically elected government in Nigeria, the region's potential giant.

The profound political transformations of the 1990s were born out of a particular constellation. At least six factors may be adduced to explain them:

- the example of the revolutionary wave in Eastern Europe;
- the end of the Cold War which diminished the enthusiasm of Western governments for supporting regimes, however repressive, as long as they toed the anti-Moscow line;
- the demise of the *apartheid* regime in South Africa which refocused attention on repression elsewhere on the continent;
- the severe economic crisis of the 1980s which drastically reduced the spoils of office available to reward supporters;
- external pressures to deal with the economic crisis by retrenchments which hit the urban sector particularly hard and led to the mobilization of urban workers and trade unions;
- the demonstration effect of revolutions, beginning with the 'velvet revolution' in Benin and spreading across the continent.

This extraordinary combination of factors released the wave of democratization that swept across the subcontinent. The results varied greatly. A number of autocrats have managed to entrench themselves afresh. Still, the contemporary setting is different from the 1960s when democratic institutions bequeathed by the departing colonial rulers crumbled in rapid succession, and there would appear to be cause for a guarded optimism. Three major changes have been particularly important: political accountability has increased, political mobilization has become more effective, and civil society has been strengthened.

A huge expansion in the educational system over the last generation, while marred by declining standards, has produced a better informed and more critical citizenry. New developments in communications technology allow it to bypass government-controlled media. Memory of the abuses of the past has sharpened people's eyes for new transgressions. And the revolutions that finally brought corrupt and repressive regimes to account are likely to be remembered by rulers and ruled alike for a long time to come. At the same time, rapid urban growth has greatly expanded the numbers that can be mobilized in key locations, most especially the national capital. And the huge increase in student enrolments at the secondary and tertiary levels has provided an easily mobilized avant-garde for mass protests. Finally, civil society has been strengthened. It has become more difficult to muzzle the trade unions. There is a now well-established class of professionals in education, the media, health care, the law, and commerce. A business class has emerged – market-oriented policies have expanded its opportunities and given it a measure of independence *vis-à-vis* the state. The political ferment has spawned a variety of local non-governmental organizations. They, together with foreign NGOs which are increasingly well represented in the region, can rapidly mobilize foreign opinion.

Market-oriented policies came in response to the economic crisis of the 1980s. In most cases they were forced on African governments by their foreign creditors, usually led by the International Monetary Fund and the World Bank. The onus for unpopular measures thus fell on foreigners rather than on governments that had accumulated foreign debt and failed to put it to productive use. By now it is widely accepted that the economic results of the 'structural adjustment programs' fell well short of expectations, and that foreign policy makers had been amiss in not taking into account the huge social costs they entailed. These costs were exacerbated to the extent that long overdue changes were compressed into abrupt policy changes: large-scale lay-offs, especially in the public sector; the abrupt abolition of subsidies that brought huge increases in the price of food, transport, and housing; readjustments of the foreign exchange rate which multiplied the price of imported food, gas, and medical drugs. At the same time restrictions on government spending led to a further decline in public services.

Recent data indicate that economic growth is beginning to outstrip population growth in Africa South of the Sahara. Still, after decades of economic decline, the region accounts for the great majority of the world's poorest countries. In 2001, the *per capita* income in the region came to about $1,600, less than five per cent of the comparable figure for the U.S.[1] Retrenchment in government and grinding poverty make it all

1 Income in terms of gross national product measured at purchasing power parity; for explanation, see note to the table on page xii. Based on data from World Bank, *2002 World Development Indicators*.

Betrayals of Independence   the more difficult to deal with the modern-day plague that is devastating the region: AIDS killed an estimated 2.4 million people in Africa South of the Sahara in 2002, and 29 million are thought to be infected by HIV/AIDS – they account for 70 per cent of victims world-wide.

The four films we are about to examine, set in Nigeria/Ghana, Senegal, and Guinea-Bissau, present major variations in the post-colonial experiences of African countries. In turn they denounce megalomaniac dictators, expose the neo-colonial order and the corruption it entails, suggest that religion can bring an African renewal, and remind us that the guerrillas' aspiration, to create a more egalitarian society, remains unfulfilled.

References and Further Reading

Achebe, Chinua. 1966. *A Man of the People*. London: William Heinemann; New York: John Day; London: Heinemann (African Writers Series 1). The reference is to the U.S. edition.

Berkeley, Bill. 2001. *The Graves Are Not Yet Full: Race, Tribe and Power in the Heart of Africa*. New York: Basic Books.

Chabal, Patrick. 1992. *Power in Africa: an Essay in Political Interpretation*. New York: St. Martin's Press.

Cooper, Frederick. 2002. *Africa Since 1940: The Past of the Present*. New Approaches to African History 1. Cambridge/New York/Port Melbourne/Madrid/Cape Town: Cambridge University Press.

Freund, Bill. (1984) 1998. *The Making of Contemporary Africa: The Development of African Society Since 1800*. Second edition. Boulder, CO: Lynne Rienner.

Gugler, Josef. 1996. 'Urbanization in Africa South of the Sahara: New Identities in Conflict,' in Josef Gugler (ed.) *The Urban Transformation of the Developing World*. Oxford/New York: Oxford University Press. 210-51.

Huband, Mark. 2001. The Skull Beneath the Skin: Africa after the Cold War. Boulder, CO: Westview Press.

Joseph, Richard. 1999. 'State, Conflict, and Democracy in Africa,' in Richard Joseph (ed.) *State, Conflict, and Democracy in Africa*. Boulder, CO/London: Lynne Rienner. 3–14.

Sandbrook, Richard. 1993. *The Politics of Africa's Economic Recovery. African Society Today*. Cambridge/New York/Oakleigh: Cambridge University Press.

——. 2000. *Closing the Circle: Democratization and Development in Africa*. Toronto: Between the Lines; London/New York: Zed Books.

Kongi's Harvest 1970
Traditional Splendor and Modern Oppression[1]

The divine rights of kings which ended with the decapitation of crowned heads of Europe some centuries ago, has – need I state the obvious? – been replaced by the divine right of the gun on this continent. We must now invite all our dictatorships, under no matter what camouflage, and however comparatively civilized, civilianized and domesticated they are, to set a definitive date within this century for the abandonment of this denigration of our popular will.
(Wole Soyinka [1992: 28–9] addressing Nigerian brass and foreign dignitaries on the occasion of the opening of the International Symposium on African Literature, Lagos, May 1988)

Betrayals of Independence

Wole Soyinka is perhaps the most distinguished African intellectual. Africa's foremost black playwright, he has also written several fine novels and a series of trenchant essays. His delightful autobiography, *Aké*, conveys a sense of growing up in a Christian household amid a still flourishing Yoruba culture in the 1930s. In 1986 he became the first black African to receive the Nobel Prize for Literature. Soyinka has employed his powerful voice time and again to denounce the high and mighty. He was quick to recognize new political patterns and to examine them critically in his fiction and his essays. In the middle of the jubilant celebrations of Nigeria's independence he produced *A Dance of the Forests*, a forceful exposure of the shortcomings of the new political elite and a somber view of the future of Nigeria.[2]

Soyinka's *Kongi's Harvest* had its première in Lagos in 1965. The play about dictatorship was topical as authoritarian one-man regimes imposed themselves in a number of African countries just a few years after independence. And it was to become ever more topical as such regimes spread through the region. Soyinka went on to create two more plays denouncing tyranny, *Opera Wonyosi* and *A Play of Giants*. *Kongi's Harvest* is arguably the most distinguished of the three.[3] It is, as Soyinka put it in the program notes for the première, a play 'about Power, Pomp and Ecstasy' (Adelugba, 1979: 258): the power of autocratic President Kongi, the pomp of detained king Danlola, and the ecstasy of Segi and Daodu, who oppose the dictator.[4]

Femi Osofisan (1994: 47), Soyinka's persistent critic, gives an enthusiastic account of the 'mesmerising' experience of seeing the Theatre Arts Production of *Kongi's Harvest* in 1966 as he was about to graduate from Government College, Ibadan:

> I was entranced by the scenic effects, by the costuming, the play of lights and colours, the dancing, the music. I had never seen anything like this. It brought back to sight the splendour of a world that was once ours but which we had lost; it recalled even to my young and fragile mind the poetry of my people's original essence. I felt transported, ennobled; I was thoroughly soaked in the play's spectacular universe; I didn't want it to end. For the very first time in my whole experience, I felt the surge of primordial energies, the currents of magical entrancement associated anciently with drama; and the evening was like an initiation into the secrets of what true African theatre should be (Osofisan, 1994, 47).

A decade after the first performance of *Kongi's Harvest*, Oyin Ogunba (1975: 200) observed that it was Soyinka's most popular play in Nigeria, except perhaps for *The Lion and the Jewel*.

Kongi's Harvest is the most instructive of Soyinka's plays in its analysis of the degeneration of personal rule. The accomplishment is all the more remarkable as *Kongi's Harvest* was the first literary treatment of dictatorship in Africa, written just a few years after the wave of independence swept the region. The play portrays with biting satire recurrent features of dictatorships – the sycophants surrounding the dictator, the dictator's megalomania, the ideological isms invoked to justify absolute-ism, the propaganda blared at the population, the

1 This discussion of *Kongi's Harvest* draws on Gugler (1997).

2 Soyinka's concerns proved to be well warranted. Less than five years after independence Nigeria was one of the first countries to fall under military rule in 1965. The next year regional conflicts came to a head and civil war broke out between the Federation of Nigeria and the self-proclaimed Republic of Biafra. It took more than three years to crush the secession, which brought widespread suffering to the civilian population blockaded in the ever-shrinking rebel-held region. Civilian rule was re-established in 1979, but it lasted little more than four years. The ensuing 16 years of military rule were characterized by extremes of corruption, and sometimes severe repression. Only in 1999 did Nigeria return to civilian rule. After independence Nigeria had become Africa's leading petroleum producer, but the new-found riches did little for the development of the continent's most populous country. They were squandered or plundered outright.

3 For a discussion of the perspectives on dictatorship offered by Soyinka's plays and by Nuruddin Farah's trilogy of novels 'Variations on the Theme of an African Dictatorship,' see Gugler (1988).

4 For a fine presentation of the play, see the sympathetic account of Jones ([1973] 1988). Wright (1993) stands in stark contrast.

Ossie Davis in the role of the narrator

repression of dissent, and the economic concomitants of such political features: mismanagement and corruption.

The film version of *Kongi's Harvest* was directed by Ossie Davis, the distinguished African-American actor who appears as narrator in the early scenes. He had come to Nigeria full of enthusiasm to direct what he claimed to be the first major motion picture produced on the African continent by an African film company, Francis Oladele's Calpenny-Nigeria Films.[5] Arthur DuBow of Herald Productions had raised the funds in the U.S. and Lennart Berns of Omega Film in Sweden had furnished the crew (Davis, 1970). The film was released in 1970, but never had much exposure. In the 1970s, New Line Cinema provided limited distribution in the U.S., then it was withdrawn from distribution altogether. By now it has all but disappeared. Still, the political significance of the accomplished play, and the fact that it remains the only work of the distinguished playwright to have been produced as a full-length film, more than justify the attention we give to *Kongi's Harvest*.[6]

Kongi's Harvest, like most of Soyinka's plays, is a play of performance rather than plot and character development. It is thus eminently suitable for transposition to the screen. The film conveys the pageantry of a Yoruba royal court: the royal drums, the royal dance and chant, most strikingly the praise song to the king, in Yoruba. And it departs from the play to take advantage of the opportunities the medium offers. It presents an aerial view of Ibadan – the largest metropolis in tropical Africa until the 1950s, street and market scenes, preparations for the New Yam Festival, a motorcade with motor-cycle outriders, a street barricade, the famous Olumo rock in Abeokuta, the dictator's militia singing and drinking, Oba Danlola's large retinue, and a masquerade of the Yoruba

5 Such a claim fails to acknowledge not only the large film production in Africa North of the Sahara since the 1920s, but also a sizeable number of films produced in francophone West Africa in the 1960s, most prominent amongst them those of Ousmane Sembène. Even the more modest claim that *Kongi's Harvest* was the first full-length Nigerian feature film is in dispute (Ukadike, 1994: 144), though Francis Oladele can lay claim to being the pioneer Nigerian film producer. He followed *Kongi's Harvest* with *Bullfrog in the Sun*. Directed by Hans-Jürgen Pohland, it was subsequently retitled *Things Fall Apart* for its principal source. Calpenny-Nigeria Films owed its name to investors from California, Pennsylvania, and New York who were involved in its early days, but they had quit by the time *Kongi's Harvest* was produced.

6 Soyinka's early play *The Swamp Dwellers* was produced as a short film directed by Norman Florence. An abbreviated version of his more substantive *The Strong Breed* concludes *Culture in Transition*. In this documentary, directed by Bert Lawrence, Soyinka introduces viewers to various aspects of Yoruba, Igbo, and Hausa culture. A similarly abbreviated version of this play, set

Gelede. It adds two significant scenes. Daodu denounces the superstition and oppression of the past as he introduces Segi to the palace shrine, filmed at the palace of the Alafin of Oyo. And Kongi enacts a Last Supper with his twelve advisors, recalling Nkrumah's designation as The Saviour. Still, Soyinka's script, while inspired in places, remains too beholden to the play and overburdens the film with dialogue. Endless cross-cutting and the absence of sustained dramatic sequences make the film appear disjointed. It does not come anywhere near the brilliance of the play's first part with its striking contrast of lighting, dress, music, and language between Kongi's mountain retreat and Segi's night club, as both are presented on the same stage (pp. 11–47).

The production of the film suffered from its low budget, reported at $300,000 (Ekwuazi, 1991: 25). The photography is amateurish, the editing poor. The Nigerian actors[7] had been recruited from the stage, except for Orlando Martins, in the role of Dr Gbenge (Makinde, 1971). Their acting remained theatrical with a couple of notable exceptions. Rashidi Onikoyi, as Oba Danlola, conveys the assurance, self-indulgence, and wiliness of the man entitled to rule. Soyinka's close friend Femi Johnson is superb as the Organising Secretary, manipulating his master with sycophancy, negotiating pragmatically with the opposition. Soyinka had taken on the role of Kongi in a fine display of self-irony. His Kongi dominates the film poster, reflecting the domineering role of Kongi as well as Soyinka's fame. He suggests the insecurity, austerity, and impatience of the character he created, but pushes them to the point of caricature. As for Ossie Davis, he had no formal training and little experience as a director. In 1969, he had been offered a role in *Cotton Comes to Harlem* and had wound up directing it. For that film he had $1.2 million to spend, but now he was operating with a much lower budget, in a foreign and very difficult environment.

Much of the play's rich dialogue was lost in its translation to the screen. Some was gutted when the voices of most of the actors were dubbed in England by African-American and South African actors because the original soundtrack had been damaged and/or to make the language more accessible to Western audiences (Ekwuazi, 1991: 25). And if the film is overburdened with dialogue, it still deprives us of some of the play's finest passages: the splendid perversion of the national anthem that opens the play (pp. 1–2), much of the deliberations of Kongi's advisors (pp. 11–13); the erotic exchange between Segi and Daodu on the eve of the Festival (pp. 44–6); and most of the Organising Secretary's exchange with the Captain of the Carpenters' Brigade and Dende (pp. 66–9).

In short, the film does not do justice to the magnificent play.[8] Soyinka has gone so far as to disown the film altogether, even though he had written the original script and played Kongi.[9] We are left to speculate about his reasons. He may have wanted to dissociate himself from the failed enterprise. He clearly was concerned about the political implications of the play. Perhaps most importantly, the film's ending drastically departed from Soyinka's script.

6 (cont.) in Senegal, was produced by Joseph Gaï Ramaka as *So Be It*.

7 The only non-Nigerian member of the cast was the West Indian Nina Baden-Semper in the role of Segi.

8 Gibbs (1973: 27) is more sanguine about the film, arguing that it is spectacular in a way that a stage play can never be and that several changes are distinct improvements on the play: the characters of Segi, Dende, and Daodu benefit from the development they receive; the Aweris are better in their curtailed form; and, since the details of the assassination plot are clarified, the film moves more effectively to its climax than the play.

9 The film, contrary to the U.S. distributor's blurb, does not credit the script to Soyinka, or anybody else for that matter. Soyinka (1979: 97) commented that this was because the film did not correspond to the script he wrote. Asked whether he had been involved with any films, he stated in 1973: 'No, that is, I hope that I have not made any movie which is widely distributed. I have been involved in one or two cinema disasters, and I just hope that they are not widely distributed' (Soyinka, 1975: 124).

When the play was first performed in Nigeria in 1965 there was no doubt that Kongi stood for Kwame Nkrumah, the President of Ghana, whose regime had degenerated over the years and exhibited the very traits castigated by Soyinka: the personality cult of the Supreme Leader, the manipulation of the population, the repression of the opposition, economic mismanagement, and corruption. If Nkrumah had become the Redeemer, Kongi poses as if he were Jesus Christ, and is ready to replace him on the calendar. Two features, rarely found in dictatorships then or since, related the play specifically to Nkrumah. In the play, Kongi and his advisors are clearly modeled on Nkrumah, his political pseudo-science of *Consciencism*, and the ghost writers he is reputed to have employed. And the focus of opposition to his rule was indeed a traditional kingdom, the famous Ashanti.

Nkrumah was overthrown in 1966 to popular acclaim, but many intellectuals continued to extend their sympathy to his regime. This sympathy is rooted in a recognition of Nkrumah's leading role in the nationalist struggle – in 1957 he had been the first leader to gain independence for a country in Africa South of the Sahara – an appreciation of his commitment to make his society more egalitarian, and nostalgia for his vision of a united Africa. Such sympathy was nurtured by the fact that the military who overthrew Nkrumah never had much legitimacy. If the play received relatively little attention, this may be traced, at least in part, to the widespread reluctance to denounce the fallen hero.

Soyinka refused to join the anti-Nkrumah crowd that gathered once he was overthrown. Immediately after Nkrumah's fall, Soyinka (1966: 19), while supporting Nkrumah's ousting, urged that he be recruited to play a major role in the international arena:

> Nkrumah's international presence has become crucial to the aims and the growing effectiveness of the OAU ... the effect of Nkrumah's return to the African scene is incalculable on the white supremacist nations.... Nkrumah must speak for [the] OAU at the United Nations, and more importantly, he must direct the will and the energies of the black states in the effort of liberation in these next desperate years.

When *Kongi's Harvest* was staged in Accra in 1970, in a production that curried favor with the authorities of the day by stressing the links between Kongi and Nkrumah, Soyinka refused permission and declined the royalties due to him (Gibbs, 1986: 96).[10] Before then, in the program notes for the play's 1969 production, he had emphasized that the play had a general thrust:

> The play is not about Kongi, it is about Kongism. Therefore, while it has been suggested with some justification that there are resemblances between the character of Kongi and that of ex-President Nkrumah – the play was indeed first presented in December, 1965,[11] while Nkrumah was still in power – it must be emphasized that Kongism has never been dethroned in Black Africa. (Gibbs, 1986: 97)

10 Ayi Kwei Armah, on the other hand, published *The Beautyful Ones Are Not Yet Born*, his stark denunciation of Nkrumah's betrayal of the masses he had roused in the quest for independence, two years after the fall of Nkrumah, perhaps because, as a Ghanaian, he had been closer to it all.

11 *Kongi's Harvest* was first performed in August 1965 according to Gibbs (1986: 97).

Betrayals of Independence   While working on the script, Soyinka had told David Rubadiri that he was writing a play about Hastings Kamuzu Banda of Malawi. And Kongi's order to apprehend Segi's father who has escaped jail 'I want him back – alive if possible. If not, ANY OTHER WAY!' (p. 49) recalls Banda's infamous 'Dead or Alive Search Order' issued in 1964 (Gibbs, 1993: 67–8). A production by the Negro Ensemble in New York in 1968 stressed the links between Kongi and Banda (Gibbs, 1986: 78). Still, Kongi's pseudo-science of politics and his royal opposition continue to recall Nkrumah.

The ending of the film diverges altogether from both Soyinka's play and his film script. In play and film it is preceded by the climax, the New Yam Festival. Kongi presides over it, and the opposition, led by Daodu and Segi, plans to kill him before he usurps the ritual power of Oba Danlola. Segi's father, who has just escaped from prison, insists on doing the deed. In the play, he is intercepted and killed. Segi persuades Daodu that the feast should proceed nevertheless, and the stage directions instruct:

> It is the signal for the feast to begin. A real feast, a genuine Harvest orgy of food and drink that permits no spectators, only celebrants. The dancing, the singing are only part of it, the centre is the heart and stomach of a good feast. (p. 81)

The crowd sings and dances until the stage directions resume:

> The rhythm of pounding emerges triumphant, the dance grows frenzied. Above it all on the dais, Kongi, getting progressively inspired harangues his audience in words drowned in the bacchanal. He exhorts, declaims, reviles, cajoles, damns, curses, vilifies, excommunicates, execrates until he is a demonic mass of sweat and foam at the lips.
>   Segi returns, disappears into the area of pestles. A copper salver is raised suddenly high; it passes from hands to hands above the women's heads; they dance with it on their heads; it is thrown from one to the other until at last it reaches Kongi's table and Segi throws open the lid.
>   In it, the head of an old man [i.e. of Segi's father].
>   In the ensuing scramble, no one is left but Kongi and the head, Kongi's mouth wide open in speechless terror.
>   A sudden blackout on both. (pp. 83–4)

After this scene the published text concludes with an epilogue. The Organising Secretary and Oba Danlola discuss the developments ensuing from Segi's dramatic gesture, while Dende partakes in a rather passive fashion. The reader/spectator is thus informed about the consequences of Segi's act of deviance and presented with an assessment of these consequences by two principal characters. Kongi remains in power. His Organising Secretary flees his wrath. Members of the opposition try to force their leaders to seek safety in exile. And the final stage directions indicate that Kongi's regime has silenced the music of both the court and the nation, and imprisoned all:

> A mixture of the royal music and the anthem rises loudly, plays for a short while, comes to an abrupt halt as the iron grating descends and hits the ground with a loud, final clang. (p. 90)

When, however, the play is performed without the epilogue – and in Soyinka's productions it has generally been cut (Gibbs, 1986: 94) – the effect of ending with the climax is quite different. We see a scene where Kongi is left alone, deserted by his retinue, gasping in horror at the head presented to him, and we are left to wonder whether anyone is prepared to answer his call henceforth.[12]

Soyinka's (n.d.) script follows the play quite closely, but it ends in strikingly different fashion: the tyrannicide succeeds.[13] As Segi's father Dr Gbenge, the leader of the opposition, steps forward to take power, he is confronted by the Captain of the Carpenters' Brigade:

CAPTAIN: You overlooked something – the Brigade.
SEGI'S FATHER: Are you able to take control?
CAPTAIN: Neither are you. Not without us.

The scene ends, and the script concludes:

The Captain's slight, lop-sided smile says 'I have your soul in my hands.'
SEGI'S FATHER: The situation has changed
CAPTAIN: Not for us.
Segi, Daodu, Secretary, Danlola have not moved or changed position.
CAPTAIN: You haven't much time.
The trio on dais [Segi's father, the Captain, and Kongi's body] remain point of converging gazes of the hushed expectant crowd.
THEME MUSIC AS SHOT WIDENS TO AERIAL VIEW OF CITY.

The film follows the script up to the confrontation between Dr Gbenge and the Captain, but then there is an abrupt shift to a final scene where Dr Gbenge takes on the dictator's role, repeating the very same megalomaniac slogans:

The will of the State is supreme, destiny has entrusted in our hands the will of the State, the will of the State is supreme.

The published play, performances of the truncated version of the play, the script, and the film, each present a different conclusion to the denunciation of dictatorship. The anti-climax of the epilogue in the published play emphasizes the staying power of dictators. The reader is forewarned by the epilogue's title, 'Hangover.' And the spectator is prepared as the curtain rises one last time to show 'The square ... littered with the debris and the panic of last night's feast.' (p. 85) We see an opposition defeated. There is a scramble to get the leaders of the opposition to safety across the border. Oba Danlola's turning around might be interpreted to indicate that the King has decided to stay with his people but for the fact that his preceding discussion with the Organising Secretary indicated his intent to flee: he turns back only to ensure that Daodu is persuaded to go into exile.[14] Still, the opposition continues. That dictators have great staying power, and that most attempts at tyrannicide fail, are realistic positions to take. They imply an awareness of the heavy sacrifices required in the struggle against such odds.

12 The script for the first performance of the play in 1965 differed from the version published in 1967 (Gibbs, 1986: 95) and subsequent performances have been modified. Thus more than the two endings to the play I sketch here have been realized. Soyinka is indeed renowned for ensuring the topicality of his plays by modifying performances to fit the circumstances of the day and may well surprise us afresh with yet another conclusion to his denunciation of *isms*.

13 As Gibbs (1986: 95) has pointed out, the play's climax presents major problems: a convincing property head is difficult to produce and the audience has no clue that it is Segi's father's. The scene could have been produced quite realistically in the film, and the viewers would have recognized Segi's father, who appeared twice before as Dr. Gbenge. However, Segi's gesture would risk appearing altogether theatrical on the screen.

14 There have been alternative interpretations of the epilogue. Booth (1981: 169) reads the epilogue to indicate that Kongi has been discredited, his power destroyed. Moore ([1971] 1978: 63) reckons that Kongi is probably finished as a political force.

Betrayals of Independence

The ending of Kongi's Harvest
according to Wole Soyinka's script

The effect of a performance of *Kongi's Harvest* that concludes with the curtain falling on Kongi, his mouth wide open in speechless horror, left alone with the head of Segi's father, must be dramatic. It is also open-ended. Spectators are left to construct their own epilogues, to interpret on the basis of their own experience and context. Was Segi's an empty gesture, or did she – and Daodu's speech denouncing Kongi, and the presence of Oba Danlola – accomplish what her father failed to achieve: the destruction of the regime? They may take their cue from the fact that Kongi has been deserted and take this to suggest that he has lost his power. They may conclude that moral outrage can bring down dictators. In a similar vein, the opposition in *Sweet and Sour Milk*, Nuruddin Farah's novel about dictatorship in Somalia, acts on the assumption that to disseminate information about the regime's misdeeds will bring about chaos, that people will turn to join the opposition, and that the tyrant will fall.

Such propositions used to be thought utterly naïve – until popular protests in Eastern Europe brought down one regime after another. Intellectuals usually played an important role. They eroded the legitimacy of regimes as they denounced oppression, mismanagement, and corruption. In most countries barely a shot was fired. In Rumania, Nicolae Ceauşescu was confronted with the blood he had shed – quite like Kongi gasping at the head in the salver. The fall of his regime was set in motion on that December day in 1989 when people at the back of the crowd corralled to listen to his harangue began to shout Timişoara! Timişoara! Timişoara! – confronting the dictator with the blood of his repression in Timişoara a few days earlier. And Ceauşescu, like Kongi, was left speechless. That same month strikes and mass demonstrations began that within a couple of months brought a 'velvet revolution' to Benin, Nigeria's immediate neighbor. In the following months popular movements swept autocratic regimes away in a number of African countries or forced them to make major concessions.

If the ending of the script is altogether different, it also remains open-ended. Soyinka suggests the limitations of tyrannicide. While it does away with the tyrant, it leaves his very apparatus of oppression in place. A stage direction in the script indicates that at least half of the Carpenters' Brigade should be armed, including a sprinkling of sub-machine guns. A power struggle between those who command the guns and the unarmed opposition is in the offing. We are left with a 'hushed expectant crowd.'

The stunning reversal in the film is highly effective in shocking the viewer and dramatizing the point that power corrupts – a recurrent theme in Soyinka's work. However, the eclipse of the process of moral renewal that might be expected to come with a new revolutionary regime seems all too cynical. The author has cautioned us against such a simplistic approach. He has Segi observe that, at some point in the past, 'Kongi *was* a great man' (p. 45). Likewise we should expect Dr Gbenge to have a time of greatness before his regime deteriorates.

Wole Soyinka was reported to be on his way to Sweden as *Kongi's Harvest* was being edited there (Anonymous, 1970a), but there is no information as to what extent he was involved in the editing, if at all. And if he can be taken to have countenanced most of the film by acting the role of Kongi, his act came to an end with Kongi's demise. Indeed, the final scene appears tagged on: the transition to that scene is unlike any other in the film, the setting is new, and even the color of the film is different; Orlando Martins, playing Dr Gbenge, provides the only continuity. We may surmise that the film's ending was unacceptable to Soyinka and the key reason that he disavowed the film.

A play such as *Kongi's Harvest* is political in more than one sense. So far I have looked at it as a statement about politics, about the politics of autocratic rule. But such a play is meant to have political consequences, to have an impact on the spectators of the performance, on the readers of the text. The political impact of a film is potentially even greater. When the play was first performed in Lagos in August 1965, the coalition government ruling the Federation of Nigeria had manipulated elections, repressed opposition, and spread corruption. *Kongi's Harvest* thus appears to warn its Nigerian audience against the usurpation and abuse of power, a warning based on the experience of Nigeria's closest anglophone neighbor, Ghana, a country that was thought to be a few steps ahead of Nigeria in those days.[15] Indeed, the program for the Lagos première featured revealing quotations from Nigerian as well as foreign politicians (Duerden, 1966). The play in its full version could then be seen to forewarn that dictatorship, once established, is most difficult to dislodge.

In March 1966, Soyinka had the play conclude without the epilogue

15 If *Kongi's Harvest* could be seen in August 1965 as a warning against encroaching dictatorship in Nigeria, it had its parallel in the warnings of another Nigerian Cassandra. Chinua Achebe's novel *A Man of the People* appeared in January 1966 to denounce the country's corruption and lawlessness and to warn of the consequences – too late, as it turned out: the military coup it predicted took place that very same month.

Betrayals of Independence

at the University of Ibadan Arts Theatre (Berry, [1966] 1980). His decision can be seen as a response to the recent dramatic events in Nigeria. In January a military coup had swept away the corrupt and oppressive civilian regime. The discouraging 'Hangover' epilogue did not fit these times. The play's climax served to remind the military regime of the importance of legitimacy. Beyond that, the spectator in March 1966 may have seen in Segi's dramatic yet peaceful gesture a denunciation of the military's brutality: the coup leaders had gratuitously killed many of the leaders of the First Republic, including Abubakar Tafawa Balewa, the untainted and widely respected Prime Minister of the Republic.

If the military regime that took over from the plotters of the first coup held out some promise, the leaders of the second coup in June failed to stop the ethnic massacres in 1966, took Nigeria into civil war, and detained Soyinka for more than two years over his attempts at the very beginning of the war to persuade leaders and the population at large to halt the bloodshed. Shortly after his release, Soyinka opted again for the truncated version of the play in performances in Ibadan in 1969 and at the Ife Arts Festival in 1970. He made the reference to contemporary Nigeria explicit by having Kongi in military uniform and his mountain retreat designed as a military headquarters (Gibbs, 1973: 2).

Soyinka completed the film script presumably at about that time – the film was shot in early 1970 (Anonymous, 1970b). He now explored the implications of tyrannicide and focused on the problem that an unarmed opposition is constrained to compromise with those who carry guns – and have served the tyrant. The parallel with Nuruddin Farah's explorations in his trilogy 'Variations on the Theme of an African Dictatorship' is striking: if in *Sweet and Sour Milk*, the first volume, the conspirators seek to delegitimize the regime, in *Close Sesame*, the last volume, an old man seeks to kill the tyrant single-handedly.

The three versions of *Kongi's Harvest* under Soyinka's control all end rather inconclusively, as is the author's wont. The film, in stark contrast, concludes firmly on history repeating itself. Of course, a film, unlike a play, cannot be modified to suit a particular audience. It is released to be shown in different settings in the indeterminate future. The dramatic warning against the corruption of power is quite appropriate to these uncertain circumstances. We might conclude that the film is in accord with the pessimism Soyinka conveys when the Organising Secretary comments on the death of Segi's father in the play: 'Doesn't anyone know it's never any use' (p. 80) – declaring futile all attempts to confront oppression. A pessimism conveyed already in the prologue: its very title, 'Hemlock,' signaled that Danlola was doomed with all he stood for, and at the prologue's end the King dances:

> Delve with the left foot
> For ill-luck; with the left
> Again for ill-luck; once more
> With the left alone, for disaster
> Is the only certainty we know. (p. 10)

Such a conclusion would fail to acknowledge that Soyinka stands as an inspiring example of the commitment to struggle, constant struggle, against oppression and the *isms* invoked to justify it.[16] Soyinka has animated the stage with *Kongi's Harvest*, *Opera Wonyosi*, and *A Play of Giants* to denounce the lust for power. In *Kongi's Harvest*, neither the Secretary compromised by serving the dictator, nor the King perceiving the end of royal glory, represents Soyinka's position. Rather, it is elaborated by the next generation, by Segi who persuades Daodu to preach life rather than hatred (p. 45), and by Daodu who takes the pulpit to counsel us that 'pain may be endured only in the pursuit of ending pain and fighting terror' (p. 79). Soyinka, of course, has taken the pulpit time and again. On the occasion of the Symposium on African Literatures, he eloquently proclaimed to the assembled brass 'our popular will.'

The film presents a cynical circular view of history, or perhaps just African history, that would be agreeable to many in the film's intended U.S. audience. It is subject to charges of conservatism and racism. As Ekwuazi (1991: 24) put it:

> *Kongi's Harvest* is a film that fosters the West's stereotype about the rest of us. Political demise, it avows, stems out of an endemic corruption; political power, out of the barrel of the gun...

Ossie Davis is a most unlikely target for such charges.[17] Soyinka has castigated anglophone African films as in the worst Hollywood taste. His specific comments – the producer's subservience to financial sponsors and the potential U.S. audience, the producer's dominant position *vis-à-vis* the editor, technological and commercial problems, and the amateurishness of some of the techniques – presumably were informed by his experience as a participant in the production of *Kongi's Harvest* (Soyinka, 1975: 124–5). When *Kongi's Harvest* was released, Soyinka was reported to have complained that the film had been 'badly butchered' by the overseas partners of Calpenny-Nigeria Films (Anonymous, 1971). Presumably that's where the playwright, scriptwriter, and lead actor puts the blame. It would appear that the foreign producers short-changed the production of a major play by the pre-eminent African playwright with insufficient finance and insisted on subverting the authorial intent.

16 On the Nigerian pop music scene Fela Kuti was Soyinka's worthy counterpart. In spite of severe repression – he was imprisoned twice, his mother died in a police assault on his house – he persevered in his denunciation of government corruption and repression. His song 'Beasts of No Nation,' written in pidgin English, went:

Animal talk done start again:
'Dash them human rights.'
How animal go know say they no born me as slave?
How animal go know say slave trade done pass?
And they want us dash us human rights...
Human rights na my property
You can't dash me my property.
(Sandbrook, 1993:113)

17 In the joint autobiography Davis wrote with Ruby Dee, he dedicated several pages to the production of *Kongi's Harvest*, but had nothing to say about the drastic change imposed on Soyinka's script. He acknowledged that the film did not do well at the box office in the U.S. and that it failed in Nigeria as well, but the only problems he mentioned concern language. All his directions to the Swedish crew had to be translated; and a few of the actors were not comfortable in English: they lost their naturalness and fluidity the moment the camera rolled and became like puppets with a British attitude and accent (Davis and Dee, 1998: 341–4).

Davis returned to Nigeria a few years later, with financing from Delta Sigma Theta Sorority, to direct *Countdown at Kusini*. The film featured an African-American cast including Ruby Dee and Davis. He appears to have been surprised, on this, his second venture in Nigeria, by the difficulties he encountered with both local conditions and his American crew. Cost overruns were huge. At the box office *Countdown at Kusini* failed, in Davis's words, 'swiftly and completely' (Davis and Dee, 1998: 372).

References and Further Reading

Achebe, Chinua. 1966. *A Man of the People*. London: Heinemann.

Adelugba, Dapo. 1979. 'Wole Soyinka's Kongi's Harvest: production and exegesis,' in *Colloque sur littérature et esthétique négro-africaines*. Abidjan/Dakar: Les Nouvelles Editions Africaines. 257–75.

Anonymous. 1970a. *Cultural Events in Africa* 63: 6. [London: The Transcription Center.]

——. 1970b. 'Kongi on Film,' *West Africa*, 15 August, 2775: 950.

——. 1971. 'People,' *West Africa*, 9 July, 2821: 775.

Armah, Ayi Kwei. 1968. *The Beautyful Ones Are Not Yet Born*. Boston: Houghton Mifflin.

Berry, Boyd M. (1966) 1980. 'Kongi's Harvest (A Review),' *Ibadan*: 23: 53–5. Reprinted in James Gibbs (ed.) *Critical Perspectives on Wole Soyinka*. Washington, D.C.: Three Continents Press; London: Heinemann. 87–9.

Booth, James. 1981. *Writers and Politics in Nigeria*. London: Hodder; New York: Africana Publishing Company.

Bullfrog in the Sun/Things Fall Apart. 1971. Film directed by Hans-Jürgen Pohland. Produced by Nigram, Calpenny-Nigeria Films Ltd, and Cine 3.

Cotton Comes to Harlem. 1970. Film directed by Ossie Davis. Produced by Samuel Goldwyn Jr. (USA). Distributed in the U.S. by Swank Motion Pictures. 97 minutes.

Countdown at Kusini. 1976. Film directed by Ossie Davis, written by Ossie Davis, John Storm Roberts, and Al Freeman, Jr. Produced by Ladi Ladebo Nigeria. 99 minutes.

Culture in Transition. 1964. Documentary produced and directed by Bert Lawrence, scripted and narrated by Wole Soyinka. Part of the World Theatre series produced by Standard Oil (now Exxon, USA). 59 minutes.

Davis, Ossie. 1970. 'When is a Camera a Weapon?' *New York Times*, 20 September, II, pages 17 and 24.

—— and Ruby Dee. 1998. *With Ossie Davis and Ruby: In This Life Together*. New York: William Morrow.

Diamond, Larry. 1988. *Class, Ethnicity and Democracy in Nigeria: The Failure of the First Republic*. Syracuse, NY: Syracuse University Press.

Duerden, Dennis. 1966. 'African Sharpshooter,' *New Society*, 8 December, page 879.

Ekwuazi, Hyginus O. 1991 (1987). *Film in Nigeria*. Second edition. Jos: Nigerian Film Corporation.

Farah, Nuruddin. 1979. *Sweet and Sour Milk*. London: Allison and Busby.

——. 1981. *Sardines*. London: Allison and Busby.

——. 1983. *Close Sesame*. London: Allison and Busby.

Gibbs, James. 1973. *Study Guide to Kongi's Harvest*. London: Rex Collings.

——. 1986. *Wole Soyinka*. Macmillan Modern Dramatists. Basingstoke/London: Macmillan.

——. 1993. 'The Masks Hatched Out,' in James Gibbs and Bernth Lindfors (eds) *Research on Wole Soyinka*. Trenton, NJ: Africa World Press. 51–79.

Gugler, Josef. 1988. 'African Literary Comment on Dictators: Wole Soyinka's Plays and Nuruddin Farah's Novels,' *The Journal of Modern African Studies* 26: 171–7.

——. 1997. 'Wole Soyinka's *Kongi's Harvest* from Stage to Screen: Four Endings to Tyranny. *Canadian Journal of African Studies* 31: 32–49.

Jones, Eldred Durosimi. (1973) 1988. *The Writing of Wole Soyinka*. Third edition. London: James Currey; Portsmouth, NH: Heinemann.

Kongi's Harvest. 1970. Film directed by Ossie Davis. Produced by Calpenny-Nigeria Films Ltd, Omega Film (Sweden), and Herald Productions (USA). Licensed by All Channel films. Available for viewing at the Film Archives of the Institute of African Studies, University of Ibadan. 85 minutes.

Kuti, Fela Anikulapo. n.d. (late 1980s) *Beasts of No Nation*.

Makinde, Olutade. 1971. 'Man Who Waited for Five Years to Make One Film.' *Sunday Post*, 25 April, pp. 8–9.

Moore, Gerald. (1971) 1978. *Wole Soyinka*. Modern African Writers. Second edition. London/Ibadan: Evans Brothers.

Ogunba, Oyin. 1975. *The Movement of Transition: a Study of the Plays of Wole Soyinka*. Ibadan: Ibadan University Press.

Osofisan, Femi. 1994. 'Wole Soyinka and a Living Dramatist: a Playwright's Encounter with Soyinka's Dream.' *Wole Soyinka: An Appraisal*, edited by Adewale Maja-Pearce. Oxford/Portsmouth, New Hampshire/Ibadan/Gaborone: Heinemann.

Owusu, Maxwell. 1970. *Uses and Abuses of Political Power: A Case Study of Continuity and Change in the Politics of Ghana*. Chicago: University of Chicago Press.

Sandbrook, Richard. 1993. *The Politics of Africa's Economic Recovery*. African Society Today. Cambridge/New York/Oakleigh: Cambridge University Press.

So Be It. 1997. Film written and directed by Joseph Gaï Ramaka. Produced by Les Atéliers de L'Arche (France). Distributed in the U.S. by California Newsreel as part of *Africa Dreaming*. 32 minutes.

Soyinka, Wole. 1963. *The Swamp Dwellers*. In *Three Plays*. Ibadan: Mbari. (First produced in 1958.)

____. 1963. *The Lion and the Jewel*. London/Ibadan: Oxford University Press. (First produced in 1959.)

——. 1963. *A Dance of the Forests*. London/Ibadan: Oxford University Press. (First produced in 1960.)

——. 1963. *The Strong Breed*. In *Three Plays*. Ibadan: Mbari. (First produced in 1966.)

——. 1966. 'Of Power and Change.' *African Statesman* 1 (3): 17–19. (Soyinka stated erroneously that this statement had appeared in *The Nigerian Statesman*, June 1966, in the letter reproduced by Gibbs [1973].)

——. 1967. *Kongi's Harvest*. London/Ibadan/Nairobi: Oxford University Press. (First produced in 1965.)

——. n.d. (about 1969). 'Kongi's Harvest by Wole Soyinka'. Typescript. Kenneth Dike Library, University of Ibadan.

——. 1975. 'Class Discussion.' *In Person: Achebe, Awoonor, and Soyinka at the University of Washington*, edited by Karen L. Morell. Seattle, WA: African Studies Program, Institute for Comparative and Foreign Area Studies, University of Washington. 108–30.

——. 1979. 'Theatre and the Emergence of the Nigerian Film Industry.' *The Development and Growth of the Film Industry in Nigeria: Proceedings of a Seminar on the Film Industry and Cultural Identity in Nigeria*, edited by Alfred E. Opubor and Onuora E. Nwuneli. Lagos/New York: Third Press International. 97–103.

——. 1981. *Aké: The Years of Childhood*. London: Rex Collings; New York: Random House.

——. 1981. *Opera Wonyosi*. London: Rex Collings; Bloomington: Indiana University Press. (First produced in 1977.)

——. 1984. *A Play of Giants*. London/New York: Methuen. (First produced in 1984.)

——. 1992. 'Power and Creative Strategies,' in Femi Osofisan, Nicole Medjigbodo, Sam Asein and G. G. Darah (eds) *200 écrivains africains à Lagos*. Ivry: Editions Nouvelles du Sud. 23–9.

The Swamp Dwellers. 1967. Film directed by Norman Florence. Produced by Transcription Centre (Britain). Distributed by Phoenix Films. 53 minutes.

Ukadike, Nwachukwu Frank. 1994. *Black African Cinema*. Berkeley/Los Angeles/London: University of California Press.

Wright, Derek. 1993. *Wole Soyinka Revisited*. New York: Twayne Publishers.

Xala 1974
Impotence Sexual, Cultural, Economic, and Political[1]

I am going to make a film on a Senegalese big businessman, on the birth of the black bourgeoisie ... we're witnessing the birth of an aborted child and some of these circumstances are very dangerous – too dangerous because they are being manipulated from the outside, from Europe....
(Ousmane Sembène in an interview with Weaver, 1972: 31)

1 This discussion of *Xala* draws on Gugler and Diop (1998).

2 Sembène Ousmane is the name his novels and films usually indicate. We follow here more recent convention in putting his patronymic last.

3 Woll (2004) explores the functional, thematic, and aesthetic affinities between Ousmane Sembène's work and Soviet film.

4 Rosenbaum (1993), a distinguished U.S. film critic, lists Sembène as one of the twelve greatest living narrative film makers.

5 The pronunciation of *xala* approximates 'hala;' pronouncing the 'x' like the 'ch' in 'chutzpah' comes closer.

6 In a critical discussion of francophone African films, Serceau (1995) mentions *Xala* as one of three films distinguished by greater complexity of characters and plot. For a summary of critical comment on the film, see Pfaff (1988: 212–13).

7 The reader/viewer skeptical of the power of the *xala* may detect that Sembène offers an alternative psychological interpretation as well. That El Hadji should be impotent on his wedding night is not all that surprising considering how Rama had denounced his polygamy, how he had been put down by Oumi, how the *badiène* and

Ousmane Sembène[2] is unique among African filmmakers in that he is also a major writer. The former dock worker had written one of the great classics in African literature, *God's Bits of Wood*, before he turned to film as the medium that would reach a wider African public. In 1962, nearly forty years old, he spent a year at the Gorki Studio in Moscow with Sergei Gerassimov and Mark Donskoy.[3] The very next year he released *Borom Sarret*, the most important of the early feature films produced by black Africans in Africa. He went on to become the premier filmmaker in Africa South of the Sahara.[4]

Xala[5] is arguably the finest among Sembène's many film productions. The film is complex in plot, diverse in characterizations, and rich in satirical detail, longer than any of Sembène's previous films. It is beautifully crafted by the accomplished director, supported by an experienced crew, including Paulin Soumanou Vieyra, the pioneer filmmaker. The film successfully marries the seductive lure of the medium to the director's didactic purpose. With about $130,000 (Pfaff, 1988: 241; Vieyra, 1983: 87), a small budget even at that time, Sembène produced a *chef-d'œuvre*.[6]

Xala offers an excellent opportunity to compare Sembène's approaches to his two chosen media. Even though the film was released just one year after the publication of his novel *Xala* in 1973, it presents a major departure from it. Some of the differences between the novel and the film can be understood as Sembène's judicious adaptations to the different medium. But there is also a clear shift in emphasis – from denouncing the parasitic Senegalese bourgeoisie to exposing the neo-colonial political regime – that defies explanation in terms of the different requirements of the two media. The artist's mirrors reflect different perspectives on the problems, the struggles, and the hopes of his people. He addresses different audiences.

Novel and film are set in Dakar, the capital of Senegal and its only major city. Both tell of affliction. The curse of the *xala* that has inflicted impotence on El Hadji Abdou Kader Bèye on his wedding night with his third wife mirrors the impotence that afflicts the emerging Senegalese bourgeoisie.[7] The story of El Hadji's *xala* becomes an allegory. He represents, experiences, and eventually articulates the impotence of his class. Sembène entertains us with the satirical account of El Hadji's physical impotence, but eventually confronts us with the economic and cultural impotence of the bourgeoisie that cripples the nation.[8]

The Senegalese bourgeoisie fails to perform a productive function. Its representatives are looking for quick profits, whatever the means. They are parasites trafficking in allotments of subsidized rice and diverting

7 (cont.) two of his fellow business-men had put his virility in doubt. Physically as well the elderly man must have been quite exhausted, retiring to the nuptial chamber at 4 am after a long wedding feast. In the quiet of a rural setting the soothing prayer of Modu's *marabout* helps him regain his manhood. El Hadji becomes impotent yet again after his commerce has been foreclosed and Modu tells him that the *xala* has been put back on him. The story has a subconscious dimension as well. El Hadji senses the responsibility of the beggars for his affliction – he explodes in anger at the beggars at the very moment when he tries to answer the President's ques-tion: who inflicted the *xala* on him?

8 For a study of the world of Senegalese business in the late 1960s, see Amin (1969) who emphasizes the neo-colonial context. Boone provides a detailed account of the relationship between business interests and the state up to the 1980s. Of particular interest to the reader/viewer of *Xala* is her account of the political crisis of 1968–70 and of the regime's response, which included the promo-tion of a *rentier* class rooted in *ad hoc*, speculative, and state-mediated busi-ness opportunities (Boone, 1992: 165–72, 182–97).

One specific response was the transformation of the European-domi-nated Chambre de Commerce, d'Agriculture et d'Industrie de Dakar into an African-dominated Chambre de Commerce d'Industrie et d'Arti-sanat de la Région du Cap-Vert – of the wider Dakar region – in 1969. As in *Xala*, the transition was abrupt, even if it proceeded in a more decorous fashion. There was remarkable con-tinuity between the two bodies in one respect: out of seven, then eight commissions only one met regularly. It was concerned with imports, and thus with gaining access to govern-ment-controlled opportunities for large legitimate and illegitimate gains (Anonymous, 1968; Diagne and Decupper, 1974; and various *Bulletins* of the two Chambers of Commerce).

The Lebanese community is the third major player in the Senegalese economy. It holds an important role in

FILMI DOMIREEW DAKAR — SOCIÉTÉ NATIONALE DE CINEMATOGRAPHIE D.
présentent

XALA

un film de
SEMBENE OUSMANE

avec

TIERNO LEYE   FATIM DIAGNE
SEUNE SAMB   DOUTA SECK
YOUNOUSS SEYE   MARTIN SOW
MIRIAM NIANG   DIEYNABA NIANG
MOUSTAPHA TOURÉ   FARBA SARR

un film de
SEMBENE OUSMANE
"XALA"
Notes Ed. Présence Africaine Paris

MAKHOUREDIA GUEYE ● ABDOULAYE SECK ● ILIMANE SAGNA
PAUL ANDRÉ PELLEGRIN ● JEAN-PAUL SALAÜN ● MARCEL BEZI...
avec la participation de
régie : IBRAHIMA BARRO   images : GEORGES CARISTAN
son : EL HADJI MBOW
directeur de production : PAULIN SOUMANOU VIEYRA

Betrayals of Independence

8 (cont.) El Hadji's economic ascension in the novel, but is mentioned only in passing (p. 10). It is omitted from the film altogether.

The film does touch on one other foreign element in Senegalese commerce. Ahmed Fall is a Mauritanian, a representative of the immigrant group that dominated the retail grocery trade. El Hadji's exchange with him reflects the ethnic distance separating them and the underlying tension. His proposal to establish shops in every neighborhood, while a blatant attempt to get his bank to provide him with funds, presents itself as a nationalist project. In 1989 that project was realized to some extent in a very different way: riots directed against Mauritanians led to their exodus.

9 Sembène's most recent film, *Faat Kine*, offers a stark contrast to *Xala*. It presents a positive image of an entrepreneur who made it in spite of the abuse she and her mother suffered at the hands of men. Her charity towards the poor is part of that image. The only cripple we see has been the beneficiary of a wheelchair provided by her and her friends. He does not appear as destitute as his counterparts in *Xala*, and he does not contest the established order; rather, he kills a homeless couple who stole his chair and his other belongings. As for Sembène's denunciation of neo-colonialism, the entrepreneur's well-kept and efficient gas station is an advertisement for Total, based in France, which contributed to the financing of the film.

10 El Hadji's analysis echoes a statement made by the Union des Groupements Economiques Sénégalais (UNIGES) in the report of its first congress in 1968: '[Commerce, industry and banking in Senegal] are the *chasses gardées* of foreigners [resting upon] their colonial privileges while Senegalese vegetate in marginal sectors of the economy' (Boone, 1992: 168). UNIGES had 2,600 members, mainly small-scale traders, transporters, and artisans, and played a major role in the 1968–70 crisis.

supplies intended for drought victims. These avowed businessmen got where they are by exploiting others – El Hadji defrauded his non-literate kin. Instead of making productive investments, they spend their ill-gotten resources lavishly in absurd imitations of foreign consumer culture – to the point where El Hadji bankrupts himself. Sembène's acerbic account of their transgressions makes us agree that they deserve to be spat upon.[9]

The story demonstrates that the members of the Chamber of Commerce constitute only a pseudo-bourgeoisie. They are crippled themselves. The impotence of these *compradores* is poignantly portrayed in El Hadji's *cri de cœur* as he faces the expulsion from the Chamber of Commerce that will seal his ruin:

> We are dirt grubbers! Who owns the banks? The insurance companies? The factories? The construction companies? The wholesale trade? The movie theaters? The book shops? The hotels? etc., etc., etc. All these and more besides are out of our control. Here, we are just crabs in a basket. We wanted the colonialist's place. We got it. This Chamber is the proof. What has changed, in general or in particular? Nothing. The colonialist has become stronger, more powerful, hidden inside us, as we are here assembled. He promises us the left-overs of the feast if we behave ourselves. Beware anyone who wants to upset his digestion, who wants a bigger slice of the profit. And we?... Dirt grubbers, agents, distributors, in our fatuity we call ourselves 'businessmen.' Businessmen without funds.[10] (p. 139, my translation)

El Hadji's request for a bank loan of CFA500,000, equivalent – even allowing for nearly three decades of inflation – to less than $10,000 today, conveys the limited nature of the resources of a member of the now all-African Chamber of Commerce. The film, unlike the novel, does not make explicit what Senegalese viewers readily assume, that El Hadji is at the local branch of a French bank and that the ultimate decision over his future lies with the French boss of the bank officer he implores.

Women are central to the story: some demonstrate the cultural alienation of the *nouveaux riches*, others present alternative models.[11] The men, in one of the rare instances where they draw on their cultural heritage, affirm their commitment to polygamy. Their polygamy, however, no longer serves traditional ends: to bring labor to the kinship group and assure its continuity. Beyond sexual pleasure,[12] El Hadji's second wife Oumi N'Doye served to project the image of a 'modern' Westernized couple, and his third wife N'Goné now confirms his economic success and satisfies his vanity.[13] And unlike their forebears, these co-wives no longer operate a joint household.[14]

Sembène presents two female characters of integrity who stand in sharp contrast to Oumi and N'Goné. One stands for tradition, the other for an African modernity. Adja Awa Astou,[15] El Hadji's first wife, portrays quiet dignity, patient devotion to the principles of a Muslim marriage, loyalty to her husband even in his ruin. Rama, their daughter, shares her mother's dignity, but she embodies the future, reborn Africa, a society that will draw on its own language and culture while emancipating women from patriarchal traditions.[16]

The beggars constitute the counterpart to the bourgeoisie.[17] Their poverty provides a telling contrast to the conspicuous consumption of the *nouveaux riches*. They have been reduced to the status of pariahs by the greed, abuse of power, and cultural alienation of the *arrivistes*. They can be seen to represent an extreme image of the masses who are similarly cheated and robbed. But in this story the beggars have a measure of power: their blind leader, Gorgui, has put the *xala* on El Hadji, and he can take it away again. Sembène's portrayal of the beggars echoes Frantz Fanon's faith in the revolutionary potential of the *lumpen proletariat* rather than Karl Marx's dismissive view of it.[18]

Novel and film are similar in style. The novel is written in a naturalistic genre, and most of the film presents the story in a realistic vein. Working with amateurs, Sembène had little choice in the matter.[19] In any case, the naturalistic novel and the realistic film are quite appropriate to Sembène's didactic intentions, and they are the styles he invariably chooses. At times, though, he uses symbolism, caricature, and parody to dramatic effect. As Sembène put it: 'the scenes preceding the credits are simply the symbolization of that bourgeoisie' (Delmas and Delmas, 1976: 13, my translation). Here the attaché cases are made to take on a symbolic role. The French advisors hand them out like licenses to establish a business. Africans have only just declared their independence, but they are already co-opted into the neo-colonial regime as *compradores*. We are reminded of the symbolic nature of the attaché cases when El Hadji's attaché case is passed on to Thieli. The symbolic transaction turns into caricature when the attaché cases are found to bulge with bank notes. If they make the corruption of neo-colonialism palpable, in practice money would be channeled to *compradores* in more subtle ways, e.g. through credits never to be repaid, through privileged access to high-profit transactions such as import licences or real estate deals.

Sembène had started out writing a film script. While waiting to find funding for his film, he transformed his script into the novel. Subsequently, from the novel, he developed a new script for the film. Vieyra (1983: 87) describes the new script as 'enriched.' Presumably the delay contributed to the complexity of the plot, the diversity in characterizations, and the rich satirical detail. The novel, on the other hand, appears to have been written in a hurry and to have gone into print in a less than polished state: the text is marred by *non sequiturs* and by less than felicitous turns of phrase.

Xala represents Sembène at the height of his creative power as a filmmaker. He plays to the distinct opportunities and limitations of the medium. The film offers telling images.[20] The businessmen wear Western suits without regard to the tropical heat – except in their public display of the ousting of the French from the Chamber of Commerce. Adja, Oumi, and Rama dress in strikingly different ways. The top of the wedding cake features a European couple. A bottle of Evian water imported from France serves to wash El Hadji's Mercedes, another to fill its radiator. Many of the beggars are severely crippled. The freeze frame that concludes the film is not easily forgotten.

11 For detailed discussions of the female characters in the film, see Pfaff (1984: 150–62) and Petty (1996).

12 The film plays on the sexual attractiveness of the young bride. The camera shows her semi-nude, and it keeps coming back to her topless photo on the bedroom wall. The poster displays her naked body.

13 In the novel, El Hadji also gains status by marrying into a family of traditional notability (p. 12, 23).

14 In *Mandabi*, set among the Dakar poor, Sembène shows co-wives co-operating harmoniously in a joint household. We will return to the issue of polygamy in the next section devoted to *Tableau Ferraille*.

15 She is identified as Awa, i.e. first wife, in the novel, but referred to only as Adja Assatou in the English subtitles of the film.

16 That a modern woman such as Rama should believe in a curse, as is shown when she asks her mother whether she put the *xala* on her father, comes as a surprise.

17 Aminata Sow Fall (1979) has focused afresh on the condition of beggars in Dakar. The title of her novel, *La Grève des bàttu ou Les déchets humains*, uses the very expression, human rubbish, employed by the President in the film. Sow Fall posits that a beggars' strike is effective, in an Islamic society that prescribes the giving of alms, in countering attempts to evict the beggars from the city's central administrative and business district. Hawkins (1996) suggests that Sow Fall took up the topic of poverty addressed by Sembène in *Xala*, as well as the issue of power central to Sembène's novel *Le Dernier de l'empire*, not for lack of imagination but so as to present them from a non-Marxist perspective. Sow Fall's novel was taken to the screen by Cheick Oumar Sissoko in *Bàttu*, an international production starring Isaach de Bankolé and Danny Glover.

Betrayals of Independence

18 Sembène's suggestion of the political potential of the *lumpen proletariat* in *Xala* contrasts with the celebration of the force of the proletariat in his literary *chef-d'œuvre*, *God's Bits of Wood*. The problems entailed in the latter's classic Marxist analysis (Gugler, 1994a) may well have induced Sembène to shift to a stance identified with Frantz Fanon. Or perhaps he would argue the complementary political roles of the workers and the *lumpen*.

The unity and purpose of the beggars stands in stark contrast to the portrayal of the beggars in Luis Buñuel's *Viridiana*, even while the car washer sporting the bridal crown recalls the outcast donning the bridal crown and veil.

19 Some of the actors had worked with Sembène before, but only one professional actor participated in the film: Douta Seck gives a fine performance as the blind beggar Gorgui (Pfaff, 1984: 53), and he dominates the film poster. A highly respected *griot*, Samba Diabaré Samb, took on the role of the *griot* accompanying Gorgui and singing the songs.

20 For a discussion of Sembène's technique in *Xala*, which includes swift cutting unusual in African films, and indeed in his earlier films, see Ukadike (1994: 180–1). Mowitt draws attention to Sembène's use of false match on action cuts in order to invert and (con)fuse narrative space. He suggests that the director employs two different syntaxes that correspond to the syntaxes of French and Wolof and that 'the specific texture of *Xala* derives from the dense bilingual interplay among French and Wolof "shots"' (Mowitt, 1993: 81).

21 The novel's subplot that Adja Awa Astou came from a Catholic family, and had been alienated from her father by her marriage to a Muslim, can be seen to facilitate Christian readers' identification with her.

22 The English version of *Xala* further limits the viewer because its subtitles

Poignancy and comedy are masterfully joined in the morning-after scene. Over the dejected couple hangs the photo of N'Goné in a nude profile. The *badiène* arrives accompanied by a relative who has brought a rooster and a knife along: Wolof society, like many cultures in Africa and elsewhere, attaches paramount importance to the virginity of the bride – and the *badiène* is ready to fabricate the evidence, the bed sheet stained with the virgin's blood, if need be. The scene becomes hilarious as the anguished screams of the rooster punctuate the couple's explanations and the *badiène's* recriminations.

The film's message is blunter. While the novel has Adja Awa Astou's father, Papa Jean, and Rama's fiancé Pathé, in the film's portrayal of the bourgeoisie we do not encounter a single male character with positive attributes to match Adja and Rama. The film moves away from the nuanced characterizations of the novel to contrast the principal figures more sharply. In the novel Adja Awa Astou's son asks his father for money; in the film her children are above such entreaty. The changes in the characterization of Rama are particularly striking. In the novel Rama is playful with Pathé, in the film she invariably presents an image of principled determination. She has a Fiat automobile in the novel, but in the film she rides a moped more in line with the image of her austerity. The novel has Rama support her father in the final confrontation with the beggars, telling them to leave, but in the film it falls to Adja to defend El Hadji.

The novel provides a good deal of assistance to the foreign reader. Some is given in the text, such as the explanation that El Hadji and Adja are titles honoring men/women who have made the pilgrimage to Mecca. In addition, there are a dozen footnotes that translate, explain, and even comment. The novel thus explicitly addresses a foreign public.[21] The film, in distinct contrast, makes little effort to avoid some aspects of the story being lost on foreign viewers. The *badiène's* references to N'Goné as her daughter lead foreigner viewers to assume that she is N'Goné's mother – in fact she is the sister of her father and in accord with local custom plays the principal role in her niece's marriage. The transvestite serving at the wedding party is well known to Dakarites, but his character escapes most foreigners who thus miss the irony of his subsequent comment on El Hadji's impotence: 'There are no real men today.' Most importantly, the Wolof songs, which constitute a major co-text, are not subtitled as is the Wolof dialogue.[22]

The film omits major strands of the story. Thus the viewer misses the story of the relationship between the *badiène* and N'Goné's parents and the *badiène's* machinations that ensnare El Hadji into marrying N'Goné. Also missing from the film is the estrangement of Adja Awa Astou from her parents after her conversion from Catholicism to Islam to become Abdou Kader Bèye's first wife. Finally, the relationship between Rama and her fiancé Pathé is omitted from the film. In the novel El Hadji's ruin comes after he has seen many *marabouts*, and neglected his business for about four months; it appears sudden and less plausible in the film which compresses time and shows him visiting only two *marabouts*.[23] Reducing the number of marginal characters – El Hadji has fewer children, the Chamber of Commerce fewer members – also simplifies the viewer's task.

The film omits, but it also adds several new developments to the story. The three Frenchmen of the old Chamber of Commerce reappear: two bring attaché cases full of cash for the members of the new all-African Chamber of Commerce, and one of them becomes advisor to the Chamber's President; the third commands the police detachments. An entirely new element is introduced with the peasant who has come to the city with the savings of his village to buy supplies and the transformation of Thieli (his name means vulture) from thief to El Hadji's successor at the Chamber of Commerce. New is the arrest and deportation of the beggars and their long walk back to Dakar. The last two stories are linked by the introduction of the seller of *Kaddu* (The Voice), the Wolof newspaper Ousmane Sembène edited with Pathé Diagne.[24]

There is thus a definite contrast between the kinds of elements Sembène has omitted and added. In moving from the novel to the film he has dropped from the story major strands that focus on family relationships. And he has added new elements that make the political dimension more explicit. The reappearance of the three Frenchmen makes palpable the neo-colonialism El Hadji comes eventually to denounce.[25] The police are shown as the ready tool of the bourgeoisie: to push the masses away from the fruits of independence, to deport the beggars from the city, to keep them out of the affluent neighborhood, to imprison the relative El Hadji had dispossessed.

If a police force at the beck and call of the bourgeoisie demonstrates state support for their interests, the connection between the Chamber of Commerce and the political establishment is made explicit by the government minister and the two 'deputies' – members of parliament – in the Chamber. When one of them agrees to get a tourism promoter a government contract on condition that he receive a 15 per cent cut, we witness a form of corruption typical of the political class – though here again the rapid transaction verges on caricature.

Subtly, the film takes the viewer a couple of steps further into a critique of the political regime. Already the jubilant crowd at the take-over of the Chamber of Commerce, and the motorcade accompanying its members to El Hadji's wedding reception, suggest politicians rather than businessmen. Then repeated references to the President make us wonder whether they are aimed at the President of Senegal rather than the President of the Chamber of Commerce. The Frenchman advising the Chamber's President reminds the informed viewer of Jean Collin, a naturalized Frenchman who played an eminent role in Senegalese government from the time of independence until 1990.[26] The empty slogans about 'true socialism, African socialism' heard at the first meeting of the Chamber of Commerce parody the discourse of Léopold Sédar Senghor, the first President of Senegal.[27] Indeed, the voice of the Chamber's president has the same intonation as that of Senghor according to Pfaff (1984: 74). The Chamber of Commerce and its members thus become emblematic of the state and its leaders. El Hadji's

22 (cont.) fail to convey whether the characters use Wolof or French. Viewers unable to follow the French dialogue thus miss what the film portrays so well: most people in Senegal do not know French – after all nearly two thirds of the population is illiterate (see table on page xii) – and even among bilingual people the choice of language depends on the situation, e.g. many switch to Wolof in family settings.

23 The term *marabout* denotes a range of religious notables. El Hadji seeks out *marabouts* who have a reputation as diviners and healers.

24 A total of 23 issues of *Kaddu* were published between 1971 and 1978. They varied in size from 10 to 20 pages. The last issues, in 1976–8, included some material in languages other than Wolof: Pulaar, Serer, Mandinka, and Arabic. Since then major national newspapers have come to carry sections in Wolof and other Senegalese languages every other week.

25 We might expect the novel to confront its foreign readers with a denunciation of their complicity in neo-colonialism, and the film to direct popular opposition against the bourgeoisie and the political regime rather than a distant power well beyond its reach. There is a striking parallel here to the later work of Ngũgĩ wa Thiong'o. *Petals of Blood*, published in 1977, described the emergence of the Kenyan bourgeoisie. Only three years later, *Caitaani Mũtharaba-inĩ* – expressly written, in language and in style, to be accessible to a broader, local public – embraced the neo-colonialism thesis, denouncing multinational companies in an allegorical mode (Gugler, 1994b). Perhaps both authors felt that popular wrath is more easily raised against a regime controlled by foreigners, that nationalism is a more potent force than class consciousness.

The distinguished Cameroonian writer Mongo Beti denounced French neo-colonialism in his country in a series of gripping novels. They have

Ousmane Sembène directing

25 (cont.) their counterpart in Jean-Marie Teno's documentary *Africa, I Will Fleece You.*

26 Jesus Christ, as Senegalese referred to Jean Collin, drawing on his initials, was extremely powerful by all accounts. In Senegal, he elicited strong emotions, for and against. For a discussion of his record, see Diop and Diouf (1990: 103–13).

27 At the inauguration of the Chambre de Commerce d'Industrie et d'Artisanat de la Région du Cap-Vert, Senghor (1970: 25, my translation) spoke of 'our socialism, national and democratic, realistic and humanistic at the same time.'

accusations expose not just the impotence of Senegalese businessmen but the political impotence of the newly independent nation. *Xala* becomes an acerbic critique of the new African elite, the inheritors of independence.

The images of the abrupt takeover of the Chamber of Commerce by Africans can be seen to stand for the political takeover by Africans that came with independence in 1960. The opening scene can then be understood to convey the exuberance and the joyous expectations at independence, if in the guise of tourist folklore.[28] The ejection of an assortment of political symbols of the colonial order from the Chamber of Commerce, and their careful recovery by Frenchmen who soon will reappear in the roles of advisor and police officer, now take on their full political significance. If the advisor is deferential,[29] this deference conceals his effective power as a representative of the French government which dominates newly independent Senegal, a small and desperately poor country, which accepted dependence on economic and technical assistance and even welcomed a French garrison.[30] This political domination complements the power wielded by well-entrenched French business interests.

Once the film is seen as a denunciation of not just the economic but the political regime, the peasant and his pronouncements, introduced into the film, take on their full significance. It is not just that the latest

We're all crabs in the same basket.

recruit to the Chamber of Commerce robbed a peasant; the entire political economy is geared toward the neglect and even outright exploitation of the peasantry, the large majority of Senegalese citizens, and the most severely deprived.

As Sembène exposes the political system, he also takes aim at its ideology. With sarcasm he dismisses the ideas of *négritude* closely linked to the poet-President Senghor, one of the principal founders of the *négritude* movement in the 1930s – along with its affirmation of pride in black culture and heritage, it tended to postulate a distinct African essence. The members of the Chamber of Commerce boast about their '*africanité*' as they congratulate El Hadji on his third marriage. And one of the guests at the wedding party tells of his last trip to Europe: he had gone to Switzerland rather than to Spain where there are all too many Africans: '*la négritude, hé! ça voyage*' ('*négritude*, hey! it gets around') is the ironic comment. Masks from distant cultures are used, or rather abused: a Mossi mask from Burkina Faso serves as an object of decoration in the President's office, a Yoruba mask from Nigeria is employed to collect the ballots at the Chamber of Commerce.

Instead of the undifferentiated slogans of *négritude*, Sembène posits a selective approach to both the African and the Western heritage. Rama

El Hadji Abdou Kader Bèye denounces the neo-colonial order at the Chamber of Commerce

28 Okore (1982: 268-70) details how the ten opening scenes establish the shift from nationalist leaders ascending to power and being celebrated by the people to their betrayal of the masses. If at the beginning they appear in popular dress, they will appear in Western suits ever after. The scene of police pushing the celebrants from the freshly installed elite has its parallel in the classic passage from Chinua Achebe's *A Man of the People* that serves as the epigraph for this chapter.

29 The very name of the advisor, Dupont-Durand, as common in France as Baker-Smith, conveys that he appears not as an individual but as the anonymous representative of France.

Betrayals of Independence

30 Two decades later, in *Guelwaar*, Sembène went on to denounce the beggar mentality, corruption, and political manipulation fostered by foreign aid.

31 A third poster in Rama's room pays homage to Charlie Chaplin – with it, we may surmise, Sembène claims his heritage as film director and as the advocate of the little man. Elsewhere in the house, a poster advertises Sembène's first major feature film, *Black Girl*. And in the hallway, a poster of Jimi Hendrix reminds us of the African diaspora's impact on Western music.

32 That the cultural significance of the final scene is quite similar to Western understandings, is attested to by Sembène: 'You spit because you detest him [El Hadji] ... to spit on the misery ... to spit on the bourgeoisie ... to spit, that's [an expression of] disgust' (McIntosh 1991: 140). He has, however, been contradicted on this very point (Pfaff, 1984: 47).

33 Senegal has been notable for its political stability and a certain degree of political openness. The Socialist Party managed to predominate in the regularly held elections for four decades, at times inviting opposition leaders to join the government. In 1981 Senghor passed the presidency on to his chosen successor, Abdou Diouf. Finally, in 2000, Senegal became one of the very rare African countries where the leader of the opposition, Abdoulaye Wade, acceded to the presidency through regular elections.

Manipulations such as characterize many African elections are depicted in Henri Joseph Koumba Bididi's *The Elephant Balls*. The story takes the form of a comedy laced with a large dose of cynicism. Such an approach may reach a larger public than a direct denunciation. And it probably was the only option in the political context of Gabon where the film was produced in the national studios, and where the story is clearly situated.

34 The threat that financial support would be withheld and/or the film

brings the ideals of such a synthesis alive. She makes do (in the film) with a moped, shakes hands with Modu, El Hadji's driver, refuses to drink Evian water with her father, wears African-style dress, works on the orthography of Wolof, insists on speaking Wolof, and denounces polygamy. The posters in her room claim the heritage of the anti-colonial struggles of Samory Touré and Amílcar Cabral.[31] When she confronts her father in his office, the camera focuses on her dress: it reproduces the national colors, and they match those of a map behind her, a map of an undivided Africa – in contrast to maps of Africa with its borders inherited from colonialism next to her father and at the Chamber of Commerce. The concern she expresses about her mother may also be heard as her concern about mother Africa.

The film ends with a 24-second freeze frame of the beggars spitting on the naked El Hadji.[32] We have watched such a cleansing before when, in *Fools*, Zamani found, perhaps, his redemption. Here we are similarly left to wonder how far the exorcism of El Hadji's *xala* will reach. Will his regained potency translate beyond the family into a new role in business? Or in the political arena? And we are led to ask: if the wretched of the earth, to use the phrase coined by Fanon, can curse and cleanse, are they a political force to be reckoned with? The novel seems to preclude such a revolutionary prospect as the police outside the house raise their weapons into firing position at the end.

How to explain the shift in emphasis from the denunciation of the Senegalese bourgeoisie in the novel to an attack on the political regime and a suggestion of revolt? The threat of persecution or censorship does not provide a ready explanation. In the first decade after independence, and indeed subsequently, the Senegalese authorities tolerated a level of dissent unheard of in most African countries.[33] Whatever Sembène might write, he was unlikely to be subjected to persecution. As for censorship, it was less of a threat to a novel published in France than to a film produced and to be shown in Senegal – as was soon to become evident.

There was, however, another problem: Sembène needed to secure funding to produce the film. He had started out writing a filmscript. While waiting to find funding for his film, he transformed his script into the novel. Subsequently, from the novel he developed a new script for the film. A novel that attacked the political regime explicitly might have jeopardized the financial support Sembène was seeking.[34] The Société Nationale de Cinéma had been established in 1972. Two years later four films were released that had been produced with its support, *Xala* among them. Sembène had begun shooting without outside support, and his reputation was such that the National Film Institute agreed to participate in the financing without a review of the script (Vieyra, 1983: 87).

A second explanation for the shift between the novel and the film focuses on the different audiences Sembène was seeking to reach. In the early 1960s, Sembène had turned to the film medium so as to reach a wider African public. In 1968 he had produced *Mandabi* in two versions, one in French, the other in Wolof, the language widely used throughout most of Senegal. In *Xala* he introduces some Wolof dialogue and advertises

Kaddu, omits the translations, explanations, and comment the novel provides for the foreign reader, and makes subtle references to the political context in Senegal that are lost on the foreign viewer. That the film seeks first and foremost to reach a large Senegalese public becomes all the more evident when we take into account the songs accompanying the scenes featuring the beggars.

These songs intertwine proverbs, popular sayings, and metaphors. They are sung by the *griot* who accompanies Gorgui, the blind beggar. While the novel and most of the dialogue in the film are in French, the *griot* sings in Wolof. He repeats his songs so that they stay with the audience, or rather, with those viewers that understand them: the songs, unlike the Wolof dialogue, are not subtitled. For Senegalese viewers the songs constitute a major co-text. Their lyrics, written by Sembène (Ghali, 1976: 90), sharpen the political message of the film. They move from the denunciation of the lizard, the epitome of autocratic rule, to praise for the lion, the symbol of selflessness and courage, and a revolutionary call for Senegalese viewers to oppose their ruler. Outside El Hadji's office, just after Thiely has robbed the peasant, the *griot*'s song chastises the new rulers whose autocratic conception of government is reminiscent of the lizard who brooks nobody else around him:

A ruler should not be like a lizard.
The lizard's character is no good.
If you follow him, he complains that you are stepping on his tail.
If you walk side by side with him, he questions your pretense to be his equal.
And if you walk ahead of him, you hear him say, you are scaring away my insects.[35]

He sings of the necessity and the inevitability of change, equates inaction with worthlessness, and extols the courage of the lion:

Instead of crying, you have to find a solution for your problems.
The cursed ones are those whose offspring are worthless.
For everything there is a season.
Everybody will have their turn.
The lion cannot be deprived of the object of his desire for lack of courage.

As the beggars march to El Hadji's villa to exact retribution, the *griot*'s song reinforces the metaphor of the lion whose determination and courage will triumph over the lizard:

The lion is courageous.
The lion is honest.
The lion cannot be deprived of the object of his desire for lack of courage.

The authorities let the film be shown in Senegal but imposed ten cuts.[36] Senegalese audiences were not to see the unceremonious removal of the bust of Marianne, the symbol of the French Republic, from the Chamber of Commerce; the Frenchman ordering police to push back the crowd in front of the Chamber; the members of the Chamber opening their attaché cases to find them stuffed with cash; the Frenchman

34 (cont.) would be censored appears to have weighed on Sembène when the film was shot. According to Samba Dione (1994), the resemblance between the actor playing the European commanding a police detachment and Collin, who was Minister of the Interior for more than ten years, was too close for comfort: his appearance was changed and the two scenes shot again. Still, his appearances had to be cut before the government allowed the film to be shown in Senegal.

35 The text of this free translation by Oumar Cherif Diop differs from the summary given by Sembène in an interview (Ghali, 1976: 90) in phrasing but not in message.

36 If the cuts imposed on *Xala* indicate that the authorities were less than pleased with the product they had financed in large part, they nevertheless provided support for *Ceddo*, Sembène's next production (Vieyra, 1983: 95) – but then the release of that film in turn was held up for several years.
Contrast this censorship of *Xala* and *Ceddo* with the encouragement then Burkinabé President Thomas Sankara gave Gaston Kaboré to make *Zan Boko* which denounces the greed of the nouveaux riches, corruption, the abuse of power – and government censorship of television (Diawara, n.d.).

Betrayals of Independence

conducting the police raid on the beggars; El Hadji's statement to the members of the Chambers that they had the police and the army in their pockets; Gorgui lecturing Adja Awa Astou that prisoners are happier than peasants, fishermen, and workers; and the call to revolt which closes the film (Hennebelle, 1976). The authorities' *diktat* proved false the member of parliament's sarcastic comment, after El Hadji had denounced his fellow members at the Chamber of Commerce, that here they had democracy. Sembène responded by distributing flyers that detailed the scenes that had been cut.[37]

In his novel *Xala*, Sembène introduces the foreign reader to family relations among the Dakar upper-middle class even as he ridicules and denounces these *arrivistes* of early post-colonial days. In his film, Sembène departs from the novel to create powerful images and introduce song. And he recasts his story to reach first and foremost a Senegalese audience. He denounces not only the pseudo-bourgeoisie but also the political leaders in the neo-colonial order a decade after independence and calls for revolutionary change. Sembène has continued to expose and denounce, to present less than flattering mirrors to his two audiences: his Senegalese fellow citizens and their former colonial masters.

37 *Xala* was a success. In the Senegalese ratings it came second in 1975 (Murphy, 2000: 98). According to Sembène, the film's impact was such that nobody drove a Mercedes in Dakar for three months after its release (Delmas and Delmas, 1976).

References and Further Reading

Achebe, Chinua. 1966. *A Man of the People*. London: Heinemann.

Africa, I Will Fleece You/Afrique, je te plumerai. 1992. Documentary written, directed, and produced by Jean-Marie Teno. Cameroon. Distributed in the U.S. by California Newsreel. 88 minutes.

Amin, Samir. 1969. *Le Monde des affaires Sénégalaises*. Paris: Editions de Minuit.

Anonymous. 1968. 'Le mystère de la Chambre de Commerce, d'Agriculture et d'Industrie de Dakar.' *Africa* 43: 15–19, 69.

Bàttu. 2000. Film directed by Cheick Oumar Sissoko, written by Joslyn Barnes. Produced by Emet Films (France). 105 minutes.

Beti, Mongo (Alexandre Biyidi). 1974 *Perpétue et l'habitude du malheur*. Paris: Editions Buchet/Chastel. English translation by John Reed and Clive Wake (1978) *Perpetua and the Habit of Unhappiness*. African Writers Series. London: Heinemann.

——. 1974. *Remember Ruben*. Paris: Union Générale d'Editions. English translation by Gerald Moore (1979) *Remember Ruben*. African Writers Series, London/Nairobi; Ibadan: New Horn Press; Washington D.C.: Three Continents Press.

——. 1979. *La Ruine presque cocasse d'un polichinelle (Remember Ruben 2)*. Paris: Editions des Peuples Noirs. Serialized in *Peuples Noirs – Peuples africains* from 1978 to 1979. English translation by Richard Bjornson (1985) *Lament for an African Pol*. Washington, D.C.: Three Continents Press.

——. 1983. *Les Deux mères de Guillaume Ismaël Dzewatama, futur camionneur*. Paris: Editions Buchet/Chastel. Serialized in *Peuples Noirs – Peuples africains* from 1981 to 1982.

——. 1984. *La Revanche de Guillaume Ismaël Dzewatama*. Paris: Editions Buchet/Chastel. Serialized in *Peuples Noirs – Peuples africains* from 1983 to 1984.

Black Girl/La Noire de... 1966. Film written and directed by Ousmane Sembène. Produced by Les Actualités Françaises (France) and Filmi Doomireew (Senegal). Distributed in the U.S. by New Yorker Films. 60 minutes.

Boone, Catherine. 1992. *Merchant Capital and the Roots of State Power in Senegal 1930–1985*. Cambridge Studies in Comparative Politics. Cambridge/New York/Melbourne: Cambridge University Press.

Borom Sarret. 1963. Film written and directed by Ousmane Sembène. Produced by Filmi Doomireew (Senegal) and Actualités Françaises (France). Distributed in the U.S. by New Yorker Films. 22 minutes.

Ceddo. 1976. Film written and directed by Ousmane Sembène. Produced by Filmi Doomireew (Senegal). Distributed in the U.S. by New Yorker Films. 120 minutes.

Cruise O'Brien, Rita. 1979. 'Foreign Ascendance in the Economy and State,' in Rita Cruise O'Brien (ed.) *The Political Economy of Underdevelopment: Dependence in Senegal*. Sage Series on African Modernization and Development 3. Beverly Hills/London: Sage Publications. 100–25.

Delmas, Jean, and Ginette Delmas.1976. 'Ousmane Sembène: 'Un film est un débat'.' *Jeune Cinéma* 99: 13–17.

Diagne, Issa, and Joel Decupper. 1974. 'La Chambre de Commerce de Dakar va-t-elle continuer à jouer les inutilités?' *Africa* 68: 29, 31, 35.

Diawara, Manthia. n.d. 1991. 'The Place Where the Past Lies Buried.' *Library of African Cinema: A Guide to Video Resources for Colleges and Public Libraries*. San Franciso: Resolution Inc./California Newsreel. 17–18.

Dione, Samba. 1994. Personal communication.

Diop, Momor Coumba, and Mamadou Diouf. 1990. *Le Sénégal sous Abdou Diouf: Etat et Société*. Paris: Editions Karthala.

The Elephant Balls/Les Couilles de l'éléphant. 2000. Film directed by Henri Joseph Koumba Bididi, written by Henri Joseph Koumba Bididi, Pauline Sales, and Jean-Michel Isabel. Produced by the Centre National du Cinéma du Gabon, Terre Africaine (Cameroon), and Adélaïde Productions (France). 98 minutes.

Faat Kine. 1999. Film written and directed by Ousmane Sembène. Produced by Filmi Doomireew (Senegal). Distributed in the U.S. by New Yorker Films and California Newsreel. 118 minutes.

Fall, Aminata Sow. 1979. *La Grève des bàttu ou Les déchets humains*. Dakar: Les Nouvelles Editions Africaines. English translation by Dorothy S. Blair (1986) *The Beggars' Strike, or, The Dregs of Society*. Harlow: Longman.

Fanon, Frantz. 1961. *Les Damnés de la terre*. Cahiers Libres 27–28. Paris: François Maspero, English translation by Constance Farrington (1963) *The Wretched of the Earth*. New York: Grove Press.

Ghali, Noureddine. 1976. 'Ousmane Sembène, entretien.' *Cinéma* 208: 83–95. English translation by John D. H. Downing (1987) 'An interview with Sembene Ousmane,' in John D. H. Downing (ed.) *Film and Politics in the Third World*. Brooklyn, NY: Autonomedia. 41–54.

Guelwaar. 1992. Film written and directed by Ousmane Sembène. Produced by Filmi Doomireew (Senegal), Galatée Films (France), and FR3 Film Production (France). Distributed in the U.S. by New Yorker Films. 105 minutes.

Gugler, Josef. 1994a. 'African Literature and the Uses of Theory,' in Josef Gugler, Hans-Jürgen Lüsebrink, and Jürgen Martini (eds) *Literary Theory and African Literature. Théorie littéraire et littérature africaine*. Beiträge zur Afrikaforschung 3. Münster/Hamburg: LIT Verlag. 1–15.

——. 1994b. 'How Ngũgĩ wa Thiong'o Shifted from Class Analysis to a Neo-Colonialist Perspective.' *Journal of Modern African Studies* 32: 329–39.

——, and Oumar Cherif Diop. 1998. 'Ousmane Sembène's *Xala*: The Novel, the Film, and Their Audiences,' *Research in African Literatures* 29: 147–58.

Hawkins, Peter. 1996. 'Marxist Intertext, Islamic Reinscription? Some Common Themes in the Novels of Sembène Ousmane and Aminata Sow Fall,' in Laïla Ibnlfassi and Nicki Hitchcott (eds) *African Francophone Writing: A Critical Introduction*. Oxford/Washington, D.C.: Berg. 163–9.

Hennebelle, Guy. 1976. 'Le cinéma de Sembène Ousmane.' *Ecran* 43: 41–50.

Mandabi (The Money Order). 1968. Film written and directed by Ousmane Sembène Produced by Comptoir Français du Film (France) and Filmi Doomireew (Senegal). Distributed in the U.S. by New Yorker Films. 90 minutes.

McIntosh, Yvonne Elizabeth. 1991. 'African Literature Through the Camera's Eye'. Ph.D. dissertation, Florida State University.

Mowitt, John. 1993. 'Sembene Ousmane's *Xala*: Postcoloniality and Foreign Film Languages.' *camera obscura* 31: 73–94.

Murphy, David. 2000. *Sembene: Imagining Alternatives in Film and Fiction*. Oxford: James Currey; Trenton, NJ/Asmara: Africa World Press.

Ngũgĩ wa Thiong'o. 1977. *Petals of Blood*. London: Heinemann; New York: E. P. Dutton.

——. 1980. *Caitaani Mūtharaba–inĩ*. Nairobi: Heinemann. English translation by the author (1982) *Devil on the Cross*. London/Ibadan/Nairobi: Heinemann.

Okore, Ode. 1982. The Film World of Ousmane Sembène. Ph.D. dissertation, Columbia University.

Petty, Sheila. 1996. 'Towards a Changing Africa: Women's Roles in the Films of Ousmane Sembène,' in Sheila Petty (ed.) *A Call to Action: the Films of Ousmane Sembène*. Westport, CT: Praeger; Trowbridge: Flicks Books. 67–86.

Pfaff, Françoise. 1984. *The Cinema of Ousmane Sembene, A Pioneer of African Film*. Contributions in Afro-American and African Studies 79. Westport, CT: Greenwood Press.

——. 1988. *Twenty-Five Black African Film makers: A Critical Study, with Filmography and Bio-bibliography*. New York: Greenwood Press.

Rosenbaum, Jonathan. 1993. 'A Cinema of Uncertainty: Films by Michelangelo Atonioni,' *Chicago Reader*, 9 April. Reprinted in Jonathan Rosenbaum (1995) *Placing Movies: the Practice of Film Criticism*. Berkeley/Los Angeles/London: University of California Press. 307–14.

Sembène, Ousmane. (1962) 1960. *God's Bits of Wood*. Garden City, NY: Doubleday. Translation by Francis Price of *Les Bouts de bois de Dieu: Banty mam yall*. Paris: Le Livre Contemporain.

——. 1973. *Xala*. Paris: Présence Africaine. English translation by Clive Wake (1976) *Xala*. London: Heinemann; Westport, CT: Lawrence Hill.

——. 1981. *Le Dernier de l'empire: roman sénégalais*. 2 volumes. Paris: L'Harmattan. English translation by Adrian Adams (1983) *The Last of the Empire: A Senegalese Novel*. London/Ibadan/Nairobi: Heinemann.

Senghor, Léopold Sédar. 1970. Discourse at the inauguration of the Chambre de Commerce, d'Industrie et d'Artisanat de la Région du Cap-Vert. *Bulletin* 1 (2): 23–28.

Serceau, Michel. 1995. 'Le cinéma d'Afrique noire francophone face au modèle occidental: la rançon du refus.' *iris* 18: 39–46.

Ukadike, Nwachukwu Frank. 1994. *Black African Cinema*. Berkeley/Los Angeles/London: University of California Press.

Vieyra, Paulin Soumanou. 1983. *Le Cinéma au Sénégal*. Brussels: OCIC/L'Harmattan.

Viridiana. 1961. Film directed by Luis Buñuel, written by Luis Buñuel and Julio Alajandro. Produced by Uninci Films 59 (Spain). 90 minutes.

Weaver, Harold D., Jr. 1972. 'Film-Makers Have a Great Responsibility to Our People: An Interview with Ousmane Sembene,' *Cineaste* 6 (1): 27–31.

Woll, Josephine. 2004. 'The Russian Connection: Soviet Cinema and the Cinema of Francophone Africa.' *Focus on African Film*, edited by Françoise Pfaff. Bloomington: Indiana University Press.

Xala/The Curse. 1974. Film written and directed by Ousmane Sembène. Produced by Société Nationale de Cinématographie (Senegal) and Films Domirev (Senegal). Distributed in the U.S. by New Yorker Films. 123 minutes.

Zan Boko. 1988. Film written and directed by Gaston Kaboré. Produced by Bras de Fer (Burkina Faso). Distributed in the U.S. by California Newsreel. 94 minutes.

Tableau Ferraille 1997
The Rise and Abrupt Fall of an Honest Politician

In this film I want to say: 'Africa wake up. You are being asked to go too fast.' Africa has taken a train without knowing where it goes. I would prefer to wait for another train where we find our place and where we know the destination.

Africa ought to be the last defense of a world in danger, the last zone of refuge for humanity, where we can recover the values lost in post-modern civilization. Africa should not join this race. If Daam failed it is because he had been asked to be ferocious and to go fast. Africa has to find its proper system. That requires courage.

(Moussa Sene Absa in an interview with Barlet, 1998, my translation)

Betrayals of Independence

Moussa Sene Absa's *Tableau Ferraille* is set in Tableau Ferraille, a real life fishing village that was transformed into a poor suburb of Dakar, now a city of two million, where the director was born and grew up.[1] The name, taken from the local bus stop at a junk yard, might be translated as Junk Yard Station. Beyond Tableau Ferraille the film introduces us to the mansion of a government minister, and to the kind of restaurant and nightclub the tiny elite and tourists enjoy.

Like *Xala*, *Tableau Ferraille* tells of corruption and polygamy in Senegal. But the context of corruption has changed by the 1990s, and the motivation for polygamy is different in this story. Daam Diagne, happily married to Gagnesiri, takes Kiné as his second wife not for social status but so that she will bear him children.[2] Even more than El Hadji in *Xala*, Daam is portrayed as a weak man at the mercy of women. He might have found a devoted wife to give him children instead of letting himself be seduced by the sex appeal of Kiné.[3] Once again, Eve brings about the downfall of Adam. However, *Tableau Ferraille*, unlike *Xala*, does not reject polygamy.[4]

By the 1990s the political, economic, and cultural hegemony of French neo-colonialism denounced in *Xala* has become less salient. Africans make their own decisions now, even if they draw on the economic support of rich countries and accept the strings attached, even if foreign ideologies hold sway. Now a government minister, despairing of the 'chaos' of present-day Africa, recalls with nostalgia how Africans used to be proud even if they were colonial subjects, marching under the French flag, and singing the French anthem. Daam has made a commitment to 'extract Africa from the chaos,' but he does not articulate its symptoms and causes. Still, he and his assistant Gora are honest politicians. And they are successful. Daam is elected to the National Assembly and soon after appointed Minister of Development. Daam negotiates an aid package from Germany; Gora reconciles employers and unions; they both press for increased employment. In Sene Absa's telling, however, their story cannot have a happy ending in the context of contemporary Africa. We soon learn that Daam's fellow ministers are corrupt. But the villains of the story are the local entrepreneur nicknamed President, his Lebanese associate Diop Dollar, and his assistant Ndiaye Civilisé (Civilized Ndiaye). Daam is no match for them. They fob him off with promises that they will expand employment. Daam's attempt to defend Anta's daughter Ndoumbé falters and he leaves her with 'We have all to do our bit' – she will throw that phrase back at Daam in the end when, in his despair, he asks her to join him to denounce the man who ruined them both. President proclaims, in English, 'Time is money,' and his ideological pedigree is graphically conveyed when he presents an Uncle Sam carving – the only white face in the entire film – to Daam's first-born. President is a manager in the American mold who fires workers attempting to unionize and thus drives Ndoumbé into prostitution. He takes advantage of the weakness of African government to enrich himself through corrupt practices. The disastrous political and domestic choices of Daam converge when President, the man he let manage the factory, bribes Kiné, the

1 Daam's references to *Tableau Ferraille* as his 'village' are not descriptive but may be understood as expressions of belonging.

2 The cultural prescription that a man must have children similarly motivates Modou to take a second wife in Mariama Bâ's classic novel *So Long a Letter*, also set in Dakar.

A third motivation for polygamy, economic advantage, is illustrated by the second marriage of Biraama, the husband of Gagnesiri's friend Anta. In rural Africa, labor rather than land used to be, and often still is, the principal constraint on production. Women commonly carry the larger share of agricultural work. Hence the contribution of additional wives to the household's productive capability is an important consideration. In urban settings the earning opportunities for women tend to be more circumscribed, while they may, like Kiné, and Oumi in *Xala*, press for increased consumption. The economic advantage to Biraama apparently derives from his second wife's father rather than from her.

3 If on Gagnesiri's wedding night the couple's bloodied bed sheet is publicly displayed, for the reasons set out in the discussion of *Xala*, we are left to wonder what transpired on Kiné's wedding night.

4 Sene Absa proudly affirmed that his is a polygamous marriage at the African and Creole Film Festival in Montréal in 1997 – to the dismay of many in his audience (Castiel, 1997).

woman he let himself be seduced by. They compromise the politician who could not be corrupted, but who was weak. With President *Tableau Ferraille* denounces the free market ideology foisted on Africa by Western policy makers and the international agencies they control.

Tableau Ferraille, like *Xala*, highlights class differences. The shacks of Tableau Ferraille contrast with the minister's villa. Gagnesiri's friend Anta cannot pay a debt of CFA5,000, then about $10, while Kiné is offered a CFA100 million bribe and eventually has CFA150 million, equal to about $300,000, waiting for her in a Swiss bank account. The general climate of corruption is strikingly conveyed by the opportunism of the Baax Yaaj, the Women's Council of First Wives: they invite the wife of the freshly elected member of parliament to join them, but reject her when the machinations of President have brought her husband's career to an abrupt end. Even the time-honored profession of the *griot* has been perverted: neither historian nor collective conscience, he sings the praises of whoever is in the ascendant. And the citizenry of Tableau Ferraille follows whoever has power and money. As Gagnesiri laments, 'Money destroys people.'[5]

Xala suggested that the oppressed could put an end to corruption and extreme inequality. A different message may be decoded from the symbolism surrounding Gagnesiri and Daam. Unlike Rama in *Xala*, Gagnesiri appears rather passive, even as she affirms herself on a few occasions: insisting on stopping at the cemetery, berating Daam for his weakness in dealing with President, scolding Kiné for heavy drinking when pregnant, assaulting Kiné who has infringed on her conjugal rights, demanding that the women's association respect her as a woman if not a mother. Only at the very end does Gagnesiri take decisive action. She surprises us with a decision we did not anticipate from the village girl devoted to her husband. Having meditated on the grave of her friend Anta, and reviewed her past with Daam, she abandons him to join the chorus. We are left to ponder the significance of this turn of events. We may see the pure village girl representing a young Africa that prepares for a different future. She could not procreate with Daam, she could not create the new Africa with the man of modernity – trained overseas, seeking foreign aid, endorsing the contract awarded to competent people graduated from the best foreign universities. Daam is a naïve man who fails to fully apprehend the corruption around him; a weak man unable to confront President until it is too late. A man who has failed.

Tableau Ferraille may be literally translated as 'picture of scrap iron.' But as with *Xala* we may see a double meaning in the title of this film which tells of the wrecked expectations of independence. As Sene Absa tells it, the progress of Africa has not been stymied by technical problems, the failure is moral. When Gagnesiri joins the chorus, Senegalese viewers will already have identified them as Baye Fall,[6] a sub-branch of the Mouride Sufi order that emphasizes the spiritual value of work and submission to a religious leader.[7] And throughout the film they will have seen Sene Absa leading the chorus.[8] A dignified woman joining a group of men who are renowned for their religious commitment, hard work,

5 Chinua Achebe's novel *A Man of the People* remains the classic account of the pervasive corruption of African politics: the government minister is corrupt, the teacher is full of disdain for corrupt politicians but can easily be co-opted, and the villagers are ready to support whoever provides them with a share of the spoils. In the Nigerian context, foreign interests were marginal to these politics of patronage even in the early post-independence period.

6 The Baye Fall are distinguished by their clothing and dreadlocks, and the sessions in which they chant litanies are popular on religious occasions (Villalón, 1995: 167, 169). Sene Absa is a Baye Fall himself, and he directed a documentary on the Mourides, *Jef Jel*.

7 Touba, the religious city the Mourides established in the Senegalese countryside, the seat of their leader and the destination of their annual pilgrimage, demonstrates their economic success and their religious fervor.

8 Sena Absa started out as an actor in theater and film, and he assisted Djibril Diop Mambety. He has characterized his profession thus: 'I am not a cinéaste, a musician, a painter... I communicate, that's all!' (Duchesne, 1997, my translation)

Betrayals of Independence

Gora Junior, here's your present.
It's Uncle Sam.

Uncle Sam, President, Ndiaye Civilisé, and Daam around Gagnesiri's baby

and austerity, and indeed their economic success, promises renewal. We are left to wonder where they are headed as they set course for the open sea, while the chant that accompanied Gagnesiri continues to haunt us.

Sene Absa appears to pay homage to *Xala* when he names Gagnesiri's mother and Kiné's daughter for Rama, who promised a better future in Ousmane Sembène's novel and film. And indeed, both directors denounce the corruption of post-colonial Senegal.[9] But they present altogether different images and propose alternative paths to a better future. The college student Rama was a modern woman who selectively reaffirms her African heritage; twenty years later the college graduate Kiné presents a decadent and corrupt modernity. While *Xala* sought to raise the masses, in *Tableau Ferraille* the Mourides incarnate the prospect of a better future. If Sembène called for political change, Sene Absa seeks moral renewal on the basis of modern Islam.

Throughout *Tableau Ferraille* the chorus, led by Sene Absa, comments on the action and establishes moods. If the songs in *Xala* called for revolution, now the Wolof lyrics by Sene Absa call for remorse. The film starts out with a woman's lament 'Blues d'une femme' (A Woman's Blues) addressed to her child. In the middle section she sings:

9 Both directors appear weary of the tourism that is more significant in Senegal than in any other West African country. In *Xala* the kickback deal involves a tourism project, and in *Tableau Ferraille* the ne'er-do-well Biraama makes money in the tourism trade.

I carried you [on my back], and I fed you.
I did everything to make you happy.
I spilt my [virgin] blood.
Today I am asking, did you deserve it?
Chorus:
Why have you forgotten me?
Why did you leave me?

Now there are no more excuses.
Everything is clear.

Do we hear African mothers in despair over what their sons made of independent Africa?

While the film turns melodramatic on Friday, the day of evil spirits, Ndoumbé parading as a prostitute and Daam drowning his sorrows at the Bar of Lost Souls, the chorus urges:

Tableau Ferraille, it's time to get up.
Nothing is left in Tableau Ferraille...
Nothing is left in Tableau Ferraille...
Remember our grandeur.
And look what's left now.

When Gagnesiri leaves the cemetery, the boy who has been her silent witness, asks what he should tell Daam. As Gagnesiri sets out to sea with the Baye Fall, a woman's voice and the chorus reply with a song of love, the 'Blues à Tableau Ferraille.' Towards the end they sing:

Tell him that I have gone...
I disappear before it is too late.
But I leave him my love,
I leave him my heart, my youth, and my [virgin] blood.
Tell him that I leave, but that I will never forget him,
What I lived with him is priceless.[10]

Tableau Ferraille assumes rather sophisticated audiences.[11] The story is presented as a series of flashbacks as Gagnesiri recalls the past at the grave of her friend Anta, a construction that sets *Tableau Ferraille* apart from any other film we consider here, except for South Africa's *Mapantsula*. Here, too, the flashbacks include scenes Gagnesiri did not witness. Unlike many African films, *Tableau Ferraille* is fast-paced. And the chorus, which accompanies the rapid transitions, is without parallel in African film, although it recalls Woody Allen's *Mighty Aphrodite* released a couple of years earlier.

Tableau Ferraille aims for a broad public. Sene Absa acknowledges the influence of Western and of Indian film. He relates *Tableau Ferraille* to the storyline of Westerns: the dreams and innocence of the good man who is destroyed by society, the bad guys, and a love. He follows Indian film in seeking to please and seduce with beautiful music, magnificent actors, and technical perfection (Barlet, 1997). *Tableau Ferraille* is one of the very few African films to feature a music superstar, Ismaël Lô in the role of Daam Diagne.[12] He dominates the poster. At a time when their relationship is overshadowed by his second marriage, he serenades Gagnesiri 'This song comes from the bottom of my heart....'[13] And Sene Absa, who is a painter, makes remarkable use of color. This may have been decisive in garnering the film the Prize for Photography at FESPACO 1997. Sada Niang (1999) argues that with its theatrical dialogue, its

10 This translation of the songs by Sophie Diagne and Josef Gugler differs from the English subtitles.

11 Sene Absa promotes *Le Cafard Libéré*, the humourous, well-informed, and critical weekly modeled on the famous French *Le Canard Enchaîné*, as he shows it, rather implausibly, as the only paper people rely on for the news.

12 *La Vie est belle* is altogether focused on Papa Wemba.

13 Mansour Sora Wade's documentary *Iso Lô* follows the star on a concert tour across West Africa and retraces his career. His first screen appearance was in Ousmane Sembène's *Camp de Thiaroye* as the soldier playing a guitar.

Let there be no tears.

Daam presents food to the leader of the chorus, Moussa Sene Absa

music ranging from traditional religious tunes to contemporary popular music to jazz, its scorching social critique, and its poetic images, the film achieves a delicate balance between the carefree, grounded style of Djibril Diop Mambety and the caustic manicheanism of Ousmane Sembène.

The grace and emotional depth of Ndèye Fatou Ndaw, in the role of Gagnesiri, Daam's first wife, are remarkable. A high school student, she had dropped by at the film's casting. Her startling beauty is showcased in a variety of superb dresses and emphasized in a number of close-ups. She is featured on the poster. If there were a sizeable film industry in tropical Africa, she might well have become the region's first movie star. Instead more lucrative opportunities lured her to Europe where she now works as a model (Wonogo, 1997; Sene Absa, 2002). She remains poised throughout the film, except when she assaults Kiné. Her performance contrasts with that of the other actors who convincingly portray their characters in a realistic fashion. As she sets out to sea with the chorus, Sene Absa has a classic diva send a symbolic message about one strand of modern Islam.

Tableau Ferraille, sponsored by a European television network and French governmental and non-governmental agencies, reaches out to Western audiences. The film presents them with memorable scenes of music and dance on Gagnesiri's wedding night, a colorful market at the picturesque fish landing, a night club. It focuses on the – polygamous –

nuclear family: the final song refers to Daam as his mother's last son (the subtitle is an error) but his siblings never appear. The subplot about the radioactive waste shipped by President's business associates in the U.S., and disposed of by ignorant cart drivers, appears to respond to Western preoccupations, even if it has real life referents in Africa.[14] And the contrast between the Statue of Liberty U.S.A. 1994 painted on the cemetery wall and the cart driver's revelation invites U.S. viewers to consider the discrepancy between their ideology and the reality of U.S. involvement in Africa. While the characters use Wolof as well as French, francophone audiences are helped by French being used in some unlikely contexts, such as Gagnesiri's village.

Western viewers are apt to miss the extent to which Daam and Gagnesiri are propelled by their emotions to transgress local norms. Non-Muslim audiences are likely to miss the full import of the impropriety of a woman of Gagnesiri's age entering the cemetery, even if the film gives some clues: the comment of the cart driver and the earlier scene of the burial of Anta, when both Gagnesiri and Ndoumbé remained outside the cemetery. Similarly, what may appear cute to Western viewers, Daam's direct approach to Gagnesiri when they first meet, is quite inconceivable in the Senegalese context. And non-Muslim audiences will miss the symbolic significance of the number of flashbacks. As Sene Absa explained, well before shooting the film, he was going to have seven flashbacks because seven is a Koranic number – he interprets it as three for women, four for men, seven the union of man and woman (Saad and Garcia, 1995).

Tableau Ferraille

14 The topic of nuclear waste appeared previously in another Senegalese film, Mansour Sora Wade's short *Picc Mi.*

References and Further Reading

Achebe, Chinua. 1966. *A Man of the People*. London: Heinemann.

Bâ, Mariama. 1981 (1980). *So Long a Letter*. London: Heinemann. Translation by Modupé Bodé-Thomas of *Une si longue Lettre*. Dakar/Abidjan/Lomé: Les Nouvelles Editions Africaines.

Barlet, Olivier. 1997. 'Entretiens avec Moussa Sene Absa (Sénégal),' http://www.africultures.com/cineastes_africains/interviews/moussa_sene_absa.htm.

——. 1998. 'Entretien: Moussa Sene Absa.' *Africultures* 4: 57.

Camp de Thiaroye. 1988. Film written and directed by Ousmane Sembène and Thierno Faty Sow. Produced by Société Nouvelle de Promotion Cinématographique (Senegal), ENAPROC (Algeria), and SATPEC (Tunesia). Distributed in the U.S. by New Yorker Films. 152 minutes.

Castiel, Elie. 1997. '*Vues d'Afrique*: Intuitions féminines.' *Séquences* 191: 7–9.

Cruise O'Brien, Donal B. 1971. *The Mourides of Senegal: The Political and Economic Organization of an Islamic Brotherhood*. Oxford: Clarendon Press.

——. 1975. *Saints and Politicians: Essays in the Organization of a Senegalese Peasantry*. Cambridge: Cambridge University Press.

Duchesne, Yanick. 1997. 'Moussa Sene Absa à Vues d'Afrique.' *L'Express de Toronto*, 22 April, page 11.

Iso Lô. 1994. Documentary directed by Mansour Sora Wade. Produced by La Huit (France), Kus Production

(Senegal), Arcanal, Le Centre Culturel Français de Dakar (Senegal), and Citétélévision Villeurbanne (France). 41 minutes.

Jef Jel. 1998. Documentary directed by Moussa Sene Absa. Produced by Les Productions de la Lanterne (France). 55 minutes.

La Vie est belle, see pages 186–91.

Mapantsula, see pages 91–7.

Mighty Aphrodite. 1995. Film written and directed by Woody Allen. Produced by Sweetland Films (USA). Distributed in the U.S. by Swank Motion Pictures. 95 minutes.

Niang, Sada. 1999. 'Moussa Sene Absa. *Tableau Ferraille*.' *African Studies Review* 42 (1): 211–13.

Picc Mi. 1992. Film written and directed by Mansour Sora Wade. Produced by Kaany Productions (Senegal). Distributed in France by Médiathèque des Trois Mondes, Paris. 17 minutes.

Saad, Lamine, and Jean-Pierre Garcia. 1995. 'Tableau Ferraille de Moussa Sene Absa (Senegal).' *Le Film Africain* 18/19: 17.

Sene Absa, Moussa. 2002. Personal communication.

Tableau Ferraille. 1997. Film written and directed by Moussa Sene Absa. Produced by ADR Productions (France), La Sept Cinéma (France), MSA Productions (Senegal), Canal Horizon (France), and Kus Productions (Senegal). 85 minutes.

Villalón, Leonardo A. 1995. *Islamic Society and State Power in Senegal: Disciples and Citizens in Fatick*. African Studies 80. Cambridge/New York/Oakleigh: Cambridge University Press.

White, Douglas. 1988. 'Rethinking Polygyny.' *Current Anthropology* 29: 529–70.

Wonogo, Zoumana. 1997. 'N'deye Fatou N'daw: From the Grammar School to Cinema.' *FESPACO Newsletter* 14.

Xala, see pages 126–28.

The Blue Eyes of Yonta 1992
Was the Struggle in Vain?

PAULO DE SOUSA
APRESENTA

UDJU AZUL
DI YONTA
OS OLHOS
AZUIS
DE YONTA

UM FILME DE
FLORA GOMES

MAYSA MARTA • ANTÓNIO SIMÃO MENDES • PEDRO DIAS • DINA VAZ • MOHAMED SEIDI   BIA GOMES

SELECÇÃO OFICIAL · CANNES 1992 · UN CERTAIN REGARD

I do not suggest alternatives. As a 'contester,' I am someone who, above all, makes observations and remarks on issues.
(Flora Gomes in an interview with Ukadike, 1995: 181)

Betrayals of Independence

The African Party for the Independence of Guinea and Cape Verde (PAIGC) which liberated Portuguese Guinea was more successful than any other guerrilla movement in Africa. Its victory in 1974 brought high expectations for the new nation. They were not fulfilled. Amílcar Cabral had predicted that civil servants and office workers would inherit state power from the colonial rulers – as was the case elsewhere in Africa – because neither the bourgeoisie nor the working class were sufficiently developed to seize political power at independence, and the peasantry was too poorly educated. He had called for that 'petty bourgeoisie' to act with full regard for the problems and hopes of the ordinary people, to commit 'class suicide.' The leaders of PAIGC were indeed former civil servants and office workers, and they did become entrenched in power after independence, but they did not commit class suicide.

At independence Guinea-Bissau united with the Cape Verde Islands, another former Portuguese colony, nearly six hundred miles out in the Atlantic. The PAIGC established a one-party state characterized by a hierarchical government and party structure, party-run mass organizations, and controlled elections. The police became increasingly intrusive, the administration expanded, and corruption was widespread. Even though the population of Guinea-Bissau numbers less than a million, factional and inter-personal conflict among various sets of party, government, and military officials was rampant. In 1980, a military coup directed against the politically dominant Cape Verdeans broke up the union between Guinea-Bissau and Cape Verde. After another decade of single-party rule, political liberalization came in 1991.[1]

The attempt to implement supposedly socialist policies was a failure, and the economy floundered. This failure, and the pressure of foreign donors and international agencies, led the government to shift to liberal economic policies in the 1980s. The urban elite of party officials and government administrators was now joined by merchants and traders. Through it all the gap between the privileged few and the mass of the population widened. In *The Blue Eyes of Yonta*, the lavish wedding reception at the Sheraton Hotel – extravagant in the context of an extremely poor country such as Guinea-Bissau – illustrates the deep inequality that characterizes Guinea-Bissau less than a generation after independence was achieved at great sacrifice.

In *Those Whom Death Refused* Flora Gomes had contrasted guerrilla warfare and nonchalant bureaucrats. Four years later he created *The Blue Eyes of Yonta*, a beautiful film that reminds us of the sacrifices made during the war but focuses on the present in Bissau, the nation's capital.[2] It shows that the socialist transformation has failed to materialize: Nando, a veteran of the war, reports that nothing has changed in the countryside; the comments of Zé's uncle confirm that nothing has changed for urban workers, either. So far, the two films tell a story that has its parallels in the experiences of Zimbabwe, as portrayed in *Flame*. *The Blue Eyes of Yonta* goes on to illustrate the hardships created by the shift to economic liberalization: when the electricity supply to a refrigeration plant is cut off because of unpaid bills, fish spoils, the

1 The *Blue Eyes of Yonta* was produced during the preparations for the first multi-party elections in 1994. Two passing comments, Vicente's about political rallies and Amílcar's about the opposition, are dismissive and suggest little enthusiasm for the new politics. In the elections, 46% of the votes went to PAIG which secured 62 out of 100 seats in the National People's Assembly. In 1998, rebellious soldiers plunged the country into two months of armed conflict which entailed artillery barrages in Bissau, the country's capital and the only city in the small country. About a third of the country's population was displaced, and Flora Gomes lost 35mm copies of his three films and the substantial materials he had assembled for a film about Amílcar Cabral (Barlet, 2000).

Gomes's most recent film, *Nha Fala*, had to be shot in the Cape Verde Islands. It appears as a response to the tragedy. The musical offers comedy all the while touching on the issues confronting Guinea-Bissau and reminding viewers of the legacy of Amílcar Cabral.

2 *The Blue Eyes of Yonta* gives a good sense of the life of the urban lower middle class. Yonta and her mother enjoy the regular if limited income that comes with their jobs and her father's workshop is busy. They are not poor – by local standards, nor do they enjoy the affluence that might come with a senior position in government or commerce, a profession such as doctor, or a substantial business. José Laplaine's *Macadam Tribu* provides a more detailed panorama of everyday life of the lower middle class, in this case in Bamako, Mali.

fishmongers are left without merchandise, and the fishermen cannot sell their catch; the widow Santa, who has rented her house since independence, is evicted to suit a new owner, and a bystander wonders aloud how the new owner came by the money to buy the house. The film suggests how hard it is to find a job, and it graphically conveys the run-down poverty of the nation's capital: some settings may appear rural to Western eyes, but all the action save one short scene takes place in Bissau. The contrast between rich and poor in *The Blue Eyes of Yonta* is not as stark as in *Xala* and *Tableau Ferraille*, but the sacrifices of the war add poignancy to it, and the commitment to socialism that came with the war makes inequality less acceptable. In one of the songs, entitled 'Bissau Has Changed,' the refrain goes:

> They see everything
> They pretend not to see anything
> How Bissau has changed!

And it concludes:

> We raised the flag
> We wept hope
> We are tired of weeping
> I will weep no more
> I will not start weeping again
> (my translation from the French translation provided with the Super Mama Djombo CD)

Only a few traces remain of the past commitment to socialism in Bissau in the early 1990s. 'Comrade' serves as a form of address for men. When Ambrus sits down for a party of checkers with Vicente, he jokes 'I now play scientifically,' implicitly referring to the 'scientific socialism' that supposedly guided state and party after independence. The foreman on the dock refers to bureaucrats who come late to their offices. Most notably, the wedding of Mana and Manecas does not include a church ceremony.

The Blue Eyes of Yonta, like *Xala*, emphasizes cultural alienation. Zé copies his letter to Yonta out of a European brochure of love letters meant to be addressed to beauties with blue eyes, to be written while the snow falls. The poet wallows in his longing for the Swedish girl with the blue eyes. And even Vicente returns with presents from Portugal that follow European fashion and taste rather than African needs: a big watch to be borne on a belt by Yonta, a bottle of wine to be shared by his workers. At the same time we see a comfortable amalgamation of tradition and Western imports. We hear a few references to God and to the Pope, but we also see tradition observed with a libation of wine for the ancestors at the betrothal of Mana. Her marriage strikingly combines the transactions between the spouses' families at that traditional ceremony and a civil marriage. Mana's white bridal gown and her African hairdo beautifully demonstrate the felicitous integration of old and new.

The principal characters present different responses to the state of Guinea-Bissau nearly two decades after independence. Yonta stands at

Betrayals of Independence

the center of this comedy of misplaced affections. Her frivolity contrasts with the self-assurance and quiet dignity of her mother Belante. She reflects the city and its superficiality. She admires Vicente but does not share his dreams: 'If your ideals have been spoiled, it's not my fault. We respect the past, but we can't live in it.' In the end Yonta is rejected by both Vicente and Zé, but she remains secure in the affection of her parents and her younger brother, however much he may tease her.

Zé is moonstruck by Yonta, but when he hears the poet declaiming his love for the Swedish girl with the blue eyes, he finally realizes that he lives in a different world. Yonta's radiance bewitches him, but he rejects the conspicuous, Western-oriented consumption of Bissau she represents. He does not share the dreams of his friend who wants to emigrate to Europe, he affirms that the place he came from – Bolama, the war-time capital, symbol of the struggle for independence – is as good as Bissau, and he is prepared to return there.[3] If Yonta's glamor recalls the glittering promises that came with independence nearly two decades before, then his disappointment stands for all those whose aspirations have been frustrated.

Vicente is a war hero. Now he seeks to help the little people with a fish storage enterprise that proudly proclaims, 'Djuda cu mo' ('Help Yourself'). He encourages the fishermen from whom he buys, he keeps fish to sell to the market women even though the wholesaler – the beneficiary of the new liberal economic policies – offers him a better price.[4] But he has not been able to stick to the ideals he fought for: 'money is the weapon now,' he tells Amílcar, 'the war is over.' When he is finally reunited with Nando, his comrade-in-arms, he observes resignedly: 'In the jungle we thought it would be for everyone. But it's not. What can I do?' The fruits of independence have come to some, here in the capital, and Vicente invites Nando to join him to get his share. But Nando has been marked even more profoundly by the struggle, mentally as well as physically – we catch a brief glimpse of his scarred left face, presumably it is because of his injury that he draws a pension. He wants no part of Bissau and returns to Catio, once at the center of the war for liberation. His quiet departure, his old hat left behind as a reminder of their common past, confronts Vicente with the failure of their struggle. As he dances to circling vultures and talks to Nha Padidor, the statue of his deceased mother he cradles, we wonder whether he has gone out of his mind. When we last see him, sitting alone at the hotel's swimming pool, his feet in the water, the question remains unanswered.

Vicente asks Nha Padidor whether the future he dreams of is still possible. When he dances to circling vultures, we recall that the card reader has told Santa and Belante that vultures only take what is already dead and wonder whether Gomes is telling us that Vicente's dreams are dead. But we also hear her say: 'To-morrow everything will change. For you, for all of us.' Gomes dedicates his film to his son Lennart and to the children of Guinea-Bissau, and the children in *The Blue Eyes of Yonta* suggest an optimistic interpretation. At the beginning of the film, as they roll old tires and inner tubes numbered from the year of independence to

3 Emigration is a recurrent minor theme in *The Blue Eyes of Yonta*. Santa's son lives in Portugal, the driver of the fuel truck has emigrated, and Amílcar dreams of playing soccer in Portugal. Given the huge gap between the standard of living of most Africans and that of even low-wage earners in rich countries, the lure of emigration is strong. Mostéfa Djadjam's *Borders* emphasizes the diverse motivations of a group of West Africans trying to make their way to Europe as illegal immigrants. It accompanies them on their journey through Mauritania, Algeria, and Morocco until they finally cross the Strait of Gibraltar and reach Spain. At the mercy of their handlers and the elements, they endure hardships and risk their lives. Hundreds like them perish every year along the way, some in the Sahara, most in the attempt to traverse the less than ten miles that separate Africa from Europe at Gibraltar.

4 Vicente's beat-up Volvo is presumably a leftover from the fleet of Volvos Sweden offered to Guinea-Bissau after independence.

You won't find what we fought for in your village

Nando and Vicente discuss the aftermath of their struggle for independence

the year 2000 down the road, they demonstrate that they have not forgotten the country's history and that they are thinking about the future. And they close the film, dancing joyously into the future. The children are joined by Yonta who has been castigated by Vicente for replacing ideals with cars, clothes, and discos, who has been rejected by Zé: we are left to surmise that she is making a fresh start.

Gomes names his youngest protagonist for Amílcar Cabral, the distinguished guerrilla leader and intellectual. Young Amílcar leads the children's parade, his inner tubes marked for the year 2000. He is quick and witty, boisterous and ingenious, full of initiative, mischief, and energy. Amílcar is consumed by his enthusiasm for soccer; Diego Maradona, the legendary Argentine soccer player, is his idol; and he dreams of playing in Portugal. But he also shows signs of following in the steps of his famous namesake. He is afraid of no one: his older sister, the truck driver, government authority – he leads the children in putting Santa back into her house. This rebellion against the callous disregard of people's needs, and the children's dance concluding the film, suggest the prospect of a better future.

Gomes went to high school in Cuba while his country was at war and learned his craft at Cuba's Instituto Superior de Arte with Santiago Alvarez, before training with Paulin Soumanou Vieyra in Senegal, but he does not tell us what a better future for Guinea-Bissau might look like: 'I do not suggest alternatives.' Still, with Nando and Zé Gomes he has firmly established that the country at large rejects the compromises that mark the capital.

Betrayals of Independence

While Gomes tells of the labors of recently independent Guinea-Bissau, he keeps us entertained with a beautiful and funny film. We follow the entanglements of our protagonists, relish their beauty and grace, enjoy the dance rhythms,[5] and discover Bissau. Through most of the film we revel in the caring among the adults and the prospect of romance among the young. Then, in the last fifteen minutes, the idyll unravels: Nando confronts Vicente with the betrayal of the ideals for which they fought, Vicente denounces Yonta and the consumer culture she represents, and Zé rejects Yonta in turn.

The film comes to a surreal ending on the morning after the wedding party. The guests are asleep; the two fishermen stand in the hotel pool dredging the water with their large nets; Vicente sits on the edge of the pool, his feet dangling in the water; Amílcar's parents dance slowly; and Amílcar floats on his tube 2000. Perhaps we are to conclude that Bissau's middle class has become oblivious of the country's realities? We may see the fishermen, so totally out of place, as bringing home the contrast between the empty consumption the hotel pool represents and their productive labor. We may wonder whether Vicente and Amílcar's parents are lost in dreams of the past. May see the future afloat. And then, as we ponder, the scene springs into life. A food cart with the wedding cake tumbles into the pool and the children emerge from under it. Off they dance, Yonta amongst them, to a future they will shape.

The actors Gomes chose and trained are key to the success of his film. Bia Gomes, who appears in the role of Yonta's mother Belante, had played a lead role in *Those Whom Death Refused* – which earned her the prize for the best female interpretation at FESPACO. But most of the actors in *The Blue Eyes of Yonta* were rank amateurs. Soon after he had completed *Those Whom Death Refused*, Gomes set out to search for actors amongst his friends, in the women's associations, in the schools, in poor neighborhoods, and also in some government ministries. He then spent nine months with the actors in regular work sessions (Deffontaines, 1992). Maysa Marta, a student, tells how Gomes met her talking in the street to a mutual friend – and how hard he made her work to become Yonta (Anonymous, 1992). If she makes the young men's eyes turn in the film, she is also, of course, featured on the film poster.[6] Gomes complemented the beauty of his actors by using soft colors to good advantage. With a budget less than $1 million he created an accomplished film.

If Bissau appears run down in *The Blue Eyes of Yonta*, conditions in the countryside are even worse, not just in Guinea-Bissau, but throughout Africa South of the Sahara. To this issue, perhaps the most important in contemporary Africa, we will now turn.

5 The joyful dance rhythms are tinged with melancholy for those who understand the creole lyrics. The music, written, scored, and orchestrated by Adrian-G. Ferreira-Atchutchi, also known as Adriano Atchutchi, and played by his band, Super Mama Djombo, has been released on CD. The band, formed shortly after independence and close to the ruling party, attained star status. However, the recordings it released in the early 1980s included, alongside the songs glorifying the ruling party, other songs mocking corruption in the very same party – and Super Mama Djombo began running into difficulties, such as finding a stage for performances, or even a room for rehearsals (Klein, 1999).

6 The actors use the language they are comfortable with, the Creole that has evolved over three centuries. The poster gives the film's title in both Creole and Portuguese, illustrating the extent to which the two languages have diverged. The lusophone market required a version subtitled in Portuguese.

*Flora Gomes, on the left,
during the shooting*

References and Further Reading

Anonymous (C. K. M.). 1992. 'Maysa Marta.' *Ecrans d'Afrique* 2: 36–8.

Barlet, Olivier. 2000. ''Nous coupons une partie de nous-mêmes pour la vendre': Entretien avec Flora Gomes, cinéaste.' *Africultures* 26: 73–5.

The Blue Eyes of Yonta/Udju azul di Yonta. 1992. Film directed by Flora Gomes, written by Flora Gomes, Ina Césair, David Lang, and Manuel Rambout Barcelos. Produced by Vermedia (Portugal), Cooperativa Cultural Arco-Iris (Guinea-Bissau), Eurocréation Production (France), and Rádiotelevisão Portuguesa (Portugal). Distributed in the U.S. by California Newsreel. 90 minutes.

Borders/Frontières. 2001. Film directed by Mostéfa Djadjam, written by Mostéfa Djadjam and Agnès de Sacy. Produced by Vertigo Productions (France). Distributed in the U.S. by Art Mattan. 105 minutes.

Cabral, Amílcar. 1979. *Unity and Struggle: Speeches and Writings*. New York/London: Monthly Review Press.

Chabal, Patrick. 1983. *Amilcar Cabral: Revolutionary Leadership and People's War*. Cambridge/New York:

Cambridge University Press.

Klein, Guus de. 1999. 'Guinea-Bissau: The Backyard Beats of Gumbe.' *World Music 1: Africa, Europe and the Middle East*, edited by Simon Broughton, Mark Ellingham, and Richard Trillo. London: The Rough Guides. Pages 499–504.

Deffontaines, Thérèse-Marie. 1992. 'Les Yeux bleus de Yonta.' *Ecrans d'Afrique* 1: 76–9.

Flame, see pages 57–63.

Forrest, Joshua B. 2002. 'Guinea-Bissau.' Patrick Chabal with others, *A History of Postcolonial Lusophone Africa*. Bloomington/Indianapolis: Indiana University Press. 236–63. Nations of Contemporary Africa. Boulder, CO, San Francisco, Oxford: Westview Press.

Macadam Tribu (Asphalt Tribe). 1996. Film written and directed by José Laplaine. Produced by Flamingo Films (France), Bakia Films (Congo/Zaïre), Centre National de Production Cinématographique du Mali, and Animatografo (Portugal). Distributed in France by Médiathèque des Trois Mondes, Paris. Available for viewing at Cinémathèque Afrique, Paris. 90 minutes.

Nha Fala (My Voice). 2002. Film directed by Flora Gomes, written by Flora Gomes and Franck Moinard. Produced by Fado Filmes (Portugal), Les Films de Mai (France), and Samsa Film (Luxemburg). 90 minutes.

Super Mama Djombo. 1996. *Les yeux bleus de Yonta/Udju azul di Yonta*. Cobalt. CD.

Those Whom Death Refused/Mortu Nega. 1988. Film directed by Flora Gomes. Guinea-Bissau. Distributed in the U.S. by California Newsreel. 93 minutes.

Ukadike, N. Frank. 1995. 'In Guinea-Bissau, Cinema Trickles Down: an Interview with Flora Gomes.' *Research in African Literatures* 26 (3): 179–85.

Xala, see pages 126–38.

*President Julius Nyerere (center)
visiting an* ujamaa *village near
Dodoma in 1970*

5 The Exploited & Neglected Peasantry

The films on the post-independence era we have explored so far have all been situated in urban areas – even if many of the settings look rural to Western eyes. They obscure an important characteristic of contemporary Africa: two thirds of Africans South of the Sahara continue to live in the countryside (see table on page xii). We now turn our attention to them to see how the problems faced by contemporary peasants have been neglected not only by most filmmakers but also, more importantly, by policy makers. Government policies have been geared primarily toward extracting resources from the rural sector, and their impact has been exacerbated by corruption.

Africa South of the Sahara continues to be one of the least urbanized regions in the world, but over the last four decades Africa has been transformed by a rate of urban growth faster than that experienced in any other region. One of the contributing factors has been natural population growth. Rates of population growth in Africa South of the Sahara are among the world's highest. Population growth accelerated as improved health conditions brought about not only a decline in mortality but also an increase in fertility. Mortality rates have rebounded in some countries, however, with the decline in living conditions brought on by severe economic crises and the onslaught of the AIDS epidemic.

Large-scale rural–urban migration is the other factor that has fueled a veritable urban explosion. It is the key factor increasing the level of urbanization in the region. Urbanization and industrialization are frequently assumed to be intimately connected, with urbanization seen as a prerequisite for development. Such assumptions are problematic. Not only do cities predate industrial manufacture by several millennia, but even today only a small proportion of urban dwellers work in industry. Most cities are, in the first place, centers of public administration and commerce. And while the more urbanized countries show greater development, whether measured in terms of economic output or human welfare, this correlation does not establish the direction of causality. It is easily assumed that a larger, more productive urban population creates higher incomes. However, the reverse causal relationship is quite plausible. The richer countries tend to concentrate greater resources in urban areas: they invest more in urban public works, they maintain larger urban-based public bureaucracies, and they have a larger middle class which supports a vast service sector.

I thought I should go to the capital of Kenya to look for work. Why? Because when money is borrowed from foreign lands, it goes to build Nairobi and the other big towns. When peasants grow food, it goes to Nairobi and to the other big towns. As far as we peasants are concerned, all our labour goes to fatten Nairobi and the big towns.
(A woman in Ngũgĩ wa Thiong'o's novel Devil on the Cross, pp. 41–2)

The Exploited and Neglected Peasantry

The assumption that the transition from a rural to an urban society is conducive to the transformation from 'traditional' to 'modern' in terms of both the technology of production and the orientation of individuals and social institutions is grounded in 'modernization theory.' However, in Africa South of the Sahara, a rapid increase in the level of urbanization stands in stark contrast to the economic stagnation of the region. The 'urban bias' approach provides a more compelling interpretation for this urban explosion. Its proponents argue that policy makers have favored urban areas over rural, and that they disproportionately allocated resources to the cities, especially capital cities, with results that are both inequitable and inefficient. In this view, rural–urban migration was fostered by the exploitation and neglect of the peasantry: this induced peasants to move to urban areas, which offered greater economic rewards, better educational opportunities, and a modicum of medical facilities.

The issue was raised soon after independence. Julius Nyerere, the leader of the independence movement in Tanganyika and first President of what was eventually to become Tanzania, was the most prominent statesman to address it. In 1967, the leaders of the Tanganyika African National Union (TANU) issued the famous *Arusha Declaration* warning:

> Although when we talk of exploitation we usually think of capitalists, we should not forget that there are many fish in the sea. They eat each other. The large ones eat the small ones, and small ones eat those who are even smaller. There are two possible ways of dividing the people in our country. We can put the capitalists and feudalists on one side, and the farmers and workers on the other. But we can also divide the people into urban dwellers on one side and those who live in rural areas on the other. If we are not careful we might get to the position where the real exploitation in Tanzania is that of the town dwellers exploiting the peasants. (from the revised English translation of the Swahili original, Nyerere, 1968: 28)

But in Tanzania, as elsewhere, resources were increasingly drained out of agriculture to support a proliferating, unproductive state and parastatal bureaucracy.

The rural sector was squeezed in a number of ways throughout Africa. Peasants were taxed. Prices for agricultural products where fixed by the government. Peasants were thus made to provide cheap food to the cities. And they had to sell crops intended for export to government marketing boards at below market prices, thereby contributing disproportionately to government revenue. Furthermore, foreign exchange rates were usually overvalued so that peasant producers of export crops obtained low receipts in local currency, while low local prices for imports benefited the urban sector.

The urban sector accounts for a disproportionate share of consumption as well as investment in every African country. Usually they are even more concentrated in the national capital. Certainly, industry and modern transport find advantage in spatial concentration. They require urban infrastructure and highly trained specialists. But it appears that resources for both consumption and investment were invariably apportioned to urban areas beyond the immediate requirements of industrialization.

Investments in public works were concentrated in urban areas, urban-based public bureaucracies became bloated after independence, and some sectors of the urban labor force came to enjoy a standard of living that was high when compared to the condition of the peasantry.

The neglect and exploitation of the peasantry arise out of a basic fact: power and privilege are centered in cities. The politicians and bureaucrats allocating resources are urban-based. They want to improve the environment in which they live and work, and to enhance their status, nationally and internationally, with public works. They seek to assure the continued collaboration of the middle class of senior civil servants, professionals, managers, and entrepreneurs. They have to placate strategically placed elements of the urban labor force such as workers at the docks and on the railroads, in utilities, and in industry. And even the urban poor have some leverage, wielding the threat of street violence: riots lead to destruction, and they scare away tourists and investors. Public resources are thus disproportionately spent on urban consumption and urban investment for the few – in the cities.

Peasants have little influence on government policy, and they are usually powerless to expose, let alone stop, the corruption of government agents. Confronted with neglect, or even outright exploitation, they are left with limited options. Many peasants sought to partake of urban privilege by moving to the city. Some peasants rebelled, but such rebellions found it difficult to reach across large rural areas, at best obtained limited concessions, and could not alter the fact that power is urban-based. Other peasants withdrew from the market and reverted to subsistence farming. As a consequence, increases in agricultural production on the subcontinent have failed to keep pace with population growth since independence. In some countries policy makers sought an accommodation so as to stimulate food supplies for the cities and the production of export crops – but usually urban-based power reasserted itself eventually. However, the economic crisis of the 1980s, and the structural adjustment programs that ensued, appear to have brought policy changes that substantially reduced urban bias.

We will examine two films. They depict quite different village settings, but in both cases the peasants' lack of power is exacerbated by military rule and urban bias is made worse by the corruption that thrives under authoritarian regimes.

References and Further Reading

Lofchie, Michael. 1997. 'The Rise and Demise of Urban-Biased Development Policies in Africa,' in Josef Gugler (ed.) *Cities in the Developing World: Issues, Theory, and Policy.* Oxford/New York: Oxford University Press. 23–39.

Ngũgĩ wa Thiong'o. 1982 (1980). *Devil on the Cross.* London: Heinemann. Translation by the author of *Caitaani Mũtharabi-inĩ.* Nairobi: Heinemann. English

Nyerere, Julius K. 1968. *Ujamaa – Essays on Socialism.* Dar es Salaam/Nairobi/London/New York: Oxford University Press.

Finzan 1990
Gender Conflict and Village Solidarity

... a cinema which works to dispel social inequalities, forms of domination which merely reduce our people to poverty. (Cheick Oumar Sissoko, quoted by Barlet, 2000: 17)

KORA films présente

FINZAN

un film de
CHEICK OUMAR SISSOKO

avec
**DIARRAH SANOGO - OUMAR NAMORY KEITA - KOTI
SAIDOU TOURE - BALLA MOUSSA KEITA - MACIRE KANTE
HELENE DIARRA - HABIB DEMBELE**
Image: CHEICK HAMALA KEITA
MAMADOU FAMAKAN COULIBALY
MOHAMED LAMINE TOURE
Son: IBRAHIM KHALIL THERA
Montage: OUOBA MOTANDI
Assistants réalisateur: IBRAHIMA TOURE
ADAMA DRABO - FASSARA SIDI DIABATE
DAVID PIERRE FILA
Collaborateur: BABOU TIMBELY

une co-production KORA films - CNPC - ZDF

Avec la partecipation du Ministère de l'Information
et des Télécommunication MALI
du Ministère de la Coopération FRANCE
du Centro Orientamento Educativo COE MILANO
SAPROSA BAMAKO et l'aimable concours de UNICEF BAMAKO
CMDT MALI-HELVETAS SUISSE BAMAKO - UNIFEM BAMAKO

Cheick Oumar Sissoko's *Finzan* introduces us, as did *Yaaba*, to a great variety of characters in village settings. And Sabugu and Konyumani, two Bamana[1] villages in Mali where most of the action takes place, look quite similar to the village we came to know in *Yaaba*. Yet *Finzan*, released only one year after *Yaaba*, portrays village life quite differently. If conflicts in *Yaaba* were personal, fed by superstition and individual shortcomings, conflict erupts in Sabugu over traditional customs imposed on women, in Konyumani over the control the chief and elders exert over nubile women. And while the village in *Yaaba* appeared to exist in isolation from the outside world, the villages in *Finzan* are part of a larger world: the peasants are affected by government, they are connected with world markets, they have gone to work in the city, and they maintain relationships with kin living in distant places.

Finzan is a Bamana term for a dance performed by men who have done exceptional deeds. With this choice of title Sissoko sought to extend it to women struggling for their freedom (Aufderheide, 1990). Two brief animal scenes at the very beginning of the film announce the film's principal theme of the devotion of mothers and the blind domination of men: a goat gives birth, a he-goat pursues a she-goat back and forth around the pole they are tethered to – throughout the film such animal scenes will appear as capsule comments on the action. And, at the end, the film carries a dedication 'To the African woman,' in Bamana as well as French and English. *Finzan* starts out with a quote from the declaration of the 1980 Copenhagen Women's Conference which connects it explicitly to feminist discourse: 'Women are 50 per cent of the world's population, do about two thirds of its work, receive barely 10 per cent of its income and own less than 1 per cent of its property.' I offer a translation here because only the French text is carried in the English version of the film, but the statement needs to be problematized. It is easy enough to agree with its general thrust, but the quantification is seriously amiss: women are more than half the world's population; women work more than men on average, but there is considerable variation across cultures and classes; women receive more than one tenth of the world's income if food and shelter among the poor, and unearned income among the aged rich, are taken into account; and they own more than one per cent of the world's property if the wealth concentrated in the hands of widows of the affluent is considered. In fact the quote from the Copenhagen conference is pertinent to *Finzan* only at the most general level: the film does little to alert us to the differential workload of men and women and does not touch on issues of income and property ownership. Rather, *Finzan* makes a dramatic plea to abandon traditional customs that oppress women. This is the film's dominant theme, and it is reflected in the film poster which shows only women.

Among the many African films that problematize the position of women, *Finzan* is the most far-reaching.[2] It is the only African feature film to date to focus on two issues that profoundly affect women in many African societies: female genital mutilation[3] and widow inheritance, part of the patrilineage's control over – and responsibility for – the women

1 The Bamana used to be referred to as Bambara. That no man appears to have more than four wives suggests that Sabugu has been Islamicized. The death ritual, however, is traditional. *Finzan* does not show the traditional sculpture that has made the Bamana famous. Sissoko may have omitted any reference to that rich artistic heritage – still alive today, if increasingly geared to the tourist market – so as not to distract from his focus on contemporary issues.

2 Sissoko is very much the activist. Political engagement led him to abandon his mathematics studies and to choose cinema as a language that would allow him to bypass the censorship of dictatorships that were silencing everybody (Hoffelt, 2003). He embarked on the study of history and sociology in France before training there at the Ecole de Cinéma Louis Lumière. All his films are politically engaged, and he played a leading role in the events that eventually led to the overthrow of Moussa Traoré in 1991. When women demonstrated against the dictator after protesters (mainly high school and college students) had been killed, he filmed the event and distributed the images worldwide. In Sophie Hoffelt's documentary *Djandjon!* he shows some of this footage and uses episodes from his feature films *Finzan*, *Genesis*, *Guimba the Tyrant*, and *Nyamanton* to provide an introduction to Mali. The popular movement against the dictator was foreshadowed in the film *Finyé* by his fellow countryman Souleymane Cissé.

The young officers who toppled the regime handed power over to civilians within a year. An activist scholar, Alpha Konaré, was elected President in 1992 and reelected in 1997. After two terms he stepped down as required by the constitution. In the 2002 elections an opposition candidate, Amadou Toumani Touré, the leader of the 1991 coup that had brought democracy to Mali, won by a large majority, and Sissoko joined a national unity government as Minister of Culture.

3 The term 'female circumcision,' in common use, is literally incorrect and, by its association with male circum-

The Exploited and Neglected Peasantry

3 (cont.) cision, diminishes the import of what continues to be imposed on an estimated two million girls every year. 'Clitoridectomy' does not cover more invasive procedures such as labiadectomy and infibulation. 'Excision' denotes a common pattern that combines various degrees of clitoridectomy and labiadectomy. Female genital mutilation was a taboo topic for most African writers until recently. Particularly notable is its absence from Chinua Achebe's classic *Things Fall Apart*, which is commonly assumed to provide a comprehensive account of pre-colonial Igbo society. In contrast, Nuruddin Farah has fiercely denounced female genital mutilation, most dramatically in *Sardines*.

4 Widow inheritance used to be part of the Judeo-Christian heritage: it is the rule in the Old Testament where it is known as the *levirate*. Even if the patrilineage is prepared to let the widow go, she will be confronted with the dilemma that her children belong to the lineage; hence the chief's comment that a woman will want to stay with her children – that is, with the lineage she married into.

5 African filmmakers seem to suggest that the tensions in polygamous households are peculiar to Westernized families, tensions strikingly portrayed in *Xala*. In *Finzan*, Bala's wives are derisive about his expectations that Nanyuma will marry him, but they might welcome her for the help she would provide in household and farm work. *Yaaba* and *Kasarmu Ce* surprise by the absence of any reference to the polygamy found in both cultural contexts.

6 *Kaddu beykat*, Safi Faye's semi-documentary portrayal of her home village, has the classic peasant comment on government. When a young man reads a politician's grandiloquent discourse from a newspaper to the villagers assembled under a baobab tree, one of the elders comments: 'All this is just your politics. My politics is that six months a year I have only one meal a day.' (My translation from the French subtitles.)

married into it and their children.[4] And while *Finzan* shows co-wives cooperating rather than in conflict,[5] it touches on an aspect of polygamy that is often overlooked: to the extent that the better established older men manage to have several wives, young men find it difficult to marry.

The struggle of the women introduces conflict into Sabugu and Konyumani. But solidarity prevails when the village confronts the district commissioner. The two conflicts remain separate, one internal, the other external. When the men face the administrators and his business associate, the women join them although this is contrary to custom. And when men and women set out together to rescue their chief, one of the elders expressly instructs them not to raise the issue of Fili's clitoridectomy: the government official is expected to oppose female genital mutilation. The unity of the village is thus maintained – and women pay the price. By producing a long film that addresses issues of both gender and government abuse, Sissoko reveals the parallels between authoritarian patriarchy and authoritarian government. And African viewers, having wholeheartedly applauded the denunciation of government abuse, may begin to reconsider customs affecting women they took for granted.

In the film *Xala*, the theft of an entire village's savings by a pickpocket symbolized the exploitation of the peasantry by the city. And the peasant victim told of rural hardship: even the city's beggars are better off than his fellow villagers. In *Finzan* we see the demands made on a village by the representative of an authoritarian government. In general, government policies in Africa have been characterized by urban bias, favoring the urban over the rural sector.[6] In this case, the peasants are required to supply millet to the government at below market prices. Supposedly, the millet will be used as a reserve for emergency supplies. More commonly, governments have imposed low prices on food so as to provide urban populations with cheap food supplies. In *Finzan*, it looks as if much of the millet the peasants are to supply will not serve any government policy at all but will be sold on the open market by the businessman in league with the corrupt district commissioner. If government intervention provides the opportunity for corruption, authoritarian government facilitates it.

Stories about how the village dealt with visiting colonial administrators, retold by one of Jigi's half-brothers, remind us that these peasants have experienced government intrusion for a long time. They were made to pay taxes, to provide forced labor, and to furnish recruits for wars in Africa, Europe, and Asia. With colonial government came the foreign language. In *Finzan* the Zangeblen, the village chief,[7] insists that the negotiations with the district commissioner proceed in Bamana – and surprises him: Bamana now has its own script. The proceedings are recorded by the village *griot*: the oral historian has become scribe. With the village's opposition to the authoritarian and corrupt government official the film inscribes itself in the opposition to Moussa Traoré who had ruled Mali as a one-party state since 1969. He was deposed in the year following the film's release after popular protests led to a military

The village confronts the District Commissioner and his business associate

takeover. That the Zangeblen should succeed in refusing to comply with the demands made upon the village and escape reprisals is rather unlikely – in the 1991 protests hundreds of people were killed. Indeed, government censors wanted Sissoko to cut the episode of the district commissioner demanding millet at a fixed price (Aufderheide, 1990).

Finzan, like *Xala*, makes its political message more explicit for local viewers who understand its language. The exchange between the village chief and the women about the porcupine and the mole may stir the curiosity of foreigners, but it is full of meaning in Mali, where a proverb has it that the mole digs the hole that the porcupine occupies. The response by the women translates as:

> No, you are not the mole at all, because if there is someone who works, it is us. Whether it rains or the wind blows, it is we who are working. All the time, all the time, all the time. And when it comes to making decisions this will never be us either. It is you. Certainly, if there is a mole, it is certainly not you. (Sissoko in Ukadike, 2002: 187)

The exchange takes on its wider political significance in Mali where the porcupine is understood to stand for the chief of state while the mole stands for the people.

In contrast to *Yaaba*, which took its village out of history, pretending that it was isolated, *Finzan* shows villages connected with the outside world in multiple ways. The Sahel has a long history of diverse societies interacting. Nanyuma hides with her friend Dikel in a Peul settlement not far from her father's Bamana village.[8] Since colonial times, if not before, the villagers have had to contend with the demands of government. They have become conversant with the prices that their products will fetch on the open market. Villagers have migrated to cities in search of work,

7 The chief is portrayed by Balla Moussa Keïta, perhaps the most prominent West African actor. Starting out in theater and radio, he came to play in most films produced in Mali during a quarter of a century. He appeared in over twenty films altogether and held leading roles in distinguished productions such as *Yeelen* and *Genesis*. Keïta died in 2001.

8 The semi-nomadic Peul cattle herders are also referred to as Fulani. Sissoko gives us glimpses of their fine wall decorations, woven mats and plates, decorated calabashes, and jewellery.

Cheick Oumar Sissoko brandishing the Stallion of (Princess) Yenenga he was awarded for Guimba the Tyrant *at FESPACO 1995; with him are Blaise Compaoré, President of Burkina Faso, and Ousmane Sembène, President of the Jury*

9 The Bala character and the boys' 'ghost' costumes are derived from the *koteba*, a popular theater tradition in rural Mali. The role is played by Oumar Namory Keïta, an established *koteba* actor. 'Bala' signifies stupidity, crudeness, and greed in Bamana (Diawara, n.d.; Diawara, 1992: 145).

among them women who find employment as maids. Others have gone overseas in pursuit of higher education and/or work. Such migrants maintain contact with their kin and most eventually return to the village. And the city offers refuge; Nanyuma would have found it had she not trusted Koman, the oldest of her deceased husband's brothers, to be less of a traditionalist than those living in the village.

Finzan provides a good deal of slapstick comedy, much of it at the expense of Bala, the village idiot who wants to marry Nanyuma, the widow of his brother. Most especially, the pranks the three boys play on Bala literally disarm him and make him an object of ridicule.[9] Farce thus lightens the mood as the film introduces us to serious conflicts. The ridicule of 'our white man' is heightened for African audiences by the fact that his is such an exceptional case. Usually a man such as he, who has been sufficiently successful in France to be able to visit home – with presents of course – would be greatly respected; other young men would want to emulate him; and the girl who gets to go overseas with him would be considered very lucky indeed.

Sissoko produced an even longer version of *Finzan* for the African market. It includes didactic sequences about the consequences of female genital mutilation as well as the treatment of diarrhoea in children – Nanyuma's daughter is the sick child. It also has a sequence of Nanyuma arriving at the market in the city and encountering working women on her way to Koman (Sissoko, 2002; Ukadike, 2002: 186). The version of *Finzan* distributed overseas appears to be aimed at both African and Western audiences. Wali, the *griot*, somewhat the counterpart of the drunkard who tells the truth in *Yaaba*, is likely to appeal to both audiences as he gently challenges the Zangeblen's patriarchal assumptions. And African and Western viewers alike will delight when two of the boys share stereotypes about Europeans farting freely. Other sequences work better for one audience than the other. The long morning sequence at the beginning appears designed to introduce foreign audiences to the village setting. On the other hand, the forest sequence with a lion chasing the village youths up the trees may be seen to provide an exotic experience for popular African audiences, rather than simply a throwback to Tarzan jungle melodrama as Ukadike (1994: 273–5) has charged.[10] Western viewers are unlikely to understand that when Nanyuma's daughter refers to her brother Jigi as her grandmother's husband, when she calls her grandmother 'old fossil,' and when her grandmother in turn addresses her as 'old witch,' this is all part of the fun and games of a joking relationship between grandchildren and grandparents.[11] And Nanyuma's lament at the end of the film ('Women bear the world...') becomes a litany of slogans apparently directed at African audiences. A cinematic version of development theatre, it sounds jarring to Western viewers who have come to see a feature film.

Finzan seeks to arouse African as well as Western opinion against the oppression of women and the exploitation of the peasantry. Addressing these very different audiences simultaneously presents problems. Most Western viewers, learning for the first time about female genital mutilation and widow inheritance, are taken aback and do not need persuading that they should reject such practices – indeed, women threatened with genital mutilation have been granted asylum in the U.S., and immigrants who had their daughters subjected to such surgery in the West have been sentenced to prison terms. But many African viewers take these traditions for granted. Sissoko has opted to mobilize such viewers by making the experiences of Nanyuma and Fili exceptional and dramatizing them.

The brother-in-law Nanyuma is to marry is a dim-wit partial to drink. She is tied up as she is escorted from the city to the village. African viewers will know that such treatment is most unusual. Western viewers, however, are prone to conclude that it is common practice. Even if they catch the truck driver's comment about the way the Bamana treat their women, they will be left with an unfounded generalization about these people.

Female genital mutilation is usually performed on young girls, with the consent of their parents, in the ritual context of a *rite de passage*. By taking the most unusual case of a grown woman, Sissoko moves beyond the pain inflicted on the girls, and the risks to their health and future

10 For the lion shots Sissoko made do with stock shots he purchased (Ukadike, 2002: 192).

11 We have already encountered an indication of a similar joking relationship between family members two generations apart in *Tableau Ferraille* when Ndoumbé's baby daughter was referred to as the 'co-wife' of her grandmother Anta.

The Exploited and Neglected Peasantry

well-being. Fili's father Koman, traditionalist that he is, had discarded custom for specific medical reasons. Now she is an adult who refuses to be circumcised, and who is articulate about the significance of her clitoris: 'It's part of what makes me a woman.' Having viewers squirm in their seats as Fili is subjected to clitoridectomy may be what it takes to mobilize African opinion, but it also reinforces Western stereotypes of 'exotic aberrations' and 'primitive barbarism.'[12] Ukadike (1994: 275) has gone so far as to affirm that '*Finzan* is a film that no African will watch and feel proud of....'

Finzan confronts its viewers with serious problems in modern-day rural Africa. But it also shows effective resistance against oppressive and corrupt government and holds out hope for progressive change. Wali does honor to his calling as *griot* by questioning what the chief takes for granted. The actions of Bengali, the man Nanyuma wants to marry, suggest that he will be a husband and father quite different from most of his peers. Fili and her brother Zan are opposed to their father Koman's treatment of Nanyuma. Koman himself ends up denouncing the villagers who insisted on 'circumcising' his daughter against his express instructions. Some women have come to support Fili, and all support Nanyuma. 'Our fathers are messed up,' the three boys conclude.[13] They, as well as Jigi's sister, just kids, stand up against the abuses perpetuated in the name of tradition. And on the train there is vehement protest against the way Nanyuma is treated.

Sissoko produced this powerful film with just $350,000. And he certainly reached his home audience: the film drew 84,000 spectators during the first three months of its release in Mali (Aufderheide, 1990).[14] It is that audience that particularly matters: much expert opinion holds that the abolition of female genital mutilation has to be pursued through local initiatives, and that outside interference risks being counter-productive. The United Nations has launched a campaign to suppress the practice and appointed Waris Dirie, a Somali who suffered female genital mutilation herself, as special ambassador.

12 The contrast with Victor Schonfeld's documentary critical of male circumcision, surgery unproblematic for Western viewers, is instructive. *It's a Boy* dwells on the suffering of babies during and after circumcision, details the complications that arise in an estimated two per cent of cases in Britain, and interviews parents whose children were seriously ill or died. But, unlike *Finzan*, it gives voice to dignified Jewish and Muslim notables and to circumcisors eloquently defending their tradition.

13 The two older boys refer to Nanyuma as their mother: she is a co-wife of the women who bore them.

14 Sissoko's first feature film, *Nyamanton*, was a popular success in Mali but had only very limited distribution in Europe (Diawara and Robinson, 1988). Likewise *Guimba the Tyrant*, his third feature film which won the Stallion of Yennenga, the Grand Prize, at FESPACO, found it difficult to gain access to European movie theaters (Barlet, 2000: 257).

References and Further Reading

Achebe, Chinua. 1958. *Things Fall Apart*. London: Heinemann.

Aufderheide, Pat. 1990. 'Interview: Cheick Oumar Sissoko,' *Black Film Review* 6 (2): 4–5, 30.

Barlet, Olivier. 2000 (1996). *African Cinemas: Decolonizing the Gaze*. London/New York: Zed Books. Revised and updated translation, by Chris Turner, of *Les cinémas d'Afrique noire: Le regard en question*. Collection Images plurielles. Paris: L'Harmattan.

Boyle, Elizabeth Heger. 2002. *Female Genital Cutting: Cultural Conflict in the Global Community*. Baltimore: Johns Hopkins University Press.

Clark, Andrew F. 2000. 'From Military Dictatorship to Democracy: the Democratization Process in Mali.' *Democracy and Development in Mali*, edited by R. James Bingen, David Robinson, and John M. Staatz. East Lansing, MI: Michigan State University Press. 251–64.

Diawara, Manthia. n.d. (1991). 'Finzan: A Call for Rebellion.' *Library of African Cinema: A Guide to Video Resources for Colleges & Public Libraries*. San Francisco: Resolution Inc./California Newsreel. 8–9.

——. 1992. *African Cinema: Politics and Culture*. Blacks in the Diaspora. Bloomington/Indianapolis: Indiana University Press.

—— and Elizabeth Robinson. 1988. 'New Perspectives in African Cinema: an Interview of Cheick Oumar Sissoko.' *Film Quarterly* 41 (2): 43–8.

Dirie, Waris, and Cathleen Miller. 1998. *Desert Flower: the Extraordinary Journey of a Desert Nomad*. New York: William Morrow; London: Virago.

Djandjon! 1999. Documentary written and directed by Sophie Hoffelt. Produced by La Luna Productions (France) and Kora Films (Mali). 58 minutes.

Farah, Nuruddin. 1981. *Sardines*. London: Allison & Busby.

Finyé/Le Vent/The Wind. 1982. Film directed by Souleymane Cissé. Produced by Filimu Sisé (Mali). Distributed in the U.S. by Kino International. 105 minutes.

Finzan. 1990. Film written and directed by Cheick Oumar Sissoko. Produced by Kora Films (Mali), Zweites Deutsches Fernsehen (Germany), and CNPC (Mali). Distributed in the U.S. by California Newsreel. 107 minutes.

Genesis/La Genèse. 1999. Film directed by Cheick Oumar Sissoko, written by Jean-Louis Sagot Duvauroux, produced by Kora Films (Mali), Balanzan, Centre National de Production Cinématographique du Mali, and Cinéma Public Films (France). Distributed in the U.S. by California Newsreel and Kino International. 102 minutes.

Gruenbaum, Ellen. 2001. *The Female Circumcision Controversy: An Anthropological Perspective*. Philadelphia: University of Pennsylvania Press.

Guimba the Tyrant/Guimba. 1995. Film written and directed by Cheick Oumar Sissoko. Produced by Kora Films (Mali). Distributed in the U.S. by California Newsreel and Kino International. 93 minutes.

Hoffelt, Sophie. 2003. 'Cheick Oumar Sissoko: "La tragique absence de nos images dans l'univers des images".' *CinémAction* 106: 122–3.

It's a Boy. 1995. Documentary produced and directed by Victor Schonfeld. Distributed in the U.S. by Filmakers Library. 52 minutes.

Kaddu beykat (Letter From My Village)/*Lettre paysanne* (Peasant Letter). 1975. Film written and directed by Safi Faye. Produced by Safi Films (Senegal). Distributed in the U.S. by Mypheduh Films. 98 minutes.

Kasarmu Ce, see pages 168–74.

Nyamanton/Garbage Boys. 1986. Film directed by Cheick Oumar Sissoko. Produced by Centre National de Production Cinématographique du Mali. 90 minutes.

Shell-Duncan, Bettina, and Ylva Hernlund (eds) 2000. *Female 'Circumcision' in Africa: Culture, Controversy, and Change*. Boulder, CO/London: Lynne Rienner.

Sissoko, Cheick Oumar. 2002. Personal communication.

Tableau Ferraille, see pages 139–46.

Ukadike, Nwachukwu Frank. 1994. *Black African Cinema*. Berkeley/Los Angeles/London: University of California Press.

——. 2002. *Questioning African Cinema: Conversations with Filmmakers*. Minneapolis/London: University of Minnesota Press.

Xala, see pages 126–38.

Yaaba, see pages 29–36.

Yeelen (Brightness). 1987. Film written and directed by Souleymane Cissé. Produced by Les Films Cissé (Mali). Distributed in the U.S. by Kino International. 105 minutes.

Kasarmu Ce 1991
Peasant Islam and Urban Corruption

A lot of the inspiration of writing the script came from certain parables in the Koran. (Saddik Balewa in an interview with Nicolas, 1993)

Kasarmu Ce is an Islamic morality play set in Northern Nigeria. Already *Tableau Ferraille*, with its chorus of Mourides, pointed towards Islamic morality as the path towards a better future. Now Islamic precepts become the leitmotif. At the very beginning of the film, before the title, Mallam (i.e. teacher), Hadi establishes the theme as he chants verses from the Koran, in Arabic, about the purification and the corruption of the soul. The subtitles end:

> By the soul and the order given it
> And its enlightenment as to right and wrong
> Truly he succeeds that purifies it
> And he fails who corrupts it.

Time and again we find Mallam Hadi in prayer with his string of beads, the *sibha* or *tasbih*. He washes the ink from Koran tablets for a solution to be used as medication, the *safara* we already encountered in the novel *Xala*. He interprets a dream in Islamic terms. And he shares his wisdom with his ward Sani.[1]

Religion is central to the Hausa village in northern Nigerian portrayed in *Kasarmu Ce*, and this element sets the film apart from most African films. The village is governed jointly by the Hakimi, the village head, and the Liman, the spiritual leader.[2] We are introduced to peasant Islam. Unlike cities that boast magnificent mosques, the village has to make do with a small mud structure. Women do not wear a veil, and they move around freely. In the courtship of Sani and Halima, it is she who repeatedly takes the initiative. The word of her grandmother is law in her family.[3] Most of the villagers are easily scared by supposed Dodo spirits even though the elders dismiss such pre-Islamic beliefs. The young men ask Mallam Hadi to find the source of the troubles by 'looking into the sands,' echoes of *Keïta!* and *Finzan*. Liquor, while frowned upon by the elders, is freely consumed: Bulus, the boozer, entertains his companions – and the film's viewers.

Apart from religion, the village in *Kasarmu Ce* differs from those portrayed in *Yaaba* and *Finzan* in two other important respects. The villagers affirm communal principles: 'One twig does not make a broom,' and we see them working together, yet they are quite mobile. Whereas village communities continue to exert a measure of control over the allocation of land in much of Africa, in densely populated Hausaland peasants can pawn and sell their land, and high rural mobility has long been established: Bulus has been born elsewhere; Karibou, 'son of magicians,' sells his land and moves away. And here we now encounter

1 Mallam Hadi is featured on the Nigerian English-language poster.

2 The religious leader of a Muslim community is more commonly referred to as Imam.

3 According to Balewa, Halima's grandmother, respected, kind, and affectionate, was to have been the major female lead in the film. However, the well-known actress who played the part was ill throughout the filming and all her scenes had to be cut at the editing stage (Bandele-Thomas, 1991). This may explain why the film is rather short.

A Saddik Balewa Film

KASARMU CE

Idan ba ka ci naman kura ba, ita ta ci naka

UMARU UBA GAYA Musa   SANI MUHAMMAD SHIRA Sani   MUSTAFA MOHAMMED Ibrahim

a resident trader. He is the only moneylender the villagers can turn to, and he controls the distribution of government-subsidized fertilizer. He is the only villager to enjoy the comforts that come with an electric generator. And, as his title indicates, Alhaji[4] Musa has made enough money off this small poor village to go on the pilgrimage to Mecca. But as he pursues his corrupt schemes, in league with Alhaji Malek, his rich and powerful patron in the city, it becomes apparent that he is anything but a good Muslim. In the end we come to see that in his heart he is a 'heathen': in his dream his crimes are expressed not in Islamic terms but in images of him destroying a sacrificial site and being confronted by a Dodo spirit. And thus it comes to pass that he will see a Dodo spirit in his final hour.

In *Finzan,* government policy to compel peasants to sell their food crop below market price was exploited for the personal profit of a government official and his crony. In *Kasarmu Ce,* a policy intended to benefit peasants with subsidized fertilizer is corrupted by the greed of the middlemen. The film adds a more spectacular element to the exploitation of the villagers. *Kasarmu Ce* may be translated as 'This Land is Ours'. The title relates to the secret scheming of Alhaji Malek, who uses the trader to buy up the village land under which a vein of

4 I follow local usage in spelling Alhaji for *Kasarmu Ce* while referring to El Hadji Abdoukader Beye in *Xala.*

Mallam Hadi praying sapphires and emeralds has been found. 'Biyi Bandele-Thomas (1991) went so far as to suggest that the film could be seen at one level as a thriller. The search for the precious stones and their discovery under cover of night contrasts strikingly with the serene chant of Mallam Hadi we hear in the distance.

Alhaji Malek appears to be a businessman who has access to the dominant political party and the government bureaucracy, perhaps he holds political office himself. He procures a voucher for government-subsidized fertilizer for the trader, and he arranges for Alhaji Musa to be the candidate of the party – presumably the locally dominant party – in the next local elections. We can be sure that the trader intends to inflate the price of the fertilizer he has hidden to the point were it will cover both the bribe he has had to pay to get delivery and a fat profit for himself. And his happy smile at the prospect of political office conveys his realization of how it will expand his opportunities to profiteer. Still, the extent of corruption is such that there is no honor among thieves: Alhaji Malek hides the discovery of the precious stones not only from the villagers, but from Alhaji Musa as well. Only Bulus is so naïve that he entrusts the deed to his land to the trader and accepts a little money for the road: chances are that the trader's toughs will bear witness that Bulus sold his land to Alhaji Musa.

The exploitative designs of Alhaji Malek are assisted by a British geologist. The only European to appear in the film, he readily lends his expertise to the machinations of a corrupt elite, but he does not wield influence. Two decades have passed since Europeans were the power behind the scene in *Xala*. But we have also moved from Senegal, in the French sphere of influence, to Nigeria, where early on the issues of colonialism and neo-colonialism lost much of the salience they held elsewhere on the continent. The experiences of the internally instigated Civil War that raged from 1967 to 1970, and the power that came with the oil boom of the 1970s may be adduced in explanation.

When the young men raise questions about the death of Sani's grandfather Mallam Ibrahim, the village elders and Mallam Hadi alike tell them to accept Fate. It remains for the young to organize and oppose the evil deeds perpetrated against the upright. But their power is circumscribed by the village. The film ends with Sani understanding the wisdom of Mallam Hadi's teaching that it is no use killing the snake unless the poisonous head is cut off. Alhaji Malek's power is undiminished, and he is bound to find another way to take advantage of the villagers. Most of them remain ignorant of the riches he seeks to appropriate, and those who do begin to understand his role cannot sanction him.[5]

In *Finzan*, the village stood united against the government official: conflict within the village was kept separate from conflict with the outside world. In *Kasarmu Ce*, the villagers choose not to recognize that what appears to them as internal conflict has been instigated from the outside, that the trader serves as the agent of Alhaji Malek. Alhaji Musa, unlike traders in many rural settings, is not an outsider. His grandfather grew onions and, the elders agree, was not to be trusted either. We may surmise that he sold onions in the city and initiated commercial exchanges. *Kasarmu Ce* develops the city connection in other ways as well: it takes us to the city as the trader visits his patron, as Sani and Korau go to buy presents for Korau's wedding, as Sani returns to get presents for Halima.

The depiction of Isa, the expert urban pickpocket, as a likeable fellow stands in stark contrast to that of the villains of the story.[6] And there is irony in the fact that two of them, Alhaji Musa and the manager of the fertilizer depot, are among his victims. There is good reason for the sympathy we are made to extend to Isa. His misdeeds don't amount to much when compared to the corruption, coercion, and outright assassination perpetrated by his victims. Yet while petty thieves, once discovered, have to run for their lives from lynching mobs, the rich and powerful are above the law. Indeed, when the film was made, Nigeria's leaders constituted the poisonous head of the snake. The military government of the day was notorious for the severity of its repression and the extent of its corruption. While Alhaji Malek was seeking to appropriate the mineral riches under the village land, the military were blatantly appropriating the petroleum riches under Nigerian lands for their private use. A glimpse of a unit of the mobile police marching by

5 The position of the villagers in *Kasarmu Ce* resembles that of the villagers in Chinua Achebe's *A Man of the People*. In the end they manage to sanction Alhaji Musa, just as Achebe's villagers sanctioned the trader Joshua. But in both stories the villagers are powerless in the wider political arena. There was, however, an important difference for the authors of the two stories: Achebe, unlike Balewa, could be explicit about the oppression and corruption of national politics in Nigeria while civilian rule lasted in the 1960s.

6 The depiction of Isa also contrasts with that of his fellow pickpockets in *Mapantsula* and *Xala*.

Saddik Balewa directing
Tom Conroy

7 The conflict between the young men and the elders over political action to be taken echoes the generational conflicts that *A Dry White Season*, *Mapantsula*, and *Fools* convey in the South African context.

8 The Hausa poster reproduced here features Sani, and its text translates as 'If you don't stop the hyena, it will surely eat you.' The British poster resembles the Hausa poster but it displays prominently 'An Anglo-Nigerian Co-Production' and omits any mention of Saddik Balewa.

serves to remind viewers of the repression of all dissent. The film, however, does not proceed to denounce corruption beyond Alhaji Malek – but then, its production was supported by the federal government through the Nigerian Council of Arts and Culture. Still, *Kasarmu Ce* appears to have ruffled the feathers of Nigeria's rulers: nearly two years after the film was supposed to have been released in Nigeria, the NCAC had kept tight control on the film, giving it only limited screenings (Bandele-Thomas, 1991; Whiteman, 1993). Perhaps this was because the film does suggest that the young can rise against oppression in spite of the acquiescence of their elders.[7] Or because *Kasarmu Ce* can also be translated as 'This State is Ours.'[8]

Balewa depicts a corrupt and murderous reality, but it is set in a moral universe where there is no room for cynicism. Mallam Hadi, after he has turned down the entreaties of the young to enquire into the death of Mallam Ibrahim, proceeds to tell Sani a story invoking the justice of the Eternal:

A thief took his son out to teach him how to steal. On a moonlit night they came to a crossroads. 'Listen my son,' said the thief, 'always look in all directions before stealing. If you see no one, it's safe to steal.' The boy pondered the words of his father. Then he pointed to the sky: 'What about looking up?' The thief looked to the heaven. He began to quake. He realized that someone powerful always watched him. He gave up stealing.

At the same time Balewa contrasts the failure of Hadi and his fellow elders to take action with the initiative of the young. Speaking of himself and his fellow African filmmakers, he has said that 'we do not offer easy solutions' (Nicolas, 1993), but we distinctly hear a message that might be summarized as 'think morally and act locally.'

Kasarmu Ce appears to have been intended for Nigerian as well as foreign audiences. Both will appreciate the lyrical moon shots and the beautiful close-ups of Mallam Hadi, Sani, Halima, and indeed Alhaji Musa. The magnificent rock landscape of the Dot Valley on Bauchi Plateau where it was filmed appeals to foreign audiences, but it holds interest for Nigerians as well: they discover one of the most stunning sights in their country, quite unlike the dry savannah where most Hausa live. The film has descriptive scenes such as the threshing of the harvested grain, that are probably of greater interest to Western than African audiences. But other features suggest that Balewa was primarily seeking to reach a Nigerian audience. Key elements in the plot take the story beyond everyday experience: the discovery of the rich deposit of precious stones, Alhaji Malek's maneuvers to appropriate the land under which they are buried, gullible peasants who believe in Dodo spirits. And at least one shot, the close-up of the spilled intestines of a goat, with flies crawling over them, puts off many Western viewers.

Kasarmu Ce was shot in Hausa, except for a little dialogue in English and pidgin. More Nigerians speak Hausa than any other language, and it serves as a *lingua franca* in much of West Africa. Indeed it is, along with Swahili, one of the two most widely spoken languages in Africa South of the Sahara, used by perhaps 50 million people. But Balewa's first feature film is only the second such film in Hausa, apart from some produced in colonial days.[9] With a budget of the order of £85,000, then about $150,000, *Kasarmu Ce* is very much a low-cost film production. A well-known actor, Kasimu Yero, put in a guest appearance as the cloth trader, other actors had various degrees of experience in theater and, to a lesser extent, in television, many were amateurs altogether. On the day shooting was to begin, after two weeks of rehearsals and a break, the lead actress did not show up. It turned out that she had left for Lagos – with a rich boyfriend (Nicolas, 1993).

Balewa, unlike other Nigerian filmmakers, enjoyed logistic support from the National Council of Arts and Culture in Nigeria and free access to the processing facilities of the National Film and Television School in Britain where he had trained (Bandele-Thomas, 1991). But such support carried its own costs: the NCAC controls the distribution of the film in Nigeria; and Balewa did not get to see 70 per cent of the material he shot until months later (Dalby and Givanni, 1993).

9 The pioneering role of Saddik Balewa in producing a film in Northern Nigeria for Hausa speakers presumably was the reason that the Nigerian government, closely tied to political leaders in that region, took the most unusual step of supporting the production of a film. That the director is a son of Abubakar Tafawa Balewa, the first Prime Minister of independent Nigeria assassinated in the first military coup in 1966, should have assured him of good connections with a regime close to his father's political allies.

The first Hausa feature film, Adamu Halilu's *Shehu Umar*, was also supported by the Nigerian government. It was based on a popular historical novella by Abubakar Tafawa Balewa, *Shaihu Umar*.

The Exploited and Neglected Peasantry

In the U.S., *Kasarmu Ce* was distributed for a while by Inter Image Video which pioneered the distribution of African films for the home video market at low prices. But at this time not a single Nigerian film, as distinct from the occasional video film, is in general distribution in the U.S.

References and Further Reading

Achebe, Chinua. 1966. *A Man of the People*. London: Heinemann.

Balewa, Abubakar Tafawa. 1955. *Shaihu Umar*. Zaria: Gaskiya. English translation by Mervin Hiskett (1967). London: Longmans; New York: Markus Wiener Publishers.

Bandele-Thomas, 'Biyi. 1991. 'This Land is Ours.' *West Africa* 3857, 12–18 August, pages 1326–7.

Dalby, Alexa, and June Givanni. 1993. 'Film Face of Africa.' *The Herald* (Glasgow), 11 May, page 16.

A Dry White Season, see pages 80–9.

Finzan, see pages 160–7.

Fools, see pages 97–106.

Kasarmu Ce (This Land is Ours). 1991. Film written and directed by Saddik Balewa. Produced by National Film and Television School (Britain) and National Council for Arts and Culture (Nigeria). Distributed by the National Film and Television School, London. Limited distribution in the U.S. by Myphedu Films. 84 minutes.

Keita! see pages 36–43.

Mapantsula, see pages 91–7.

Nicolas, Bernard. 1993. Video interview with Saddik Balewa. 30 minutes.

Shehu Umar. 1977. Film directed by Adamu Halilu, written by Adamu Halilu and Umaru Ladan. Produced by Fedfilms Nigeria. A 90 minute version is distributed by the British Film Institute. 140 minutes.

Tableau Ferraille, see pages 139–46.

Whiteman, Kay. 1993. 'Film Frustrations for Saddik.' *West Africa*, 5–11 April, page 544.

Xala, see pages 126–38.

Yaaba, see pages 29–36.

6 Between the African Mass Market & International Recognition

The plight of African filmmakers has been defined time and again in terms of the obstacles to the distribution of their films in Africa. Recently, technological change has added a new dimension to the discussion. Low-cost video production has come to Africa. It is booming already in a couple of African countries. The video industry in Nigeria is beginning to be referred to as Nollywood. Its output is indeed prodigious. In 1995, the censors reviewed 201 video films, the following year 250, and by now as many as 650 are said to be produced every year – more than the number of films produced in the U.S. Average sales are about 30,000, but the most successful releases sell as many as 150,000 copies. Most cinema theaters in Lagos, the multi-million former capital, are showing Nigerian videos (Haynes and Okome, 2000). A magazine, *Reel Stars*, was launched. In Ghana, about fifty video films were released each year in the 1990s (Meyer, 2003). Most movie houses in Accra, the capital, had switched to these indigenous productions and ceased to show any foreign films by the late 1990s (Meyer, 1999b). A popular movie would be watched by tens of thousands in Accra theaters and then sold as video cassettes for home use for ten dollars or less. One Accra video shop reported selling 30,000 copies of a particularly popular Nigerian video within six months (Meyer, 1999a). In both countries they are broadcast on television.

Nigerian videos sell all over anglophone Africa, and producers have begun to subtitle and dub videos in French for distribution in franco-phone Africa. The position of African producers of video films is in some ways analogous to that of filmmakers in other poor countries such as India and Egypt. They produce large numbers of features that are commercially successful at home. They export beyond the national borders, but do not even attempt to access Western markets. Such distribution as exists overseas serves Africans through the Internet and in stores cater-ing to the expatriate African community. Britain has a large enough number of fans to prompt the publication of the magazine *Nigerian Videos*.

These videos were pioneered by producers without prior experience with film and by directors without formal training. They operated on extremely low budgets: the cost of producing a video film came to about $10,000 in Ghana in the 1990s (Meyer, 1999b). The scripts were rudi-mentary, the shooting completed in a week or two, the technical quality poor. Over the years directors acquired expertise. In Ghana, the Ghana

My ambition is for my films to be seen in Africa and elsewhere in the world, that the public choose them as films, and not because my films are 'African'.
(Ouedraogo, 1995: 338, my translation)

Between the African Mass Market and International Recognition

Film Industry Corporation began producing video films, and a number of its trained filmmakers left to venture out on their own after it was privatized. Now experienced professionals produce technically sophisticated video films with spectacular special effects (Meyer, 2003).

The content of the video films produced in Nigeria and Ghana is market-driven.[1] Most exhibit the trappings of affluent settings – like so many Hollywood films. Many respond to their viewers' preoccupation with occult forces by giving them major play. Special effects allow them to make the invisible forces visible: audiences witness ghostly apparitions; they may watch a woman leave her body and transform herself into a vulture/witch. This revelation of the occult confirms its existence, enhancing the credibility of beliefs in the occult. The occult is usually represented as Evil, and often it is ultimately defeated by Christian forces of Good. The videos resemble soap operas in that they tend to focus on domestic issues. Most reject polygamy and extra-marital affairs, and affirm the priority of the nuclear over the extended family. Such films hold particular appeal for women who are eager to take their husbands and boy friends to the movies to implant the message (Meyer, 2003).

Human sacrifice which brings great wealth is a recurring theme in such video films. In their distorted fashion these stories reflect a reality. Much wealth is ill-gotten by means that bring death. Violent crime, rampant in many cities, is the most obvious example, but greater wealth is amassed through schemes that kill many more, if less obviously. In *Xala* we heard of food meant for famine relief being diverted to the black market, and we can imagine the consequences. Corruption that empties government coffers deprives people of necessities, most strikingly when people are denied the most basic preventive and curative health services. Where many African films present a critique of political processes that engender extreme inequalities, these videos films promote an altogether divergent interpretation.

Quite different stories are characteristic of Hausa video films in northern Nigeria. They have displaced the once predominant Indian films while drawing on them in theme and aesthetics. The typical story involves young lovers overcoming seemingly insurmountable obstacles, the imposition of an arranged marriage often prominent among them, to be united eventually. Along the way the audience is treated to loosely integrated sequences of song and dance – even if mixed-sex song sequences have come to be banned in the wake of the increased affirmation of Islamic tenents. Some of these films are based on romantic novellas which themselves were inspired by Indian films (Larkin, 2003). A major third type of video film is the epic based on oral history and myth, such as the story of Sango, the Yoruba God of Thunder.

If African filmmakers seeking to reach African audiences faced competition from popular foreign films released at low cost in a marginal market, they are now confronted with competition from these low-cost African video productions. While their budgets are puny by Hollywood standards, they are easily fifty times those of their new, indigenous competitors. Their goal of reaching African audiences appears further off

1 Summaries of several Nigerian videos films, illustrated with frames, may be found in Haynes (2000).

than ever. Some are likely to embrace video technology in the near future. It remains to be seen whether they will adopt topics and adopt interpretations that hold sufficient popular appeal to compete effectively in the mass market video producers have so successfully established.

Other African filmmakers are likely to continue pursuing international recognition. Video technology offers them the opportunity to reduce their dependence on established sponsors and consumers in rich countries: the French government, the European Union, non-government organizations in Western Europe, European television, the international festival circuit, and the college market in the U.S. For these arbiters of the prospects of African films venturing beyond Africa, the primary appeal of such films lies in their 'African' specificity. Even if video production lessens the financial dependence of African filmmakers, these thematic expectations of the restricted circle of Western consumers of their films are likely to remain salient. Additional constraints confront any attempt to break into Western mass markets. Abandoning the claim to a specifically African dimension means competing head-on with a flood of Western productions. These Western films present characters with whom Western viewers can identify much more readily. Most of them are supported by huge budgets for production and distribution. And they usually feature popular actors. So far few non-Western filmmakers, nearly all of them from East Asia, have managed to compete effectively, and the appeal of their films was usually based at least in part on the non-Western context they imaged for Western viewers.

Still, some African filmmakers have been anxious to escape the confines of producing films that present 'African stories' in an 'African mode.' Three widely acclaimed films have buttressed their claim to move beyond 'African film' by drawing on stories that, while strikingly diverse, are part of the Western canon. Cheick Oumar Sissoko's *Genesis* sets the Old Testament's fratricidal conflict between Jacob and Esau in the Sahel. *Hyenas*, the most important film of the celebrated and much-missed Djibril Diop Mambety, recreated a major play, Friedrich Dürrenmatt's *The Visit*, in a Senegalese setting to critical acclaim. And Joseph Gaï Ramaka's *Karmen Geï*, also set in Senegal, draws on the Carmen story which, in its various permutations, has gathered a large following over more than a century. As the directors claim these stories as shared stories, they give them a distinctive African imprint. They situate them in their own societies and, in varying degrees, transform them and enrich them with local cultural elements.

We will conclude our exploration by examining two outstanding efforts to move beyond 'African film' that recall well-established film genres: the buddy movie where the friendship of men is jeopardized by their relationships with women, and the musical comedy that takes its aspiring artist from rags to stardom and the woman of his dreams.

References

Dürrenmatt, Friederich. 1958 (1956). *The Visit: A Drama in Three Acts.* Adapted by Maurice Jacques Valency. New York: S. French. English translation of *Der Besuch de alten Dame: Eine tragische Komödie.* Zürich: Verlag de Arche.

Genesis/La Genèse. 1999. Film directed by Cheick Oumar Sissoko, written by Jean-Louis Sagot Duvauroux, produced by Kora Films (Mali), Balanzan, Centre National de Production Cinématographique du Mali, and Cinéma Public Films (France). Distributed in the U.S. by California Newsreel and Kino International. 102 minutes.

Haynes, Jonathan (ed.) (1997) 2000. *Nigerian Video Films,* edited by Jonathan Haynes. Revised and expanded edition. Research in International Studies. Africa Series 73. Athens, OH: Ohio University Center for International Studies.

——, and Onookome Okome. (1997) 2000. 'Evolving Popular Media: Nigerian Video Films.' *Nigerian Video Films,* edited by Jonathan Haynes. Revised and expanded edition. Research in International Studies. Africa Series 73. Athens, OH: Ohio University Center for International Studies. 51–88.

Hyenas/Hyènes. 1992. Written and directed by Djibril Diop Mambety. Produced by ADR Productions (France), Thelma Film (Switzerland), Maag Daan (Senegal), and MK2 Productions (France). Distributed in the U.S. by California Newsreel and Kino International. 113 minutes.

Karmen Geï. 2001. Film written and directed by Joseph Gaï Ramaka. Produced by Euripide (France), Mataranka (Senegal), Les Atéliers de L'Arche (France), and Zagarianka (Senegal). Distributed in the U.S. by California Newsreel. 82 minutes.

Larkin, Brian. 2003. 'Why Indians Film Travel: African Videos, Bollywood and Global Media.' *Multiculturalism, Postcoloniality and Transnational Media,* edited by Ella Shohat and Robert Stam. New Brunswick, NJ: Rutgers University Press.

Meyer, Birgit. 1999a. '"Blood Money": On the Attraction of Nigerian Movies in Ghana.' Paper presented at the 1999 Annual Meeting of the American Anthropological Association, Chicago, November.

——. 1999b. 'Popular Ghanaian Cinema and "African Heritage".' *Africa Today* 46 (2): 93–114.

——. 2003. 'Ghanaian Popular Cinema and the Magic in and of Film.' *Magic and Modernity: Interfaces of Revelation and Concealment,* edited by Birgit Meyer and Peter Pels. Stanford, CA: Stanford University Press.

Ouedraogo, Idrissa. 1995. 'Le cinéma et nous.' *L'Afrique et le Centenaire du Cinéma/Africa and the Centenary of Cinema.* Paris/Dakar: Présence Africaine. 336–41.

Xala, see pages 26–36.

Kini and Adams 1997
The Vagaries of Adult Friendship

To affirm hate, joy, violence, love for Africa is to reconstitute Africa beyond the clichés the world has established and that we have often endorsed. (Idrissa Ouedraogo in an interview with Barlet, 1997: 45, my translation)

SELECTION OFFICIELLE CANNES 1997
KINI & ADAMS
UN FILM DE IDRISSA OUÉDRAOGO

Between the African Mass Market and International Recognition

Kini and Adams, Idrissa Ouedraogo's most recent feature, represents the move away from social and political concerns to personal relationships. African directors set out to *re-image* Africa, and we were given the opportunity to *re-imagine* the continent and its people. And most of the films we have considered so far told of African struggles for liberation or the failures of post-colonial Africa. Now Ouedraogo *re-images* Africa in a quite different way: he makes us see that Africans face the same conflicts as Westerners. His story of the vicissitudes of adult friendship in a rapidly changing world is all too similar to our own experiences. At the same time Ouedraogo introduces ambiguities and transcends the manichean tendencies that often prevail in African films.

Like *Yaaba*, *Kini and Adams* tells a story of friendship. But it is a very different story. Ouedraogo has taken us from the constancy of the friendship between two children and an old woman in a village that time forgot, to two men struggling to realize their aspirations in a world that is constantly changing – even out in the countryside. Now the endurance of friendship, however profound, is no longer assured. Diverging career paths put friendship at risk. The friendship of men collides with their relationships with women. Along the way Ouedraogo explores, sometimes indirectly, a wide range of relationships between men and women. In the story of the friendship of Kini and Adams we are confronted with universal issues. *Kini and Adams* joins the genre of the buddy movie. The buddy theme is explicit in the film's title, and it is conveyed in the beautiful film poster of the two friends sitting on top of their car against the setting sun.

Ouedraogo presents a universal story, and he intends it for a universal audience.[1] On a budget of 9 million French francs (Bouzet, 1997), then about $1.8 million, Ouedraogo managed to create a heart-wrenching drama leavened by humor. With the entire dialogue in English, it reaches out to a large potential public in Africa and beyond. The magnificent photography, including dramatic close-ups of faces, is presented on widescreen. And this time Ouedraogo recruited professional actors: Kini, Adams, Ben, and Aida are played by actors well established in South African theater, television, and film. Kini is portrayed by Vusi Kunene whom we have already glimpsed in the role of Mazambane in *Fools*, and who appears in the role of Msimangu in *Cry, the Beloved Country*. John Kani, who plays Ben, is best known for his collaboration with Athol Fugard, South Africa's foremost playwright. We saw him in the role of Julius Nqukula, the Ngubenes' lawyer, in *A Dry White Season*. Ouedraogo has argued that while peasants could convey the innocence of children and old age in *Yaaba*, it required professional actors for us to get caught up in the emotions of adults (Ruelle, 1997). But we can see his choice of actors also as part of a move towards mainstream film production. The music of *Kini and Adams* is emblematic of Ouedraogo's shift away from 'African' film. Composed by Wally Badarou, who was born of African parents in France, most of it draws on the African diaspora rather than Africa.

Kini and Adams is set in rural Zimbabwe. Here we see a dispersed rural settlement pattern, unlike the compact West African villages in *Yaaba*,

1 Ouedraogo's rejection of the notion of *the* African film and his desire to produce universal films are the central issues in *Idrissa*, a documentary on his life and work by Malick Sy.

Finzan, and *Kasarmu Ce*. More importantly, the historical experiences have been very different. West African villages have enjoyed considerable stability since pre-colonial days in contrast to the series of upheavals that have marked rural Zimbabwe: the armed confrontation with European settlers at the end of the nineteenth century, the alienation of land to these settlers, and the guerrilla war for majority rule in the 1970s that we witnessed in *Flame*. These events caused profound transformations: large numbers of people had to abandon their ancestral homes, and those who stayed were driven to choose opposing sides in the conflicts that intruded on them.

With *Kini and Adams* Ouedraogo takes us to a rural setting that is very different from *Yaaba* and does not conform to Western notions of 'the African village.' At the same time *Kini and Adams* focuses, even more than the earlier film, on individuals, and conveys little sense of the local community. The village has just about disappeared. Instead we get involved with two individuals, Kini who lives with his wife Aida and their daughter Bongi, and Adams who leads a bachelor's existence. In distinct contrast to the villagers in *Yaaba*, for Kini and Adams the city, while distant, is very much part of their universe. Like so many peasants, they want to escape their rural poverty. They are rebuilding an old beat-up car that will take them to the city and, as a cab, will provide them with a livelihood. The peddler brings from the city the spare parts they need to realize their ambition. Kini and Adams are united in their efforts to make their dream of an urban future come true.

The two friends have worked on their car for five years, but their dream remains just that, a dream. Then the city suddenly arrives on their doorstep in the form of a crew that is going to work the local quarry. A troupe of prostitutes, led by their madam, follows soon. Meanwhile, a poster and a television program bring news that Big John, the musician who went off to the city, has become a star. Kini and Adams are employed when they know the right answers to the questions of Ben, the leader of the crew: What does a deaf-mute do when he wants to drink? what does a blind man do when he wants a pair of scissors? They soon become involved with the people from the city. Kini is an ambitious worker, and he becomes a foreman after he has saved the life of Ben. Adams, the dreamer, turns jealous, finds himself bossed around by Kini, and seeks solace with the independent prostitute, Binja. Thus the issue of the inequality between the countryside and the city is overshadowed by the classic theme of the contrast between a simple rural life and the temptations of the city. While Aida tries to persuade Kini to be content with their rural existence, Ben seeks to introduce him to a fast life of drink and women, and Binja brings Adams to perdition.

In the end the people of the city separate the two friends. Ben offers Kini the opportunity to move to the city, and Adams feels abandoned. He is good-hearted – earlier, he lets Kini repeat a wager until Kini wins the right to their car for the night – but now he succumbs to the lure of Binja and betrays his friend. The defining moment comes when Kini takes on all responsibility for Adams's theft, but Adams is unable to respond to his

generosity. From there on Adams's actions carry a great deal of ambivalence, and we are left to guess at his understandings and intentions.

Kini and Adams joins earthy humor and tragedy. Riddles are part of the fun. Five birds are sitting on a fence; I shoot one; how many are left on the fence? What has two thumbs, one eye, and wants to be loved like God? And then there are stories, like the story of the man who went to shit on a farmer's land. But Ouedraogo's view of friendship is bleak (there are limits to what a man will do for his friend who went to pee and encountered a snake), his take on sibling rivalry altogether dismal: when God grants a poor man a wish with the proviso that whatever he wishes for himself, his younger brother will get twofold, the elder opts to lose an eye. We are far from the solidarity of the extended family taken for granted in *Yaaba* and *Finzan*. As in *Yaaba*, Ouedraogo ends his new film with a somber realism rare in Hollywood.

Ouedraogo is arguably the most important African filmmaker of the second generation that began producing films in the 1980s. Ukadike (2002: 151) sees him as the dean of the 'new wave' in African film. To date Ouedraogo has directed eight full-length feature films. He is fêted in Burkina Faso where he has directed fifty 12-minute episodes of a sitcom, *Kadi Jolie*. Some of his films have enjoyed considerable success. *Yaaba* won the International Critics' Prize at the Cannes Film Festival, the Special Prize of the FESPACO Jury, and the Sakura Gold Prize at the Tokyo International Film Festival; *Tilaï* received the Grand Jury Prize at Cannes and the Grand Prize at FESPACO. If the village in *Yaaba* remained ahistorical, *Tilaï* dramatizes a legend explicitly set in the precolonial past. After these successes Ouedraogo sought a new style that culminated in *Kini and Adams*, 'the great work of my cinematic career, with an alternative vision and curiosity for the world' (Ukadike, 2002: 152). But without the

appeal of 'African' specificity, the film so far has enjoyed little recognition in spite of its qualities. It was selected for the official competition at the Cannes Film Festival, but it did not garner any prizes. In France, it sold only 7,000 seats in 1997 (Barlet, 2000: 254). At this time it does not have a distributor in the U.S.

John Kani and Idrissa Ouedraogo during the shooting

References and Further Reading

Barlet, Olivier. 1997. 'Entretien: Idrissa Ouedraogo (Burkina Faso).' *Africultures* 2: 45–9.
——. 2000 (1996). *African Cinemas: Decolonizing the Gaze.* London/New York: Zed Books. Revised and up-dated translation, by Chris Turner, of *Les cinémas d'Afrique noire: Le regard en question.* Collection Images plurielles. Paris: L'Harmattan.
Bouzet, A.-D. 1997. 'J'avais envie de ma liberté.' *Libération,* 22 October.
Cry, the Beloved Country. 1995. Film directed by Darrell James Roodt, written by Ronald Harwood. Produced by Anant Singh (South Africa). Distributed in the U.S. by Swank Motion Pictures. 109 minutes.
A Dry White Season, see pages 80–9.
Finzan, see pages 160–7.
Flame, see pages 57–63.
Fools, see pages 97–105.

Idrissa. 2001. Documentary directed by Malick Sy. Produced by Canal France International (France) and Stella Films (France). 52 minutes.

Kasarmu Ce, see pages 168–74.

Kini and Adams. 1997. Film directed by Idrissa Ouedraogo, written by Idrissa Ouedraogo, Olivier Lorelle, and Santiago Amigorena. Produced by Noé Productions (France), Les Films de la Plaine (France), Polar Productions (Britain), and Framework International (Zimbabwe). Distributed in Southern Africa by Media for Development International, in France by PolyGram. 93 minutes.

Ruelle, Catherine. 1997. 'Entretien avec Idrissa Ouedraogo,' in press kit *Kini and Adams.*

Tilaï. 1990. Film written and directed by Idrissa Ouedraogo. Produced by Les Films de l'Avenir (Burkina Faso), Waka Film (Switzerland), and Rhéa Films (France). Distributed in the U.S. by New Yorker Films. 81 minutes.

Ukadike, Nwachukwu Frank. 2002. *Questioning African Cinema: Conversations with Filmmakers.* Minneapolis/London: University of Minnesota Press.

Yaaba, see pages 29–36.

La Vie est belle 1987
It's a Wonderful Life

The term 'commercial' is quite pejorative, let me call it 'popular cinema.' I like to make a film that many Africans come and see and feel good with ... [and] which will feature African problems and accomplishments at the same time.
(Mweze Ngangura quoted by Ukadike, 1994: 285)

1 Papa Wemba is featured in *Sigui*, along with other artists who have found international recognition, go on concert tours across Europe and North America, and record in professional studios. The documentary contrasts them with musicians who play for expatriate African communities in Europe and produce their own recordings for that substantial market.

2 Joseph Gaï Ramaka's *Karmen Geï* is even more of a musical as well as a dance revue, Med Hondo's *West Indies* and Flora Gomes's *Nha Fala* are both full-blown musicals.

La Vie est belle is set in Kinshasa, the multi-million capital of the Congo world-famous for a music that blends traditional music with styles from the diaspora. When Senegal's music superstar Ismaël Lô appeared in the lead role in *Tableau Ferraille*, we didn't hear him sing very often. Now Congolese superstar Papa Wemba (Julius Shungu Wembadio) in the lead role sings for us time and again – and does not show his 37 years.[1] He is joined by another star, the obese Pépé Kallé (Jean Kabasele Yampanya) as himself, and the dancing dwarf Emoro (Tumba Ayila). Their songs are in Lingala, the *lingua franca* of Kinshasa and the Western Congo, except for the title song which mixes French and Lingala. It all ends in an exuberant grand finale of music and dance.[2]

La Vie est belle never ventures into politics. The directors, Benoît Lamy and Mweze Ngangura, had little choice in the matter, as Ngangura acknowledged recently: 'In a society in which it's very difficult to speak about politics or to be very critical, comedy ... [is] the only means to talk about very serious things, but in a light way' (Chiwengo, 2001: 14). The Congo (Kinshasa),[3] a country rich in mineral resources and agricultural potential, was oppressed and impoverished by the ruthless and utterly corrupt Mobutu regime which lasted from 1965 until 1997 – with a good deal of assistance from Western powers until late in the day.[4] Only as the regime crumbled could Balufu Bakupa Kanyinda's *Le Damier* show us a dictator brutal and capricious.[5]

3 The country had been rebaptized Zaïre in the name of Africanization by then President Mobutu who added Sese Soko, the All Powerful, to his name. A rebel movement led by Laurent Kabila overthrew the Mobutu regime in 1997, and the country reverted to its former name as the (Belgian) Congo: it needs to be identified by its capital Kinshasa in order to distinguish it from neighboring Congo (Brazzaville), formerly a French colony. Formally, the Congo (Kinshasa) is known as the Democratic Republic of Congo, Congo (Brazzaville) as the Republic of the Congo. The two capitals are just across the Congo/Zaïre river from each other, and traders such as Mamu commonly make the crossing to take advantage of different market conditions in the two countries.

In *La Vie est belle* we hear people addressing each other as *citoyen* (*citoyenne* for women), i.e. citizen. This form of address, derived from the French Revolution, was imposed by Mobutu.

4 The regime is portrayed in Thierry Michel's *Mobutu, King of Zaïre*. The actors in the current drama in Congo are African, in particular five countries that have sent soldiers to do battle and pilfer a country rich in resources. Still, the desperate situation is a direct consequence of Western support for the Mobutu regime and the refusal of Western powers to intervene in the 1994 massacre in Rwanda and its aftermath.

5 In 1996, with Mobutu still in power, José Laplaine made his first film, *Macadam Tribu*, in Mali. Only Papa Wemba's songs remind us of the director's Congolese origin.

Between the African Mass Market and International Recognition

Happy ending

6 The subtitles' 'Mister Nganga' is in error. *Nganga* designates a spiritual healer among the Bakongo, and the French dialogue's 'Maître' expresses a degree of respect that 'Mister' fails to convey.

7 For viewers familiar with Papa Wemba there is the added kick of seeing him in rags. The star prides himself on being the most elegantly dressed man around. In local parlance such well-dressed people are referred to as *sapeurs*, or members of the Société des ambianceurs et des personnes élégantes (Society of People of Ambience and Elegance). Papa Wemba has been known as Le Roi de la Sape, King of the Sape. The film touches on Kinshasa fashion when Mongali shows off his black-and-white shoes to Kuru.

Precisely because it could not enter the political arena, *La Vie est belle* is an early example of an African film that forsakes 'African' issues to join the mainstream. While *La Vie est belle* was released in the U.S. under its original French title, which literally translates as 'Life is Beautiful,' distributors refer to it as *Life is Rosy*. The English subtitles likewise translate Emoro's recurrent exclamations 'La vie est belle' as 'Life is Rosy.' This translation conveys the fairy tale character of the film. And what a tale it is! The skirt chaser Nvuandu learns his lesson; his wife Mamu spins an intrigue that wins him back; her gigolo Mongali links up with Kabibi's envious neighbor Nzazi; Kuru makes it from village musician to the Kinshasa music scene – unlike Papa Wemba who grew up in Kinshasa, but like that other creation of fiction, Big John in *Kini and Adams*; and he will, you may rest assured, live with beautiful Kabibi happily ever after. Master Nganga,[6] the 'witch doctor', and the 'tribal' dance he organizes, provide a dose of exoticism and add comic effects. Similar stories with a famous entertainer in the role of a backwoods boy who finds success,[7] similar comedies of romantic entanglements – indeed three connected triangles of six characters in love requited, unrequited or capricious – have been produced in Hollywood, Paris, Cairo, and Bollywood many times. Ngangura, however, has emphasized the film's roots in popular theater and television which draw on the *Commedia dell'Arte*. If Papa Wemba, Pépé Kallé, and Emoro assured the film's popular appeal, it was reinforced by the selection of professional theater actors for a range of minor roles (Ukadike, 2002: 138).

Ngangura had trained at the Institut des Arts de Diffusion in Belgium. He showed his script to his former teacher Lamy who encouraged him to move beyond the 16mm production with local resources he had envisaged. Eventually *La Vie est belle* secured relatively generous funding,

1.3 million dollars. The largest share came from the Belgian Ministry of Culture – with strings attached: the non-Belgian novice filmmaker had to find an established Belgian co-director (Nagbou, 1988). The product of this most unusual arrangement was a success, and the investment paid off. *La Vie est belle* found a large audience in Africa and beyond. In Kinshasa it ran continuously in the big theaters for the better part of a year (Aufderheide, 1988).[8] In the francophone world its appeal was enhanced by a dialogue virtually entirely in French, however implausible – Kuru speaking with an old villager, for example. In the U.S. it is one of the very few African films to have found wide distribution in the home video market: it has reached a public beyond the afrophile.[9]

Mweze Ngangura and Benoît Lamy celebrate the first shot of La Vie est belle

8 *La Vie est belle* was promoted in the Congo (Kinshasa) with a comic book (Baruti, 1987) telling the life of Papa Wemba.

9 The soundtrack was distributed on LP.

Between the African Mass Market and International Recognition

La Vie est belle trades on the world-wide recognition of music from the Congo. At the same time the film reminds us of issues we have encountered already on our African journey. A childless marriage is a compelling argument to take a second wife. Kuru's journey from the dusty village to the modern city provides striking contrasts in architecture, dress, and entertainment. In the city, Nvuandu's Mercedes and the fancy dresses of Mamu and her friends contrast with the poverty of the street hawkers, the shoeshine boys, and the tenants of Kabibi's mother Dingari. It is easy for a man of means such as Nvuandu to make Dingari push her daughter into marrying him. But *La Vie est belle*, instead of polemics against the rich, makes jokes at their expense (Diawara, 1992: 142). It also has a sexist streak. Screaming women tear into each other. Members of the Moziki Club boast of their extra-marital affairs as 'liberation' and we forget that theirs is after all a savings association like the Baax Yaaj in *Tableau Ferraille*.

La Vie est belle follows a formula as old as the movies – a musical comedy around a boy and a beautiful girl who, whatever the adversities, will eventually be united in a happy ending. The film poster engagingly conveys the message: the face of Kabibi dominates the suggestion of a music score and Kuru joking with his friend. We can savor the film as a happy ending to our journey of exploration. And it serves to remind us that Africans make merry like everybody else. Since it comes from a part of the world mainly known from television pictures of poverty, starvation, and death, we may take it as a celebration of the resilience of Africans. Indeed, the film is dedicated to the people of Kinshasa. In its first incarnation, the title song 'La Vie est belle' continues 'débrouillez-vous, débrouillez-vous,' which might be rendered as 'hustle and get by, hustle and get by.'

Perhaps there is something more we can take away from *La Vie est belle*. The film prods us to enjoy life as we listen to the music, follow the rags to riches story, and savor the comedy spiced with local aphorisms. *La Vie est belle* is a life-affirming film, just like the American classic *It's a Wonderful Life* – which is rendered as *La Vie est belle* in the French version. The vibrant music scene of Kinshasa in the midst of severe political oppression, rampant corruption, and economic decline suggests the question: have some of us who are privileged to live in societies affluent beyond the imagination of our forebears become so absorbed in amassing ever more material possessions that we have forgotten how to enjoy life?

References and Further Reading

Aufderheide, Pat. 1988. 'African Filmmakers in conversation.' *Black Film Review* 4: 6–16.
Baruti, Barly. 1987. *Viva la musica*. Kinshasa: Afrique Editions.
Chiwengo, Ngwarsungu. 2001. 'Mweze Ngangura – Congelese Filmmaker. Studio Interview April 28, 2000.' *ALA Bulletin* 28 (1): 108–36.
Diawara, Manthia. 1992. *African Cinema: Politics and Culture*. Blacks in the Diaspora. Bloomington/Indianapolis: Indiana University Press.

It's a Wonderful Life. 1946. Film directed by Frank Capra, written by Frances Goodrich, Albert Hackett and Jo Swerling. Produced by Liberty (USA). Distributed in the U.S. by Swank Motion Pictures. 125 minutes.

Karmen Geï. 2001. Film written and directed by Joseph Gaï Ramaka. Produced by Euripide (France), Mataranka (Senegal), Les Atéliers de l'Arche (France), and Zagarianka (Senegal). Distributed in the U.S. by California Newsreel. 82 minutes.

Kini and Adams, see pages 181–6.

Le Damier, Papa National Oyé! (The Draughtsmen Clash). 1996. Film written and directed by Balufu Bakupa Kanyinda. Produced by Dipanda Yo! (Zaïre/Congo), Centre National du Cinéma (Gabon), Centrale Productions (Gabon), and Myriapodus Films (France). Distributed in the U.S. by ArtMattan Productions. 40 minutes.

La Vie est belle (Life is Rosy). 1987. Film directed by Benoît Lamy and Mweze Ngangura, written by Mweze Ngangura, Maryse Léon, and Benoît Lamy. Produced by Lamy Films (Belgium), Stephan Films (France), and Sol'Oeil (Congo Kinshasa). Distributed in the U.S. by California Newsreel and Kino International. 85 minutes.

Macadam Tribu (Asphalt Tribe). 1996. Film written and directed by José Laplaine. Produced by Flamingo Films (France), Bakia Films (Congo/Zaïre), Centre National de Production Cinématographique du Mali, and Animatografo (Portugal). Distributed in France by Médiathèque des Trois Mondes, Paris. Available for viewing at Cinémathèque Afrique, Paris. 90 minutes.

Mobutu, King of Zaïre. 1999. Documentary written and directed by Thierry Michel. Produced by Les Films de la Passerelle (Belgium), CBA, Image Création, and Les Films d'Ici. Distributed in the U.S. by First Run/Icarus Films. 156 minutes.

Nagbou, Mustapha. 1988. 'Le réalisateur zaïrois Ngangura Mweze.' *Septième Art* 64-5: 23–4.

Nha Fala (My Voice). 2002. Film directed by Flora Gomes and Franck Moinard. Produced by Fado Filmes (Portugal), Les Films de Mai (France), and Samsa Film (Luxemburg). 90 minutes.

Schatzberg, Michael G. 1988. *The Dialectics of Oppression in Zaïre*. Bloomington : Indiana University Press.

Sigui. 1998. Documentary written and directed by Bakonga. Produced by Afro art and Afrique en créations. 52 minutes.

Stewart, Gary. 2000. *Rumba on the River: A History of the Popular Music of the Two Congos*. London/New York: Verso.

Tableau Ferraille, see pages 139–46.

Ukadike, Nwachukwu Frank. 1994. *Black African Cinema*. Berkeley/Los Angeles/London: University of California Press.

——. 2002. *Questioning African Cinema: Conversations with Filmmakers*. Minneapolis/London: University of Minnesota Press.

Young, Crawford and Thomas Turner. 1985. *The Rise and Decline of the Zairian State*. Madison: University of Wisconsin Press.

West Indies: Les Nègres marrons de la liberté. 1979. Film directed by Med (Mohamed Abib Medoun) Hondo. Produced by Soleil O (France), Yanek Sces (Mauritania), RTA (Algeria), IPC, ONCM (Mauritania). 110 minutes.

In Life on Earth *Abderrahmane Sissako starts out in a French department store. Later scenes are set in Sokolo, a small town in Mali: women fetching water at a well, a photographer at work, a radio host broadcasting the complaints of a farmer on the local radio station*

Epilogue

Re-Imagining Ourselves

We have considered seventeen films, most of them produced by Africans who have invited us to re-imagine Africa South of the Sahara. They have taken us on an exciting journey across a diverse continent. We have travelled from the founding of an ancient empire to wars of liberation, to *apartheid*, to neo-colonialism, and the afflictions of contemporary Africa; from the village that time forgot to the Soweto Uprising, from a South African urban culture shaped by Hollywood to village Islam in Northern Nigeria. As we re-imagine the Other, we are prompted to re-imagine ourselves. Thus the last film we saw, *La Vie est belle*, brought to the fore the question how our quest for material possessions relates to the enjoyment of life.

Our discovery of Africa re-imaged by its filmmakers prompts a second question: is it sufficient to watch or do we have an obligation to act? In *Life on Earth* Abderrahmane Sissako starts out in a French department store overflowing with merchandise, then takes us to the austere life of Sokolo, the small town in Mali he came from. Along the way he quotes Aimé Césaire (2000: 9), the celebrated Caribbean writer, leader with Léopold Sédar Senghor of the *négritude* movement:

Gardez-vous de vous croiser les bras	Beware of folding your arms
En l'attitude stérile du spectateur...	In the sterile stance of a spectator ...
Car la vie n'est pas un spectacle	For life is not a spectacle
Car un homme qui crie	For a man who screams
N'est pas un ours qui dance	Is not a dancing bear
	(my translation)

Can we re-imagine ourselves as citizens of the world who have a measure of responsibility towards our fellow human beings, wherever they may be, whatever their nationality, whatever their race? [1]

1 For perspective consider that in 2000 the U.S. spent $10 billion on foreign aid, most of it primarily geared to the foreign policy interests of the U.S. rather than the needs of the world's poor. That same year U.S. consumers spent $16 billion on pet food. The U.S. expenditure on foreign aid constituted about 0.1 per cent of the national income. That put the U.S. last amongst rich countries. A country such as Sweden spent eight times as much relative to its income (World Bank, 2002 World Development Indicators).

References

Césaire, Aimé. ([1956] 2000). *Cahier d'un retour au pays natal.* Paris: Présence Africaine. Edited with introduction, commentary, and notes, by Abiola Irele. Second edition. Columbus, OH: Ohio State University Press.
La Vie est belle, see pages 186–91.
Life on Earth/La Vie sur terre. 1998. Film written and directed by Abderrahmane Sissako. Part of the international '2000 Seen By ...' series by independent film makers. Produced by La Sept Arte (France) and Haut et Court (France). Distributed in the U.S. by California Newsreel. 61 minutes.

Sources and Credits

Eventually I managed to find posters of all the featured films. Unfortunately the black-and-white reproductions do not render them in all their splendor. All the shots from films are frame enlargements, except for the production still that was used for the frontispiece. Frame enlargements do not reproduce as well as stills, but they show the film image as it actually appears on the screen, and they allow selection of the exact image to be presented. Depending on availability, the frames were taken from DVD,16 mm film, laserdisc, and video. The quality of the reproductions declines in that order.

The front cover is based on the film poster of *Yaaba*, from *Nuovi Graffiti d'Africa*, Centro Orientamento Educativo, Milan, courtesy Pierre-Alain Meier, Thelma Film

Page ii Still of Sotigui Kouyaté in the role of Djéliba Kouyaté in *Keïta! The Tale of the Griot*, courtesy California Newsreel
Page x Photo of the Place des Cinéastes Africains, Ouagadougou, by permission of L. Lee McIntyre, from the Art and Life in Africa Project of the University of Iowa, © L. Lee McIntyre
Page xiv Poster FESPACO 2003, courtesy Didier Bergounhoux, © D. Bergounhoux

Chapter 1
Out of Africa
Film poster, © Universal City Studios
Yaaba
Film poster, from *Nuovi Graffiti d'Africa*, Centro Orientamento Educativo, Milan, courtesy Pierre-Alain Meier, Thelma Film
Idrissa Ouedraogo, Noufou Ouedraogo, and Fatimata Sanga during the shooting, photo by Michel Cressole, courtesy *Libération*,
  © *Libération*
Keïta!
Film poster, from *Nuovi Graffiti d'Africa*, Centro Orientamento Educativo, Milan
Dani Kouyaté directing Sotigui Kouyaté, by permission of J. Christophe Dupuy

Chapter 2
Engraving featuring Amílcar Cabral, from *Quem Moundou Matar Amílcar Cabral*, Relógio D'Agua Editores, Lisbon, 1995
Sambizanga
Czech film poster, by permission John Kisch
Sarah Maldoror during the shooting, courtesy Sarah Maldoror
Flame
Film poster, courtesy Ingrid Sinclair
Ingrid Sinclair during the shooting, courtesy Ingrid Sinclair

Chapter 3
Nelson Mandela votes in South Africa's first election with universal suffrage, 1994, photo by Walter Dhladha, courtesy ANC Archives
The Gods Must Be Crazy
U.S. film poster, 1982, © Jensen Farley Pictures
A Dry White Season
Video poster, © CBS/Fox
Euzhan Palcy directing Marlon Brando, by permission of Everett Collection
Mapantsula
British film poster
Oliver Schmitz, Juliet Mazamisa, and Thomas Mogotlane, courtesy Oliver Schmitz
Fools
Video poster, courtesy Film Resource Unit
Ramadan Suleman directing Robin Smith, courtesy JBA Production

Chapter 4
Ghanaian wall calendar, courtesy Deborah Pellow

Kongi's Harvest
Film poster, from *Nuovi Graffiti d'Africa*, Centro Orientamento Educativo, Milan, courtesy of Francis Oladele
Xala
Film poster, from *Nuovi Graffiti d'Africa*, Centro Orientamento Educativo, Milan
Ousmane Sembène directing, courtesy New Yorker Films
Tableau Ferraille
Film poster, courtesy Flach Pyramide International
The Blue Eyes of Yonta
Film poster, courtesy Festival International du Film d'Amiens
Flora Gomes during the shooting, from *Ecrans d'Afrique* 1, May 1992

Chapter 5
Julius Nyerere visiting an *ujamaa* village in 1970, by permission of Camera Press
Finzan
Film poster, from *Nuovi Graffiti d'Africa*, Centro Orientamento Educativo, Milan
Cheick Oumar Sissoko brandishing the Stallion of Yennenga he was awarded for *Guimba the Tyrant* at FESPACO 1995, from
Cinémathèque Africaine, Ouagadougou
Kasarmu Ce
Hausa film poster, courtesy Saddik Balewa
Saddik Balewa directing Tom Conroy, courtesy Saddik Balewa

Chapter 6
Cover of *Reel Stars*, courtesy Jonathan Haynes
Kini and Adams
French film poster
John Kani and Idrissa Ouedraogo during the shooting, courtesy Noé Productions
La Vie est belle
Film poster, courtesy Mweze Ngangura
Mweze Ngangura and Benoît Lamy, from cover of *Bruxelles/Wallonie* 45, September 1993, courtesy *Bruxelles/ Wallonie*

The author has made very effort to trace the copyright holders, but if I have inadvertently overlooked any, I will be pleased to make
the necessary arrangements at the first opportunity.

Some material appearing here was published previously and is used by permission:

'The Blue Eyes of Yonta,' 'Kongi's Harvest,' and 'Yaaba' in *International Dictionary of Films and Filmmakers 1: Films*, edited by Tom
Pendergast and Sara Pendergast, fourth edition, Detroit: St. James Press, 2000
'Images of Villages in Four Recent African Films' in *African Writers and Their Readers: Essays in Honor of Bernth Lindfors*, volume 2,
edited by Toyin Falola and Barbara Harlow, Trenton, NJ/Asmara, Eritrea: Africa World Press: 501–25, 2002
'African Writing Projected onto the Screen: *Sambizanga, Xala,* and *Kongi's Harvest*', *African Studies Review* 42 (1): 79–104, 1999
'Wole Soyinka's *Kongi's Harvest* from Stage to Screen: Four Endings to Tyranny', *Canadian Journal of African Studies* 31(1): 32–49,
1997
'Ousmane Sembène's *Xala*: The Novel, the Film, and Their Audiences' (with Oumar Cherif Diop) *Research in African Literatures* 29(2):
147–58, 1998

Index

The Author

Josef Gugler is Professor of Sociology and Director of the Center for Contemporary African Studies at the University of Connecticut. Previously he served as Director of Sociological Research at the Makerere Institute of Social Research, Uganda, and as Professor of Development Sociology at Bayreuth University, Germany. He has held visiting appointments in the Congo (Kinshasa), Germany, Tanzania, and the U.S. His research has taken him to Cuba, India, Kenya, Nigeria, and Tanzania. He has widely published on urbanization in Africa and beyond in the 'South,' and more recently on literature and film in Africa. Since 1991 he has regularly taught a course *Modern Africa: Re-Imagining Africa With Films and Novels*.